ETERNALIZED FRAGMENTS

COGNITIVE APPROACHES TO CULTURE
Frederick Luis Aldama, Patrick Colm Hogan, Lalita Pandit Hogan,
and Sue J. Kim, Series Editors

ETERNALIZED FRAGMENTS

RECLAIMING AESTHETICS IN CONTEMPORARY WORLD FICTION

W. MICHELLE WANG

THE OHIO STATE UNIVERSITY PRESS

COLUMBUS

Copyright © 2020 by The Ohio State University.
All rights reserved.

Library of Congress Cataloging-in-Publication Data
Names: Wang, W. Michelle, author.
Title: Eternalized fragments : reclaiming aesthetics in contemporary world fiction / W. Michelle Wang.
Other titles: Cognitive approaches to culture.
Description: Columbus : The Ohio State University Press, [2020] | Series: Cognitive approaches to culture | Includes bibliographical references and index. | Summary: "Bridges discussions of traditional aesthetics with contemporary neuroaesthetics and evolutionary psychology and analyzes texts from many cultural and national traditions (including Gabriel García Márquez, Kazuo Ishiguro, Arundhati Roy, Jeanette Winterson, Jennifer Egan, Italo Calvino, Flann O'Brien, and Alasdair Gray), identifying three dominant aesthetic modes pertinent to post-war fiction"—Provided by publisher.
Identifiers: LCCN 2019051767 | ISBN 9780814214374 (cloth) | ISBN 0814214371 (cloth) | ISBN 9780814277911 (ebook) | ISBN 0814277918 (ebook)
Subjects: LCSH: Fiction—20th century—History and criticism. | Fiction—21st century—History and criticism. | Aesthetics in literature.
Classification: LCC PN3503 .W35 2020 | DDC 809.3/04—dc23
LC record available at https://lccn.loc.gov/2019051767
Other identifiers: ISBN 978-0-8142-5585-8 (paper) | ISBN 0-814-25585-X (paper)

Cover image by Colleen Brannigan, http://www.cittainvisibili.com
Cover design by Angela Moody
Text design by Juliet Williams
Type set in Adobe Minion Pro

Ong Yew Sam

Betsy Tan CK

致　　爸妈

CONTENTS

Acknowledgments		ix
INTRODUCTION	Reclaiming Aesthetics in Literary Fiction	1

CHAPTER 1	Play (I): Formal (Dis)Order, Sensory Chaos
	   A Visit from the Goon Squad
	   The Castle of Crossed Destinies
		17

CHAPTER 2	Play (II): Postmodern Play with Possible Worlds
	   At Swim-Two-Birds
	   Lanark: A Life in Four Books
		41

CHAPTER 3	Literary Sublime (I): Imagination Reigns
	   The Third Policeman
	   Invisible Cities
		71

CHAPTER 4	Literary Sublime (II): Imaginative Engagements of Our Moralistic Minds
	   The God of Small Things
	   Blood Meridian
		97

CHAPTER 5	Muted Beauty: Complex Harmonies
	   Written on the Body
	   Never Let Me Go
		127

CODA	Between Borders *One Hundred Years of Solitude*	163
Works Cited		189
Index		207

ACKNOWLEDGMENTS

THIS BOOK was made possible by the unwavering support of five amazing lifelong teachers.

To Neil Murphy, this project's genesis likely dates back to 2008, the day I picked up *One Hundred Years of Solitude* in your classroom. In teaching me to see the beauty in books, you altered my landscape of literature forever. Thanks for believing in me before I ever did; I learn to be a better teacher, scholar, and person every day by your example.

To Brian McHale, your astute insight, steady guidance, and unfailing kindness helped me survive the most challenging aspects of this writing process. Not only were you always present to teach, inspire, and encourage, but I continue learning to see the world with renewed wonder in our conversations from literature to art to architecture. Your brilliance and generosity of spirit are a constant source of inspiration. Thank you for everything.

To James Phelan, you taught me what it is to go above and beyond as a teacher and scholar in equal measures of humor, kindness, and brilliance. You found value in every argument I struggled to articulate and, in doing so, gave me the confidence to keep plowing forward. I hope to someday be a fraction of the amazing teacher and scholar that you are.

To David Herman, who is a beacon of goodness in his gentle patience and intellectual generosity: I miss being your student. From the very beginning, you gave me the freedom and guidance I needed to pursue a project I was passionate about; I am so blessed to have met you.

To Frederick Luis Aldama, who tirelessly champions and advocates for his students, actively fostering communities of intellectual support and warm friendships that I continue to cherish years later: thank you for the opportunities, mentorship, and friendship. You've done amazing things for me that I hope to one day be able to pay forward.

I'm so grateful for the warm friendships and infinite kindness of so many during the half-decade I spent in the US (especially Erin Bahl, Leila Ben-Nasr, Matt Cariello, Kelli Fickle, Chris González, Esther Gottlieb, Kathleen Griffin, Wanlin Li, Brandon Manning, Hyesu Park, Andrew Richmond, Theresa Rojas, Erin Wagner, as well as the wonderful folks from Jim's potluck, Project Narrative, and the annual Narrative conference), while friends and colleagues at NTU English and the School of Humanities have been so welcoming and supportive—though I can't name everyone here, it's a joy and a privilege to teach, learn, and work alongside you all.

To the Cognitive Approaches to Culture series editors, Frederick Luis Aldama, Patrick Colm Hogan, Lalita Pandit Hogan, and Sue J. Kim; the outstanding team at The Ohio State University Press, including Kristen Elias Rowley, Rebecca Bostock, Tara Cyphers, Laurie Avery, and Samara Rafert; as well as the two readers of my initial manuscript (with special thanks to Christopher González): I am full of gratitude for all of your support, encouragement, and help.

I gratefully acknowledge the support of Nanyang Technological University (NTU) and Singapore's Ministry of Education, particularly through the Humanities, Arts, and Social Sciences (HASS) International Postdoctoral Fellowship; warm thanks especially to the selection committee led by Professor Alan Chan for their confidence in my work, and to Professor Mark Currie and the School of English and Drama at Queen Mary University of London for hosting my postdoctoral research.

My gratitude to artist Colleen Corradi Brannigan (www.cittainvisibili.com) for generously allowing me to use her beautiful artwork on the cover of this book; I have admired her artistic renditions of *Invis-*

ible Cities for years. Thanks to the University of Nebraska Press for permission to reproduce part of the material in chapter 2 (previously published in Alice Bell and Marie-Laure Ryan's *Possible Worlds Theory and Contemporary Narratology*) and to Routledge for permission to reproduce part of the material in chapter 4 (previously published in Daniel Jernigan, Walter Wadiak, and W. Michelle Wang's *Narrating Death: The Limit of Literature*).

Thanks be to God for blessing this journey: to Melissa and Melinda, Samuel and Pet, Godma and family, Mas and family, and Kai, for all the joy you bring. I dedicate this book to my parents, the first storytellers who read to me in two languages as a child—you gave me the world and I love you immensely.

INTRODUCTION

Reclaiming Aesthetics in Literary Fiction

> And then they understood that José Arcadio Buendía was not as crazy as the family said, but that he was the only one who had enough lucidity to sense the truth of the fact that time also stumbled and had accidents and could therefore splinter and leave an eternalized fragment in a room.
>
> —GABRIEL GARCÍA MÁRQUEZ, *ONE HUNDRED YEARS OF SOLITUDE*

THIS BOOK is about the aesthetics' stumble in time; more precisely, it explores the tension between the anti-aesthetic emphasis of postmodern and contemporary literary theory on the one hand, and readerly engagements with the aesthetic on the other. Like José Arcadio Buendía, whose clarity about the nature of his world belies the apparent derangement of his senses, my book seeks to lucidly render aesthetic energies at work in twentieth- and twenty-first-century fiction in ways that conform with our reading experiences: to elucidate the luminosity, and even the resplendence, of its splinters and fragments—particularly in light of the disjunctures, paradoxes, incongruities, destabilizations, and absurdities that characterize novels of this period.

In a press release announcing the 2015 Man Booker Prize finalists, the judging committee noted that "the novel today is in fine form: as a field of inquiry, a tribunal of history, *a map of the heart*, a probe of the psyche, a stimulus to thought, *a well of pleasure* and a laboratory of language" (emphases added).[1] In 2014, the Nobel Prize in Literature was awarded to Patrick Modiano for his evocation of "the art of memory,"[2]

---

1. http://www.themanbookerprize.com/press-releases/man-booker-international-prize-2015-finalists%E2%80%99-list-announced.
2. http://www.nobelprize.org/nobel_prizes/literature/laureates/2014/press.html.

and the Pulitzer Prize for Fiction to Donna Tartt for her "beautifully written [. . .] novel with exquisitely drawn characters."[3] What these prestigious literary prizes share in common in their articulation of fiction's value is an emphasis on literature *as art*—that is, on the artful treatment or virtuosity with which novelists handle various aspects of writing, with a particular focus on the writing's aesthetic and affective qualities among other merits.

Yet an insistently anti-aesthetic emphasis undergirds much of twentieth-century art and philosophy. From its inception, modernist arts by (now-canonical) figures such as Pablo Picasso and James Joyce were "received as being variously ugly, dissonant, obscure, scandalous, immoral, subversive, and generally 'antisocial'" (Jameson 4). Marcel Duchamp's readymades, in particular, were a critical force "in fostering the widespread reaction against beauty," and this "anti-aesthetic exploration [continued] well into the 1920s" with the Dadaists (Benezra, Viso, and Danto 20). "Mistrustful of passion, the twentieth century gradually came to doubt beauty itself. The contrast between helping the suffering and painting them, between fighting for them and writing about them, became starker and deeper" (Nehamas 3). Wary of art's ability "to transmute the greatest horrors into objects of beauty, philosophy disavowed" beauty (3). By the 1970s and '80s, "the art world became almost wholly consumed by the idea of the anti-aesthetic," with postmodern art "deliberately undermin[ing] such principles as value, order, meaning, control, and identity" (Gilbert-Rolfe, "Attractiveness" 13; Hutcheon 13; see also Shimamura 12).

This anti-aesthetic emphasis likewise extends to literary and critical theory of the same period—with the notable exception of the New Critics' focus on poetry in the 1940s and '50s. Hence, postmodernist theorists like Hal Foster and Jean-François Lyotard observe that the move from the modern to the postmodern has led to a dismantling of grand narratives, including the grand narrative of beauty (Kelly, "New Criticism"; Lyotard, *Postmodern* xxiv, 37).[4] The postmodern period,

---

3. http://www.pulitzer.org/citation/2014-Fiction.

4. Jeremy Gilbert-Rolfe suggests, "It is now quite clear that when we hear the term anti-aesthetic we mean anti-beauty, and that this is because the beautiful is regarded as inherently frivolous" ("Attractiveness" 14). Despite the dominantly anti-aesthetic emphasis in critical paradigms, postmodern theorists like Jameson and Lyotard have (re)turned to and revised the eighteenth-century aesthetic category of the sublime to characterize this moment in history—an issue I take up more fully in chapters 3 and 4 when I address the literary sublime.

Fredric Jameson notes, "has generally grown skeptical about deep phenomenological experience"—what he terms "the waning of affect in postmodern culture" (134–35, 10–11). Literary criticism of the period stresses "the heterogeneity and profound discontinuities of the work of art" through the use of strategies such as "contradiction, discontinuity, randomness, excess, short circuit," as well as "juxtaposition, interpolation, superimposition, and misattribution" (Jameson 31; McHale, *Postmodernist* 7, 45).

An apparent rift thus exists between the anti-aesthetic emphasis in philosophical, postmodernist, and contemporary literary theory on the one hand, and readerly appreciations of and engagements with the aesthetic on the other. Rex Butler observes that "the last thing one could imagine saying about art after the reign of postmodernism, [is] that it could actually be about beauty," yet beauty "returned after the intervening period of what came to be known as anti-aesthetics" (Butler 7; see also Shimamura 250). Beauty rematerialized in the field of contemporary aesthetics with a resurgence of publications such as Dave Hickey's *The Invisible Dragon: Four Essays on Beauty* (1993); Jeremy Gilbert-Rolfe's *Beauty and the Contemporary Sublime* (1999); Elaine Scarry's *On Beauty and Being Just* (1999); Neal Benezra, Olga M. Viso, and Arthur Danto's *Regarding Beauty* (1999); Richard Shusterman's *Pragmatist Aesthetics: Living Beauty* (2000); Arthur Danto's *Abuse of Beauty* (2003); Denis Donoghue's *Speaking of Beauty* (2003); Umberto Eco's *History of Beauty* (2004); Arthur Pontynen's *For the Love of Beauty: Art History and the Moral Foundations of Aesthetic Judgment* (2006); Jennifer Green-Lewis and Margaret Soltan's *Teaching Beauty in DeLillo, Woolf, and Merrill* (2008); Galen A. Johnson's *The Retrieval of the Beautiful* (2010); Alexander Nehamas's *The Place of Beauty in a World of Art* (2010); and Howard Gardner's *Truth, Beauty, and Goodness Reframed* (2012), among others.[5]

---

5. The resurgence of interest in aesthetics (and beauty) from the final decade of the twentieth century onward is well documented by Benezra, Viso, and Danto (12): Ann Goldstein curated "'Pure Beauty [. . .]' for the American Center in Paris in cooperation with the Museum of Contemporary Art, Los Angeles" in 1994. This was followed by Lynn Gumpert's "'La Belle et La Bête' (Beauty and the Beast) for the Musée d'Art Moderne de la Ville de Paris" (1995); "Dan Cameron's 'On Beauty' for the Regina Gallery in Moscow" (1996); "Mosa Martinez's 'On Life, Beauty, Translations and Other Difficulties'" for the fifth Istanbul Biennial (1997); and Benezra and Viso's "Regarding Beauty: A View of the Late Twentieth Century" at the Smithsonian's Hirshhorn Museum in Washington, DC (1999).

Furthermore, aesthetics and beauty have found a new and perhaps not unexpected home in the interrelated fields of neuroaesthetics and evolutionary psychology: John Tooby and Leda Cosmides's "Does Beauty Build Adapted Minds?" (2001); Semir Zeki's *Splendors and Miseries of the Brain* (2008); Denis Dutton's *The Art Instinct: Beauty, Pleasure, and Human Evolution* (2008); V. S. Ramachandran's *The Tell-Tale Brain: A Neuroscientist's Quest for What Makes Us Human* (2011); Arthur P. Shimamura and Stephen E. Palmer's *Aesthetic Science: Connecting Minds, Brains, and Experience* (2011); Shimamura's *Experiencing Art: In the Brain of the Beholder* (2013); G. Gabrielle Starr's *Feeling Beauty: The Neuroscience of Aesthetic Experience* (2013); and Patrick Colm Hogan's *Beauty and Sublimity: A Cognitive Aesthetics of Literature and the Arts* (2016), among other recent publications, all point to a lively, revived interest in aesthetics, beauty, and the pleasures of fiction in the twenty-first century.

This book joins the ongoing dialogue by putting aesthetic, cognitive, literary, narrative, and philosophical traditions in conversation, in order to propose a framework for understanding aesthetic impulses at work in post–world war fiction. In line with Theodor Adorno's notion that "works of art exist only in *actu*" or "lived dynamic experience"—what Hogan terms the "aesthetic event"—I adopt John Dewey's and Richard Shusterman's pragmatist stance, which assumes an *experiential* approach in treating "aesthetic concepts, including the concept of art itself," as "instruments which need to be challenged and revised when they fail to provide [or account for] the best experience" (Shusterman 18; Aldama and Hogan 131; see also Starr 17). An experiential approach further incorporates considerations of readerly roles and responses—an issue particularly pertinent to our experience of postmodern and contemporary fiction, as I show in the chapters that follow—such that aesthetic theorizations of (literary) art remain ongoing and dynamic rather than static and outdated.

Writing in 1997, Christopher Beach notes that "questions concerning the nature and role of the aesthetic stubbornly persist in our discussion of both literature and culture. In recent years, books by Michael Sprinker, Richard Shusterman, Peter de Bolla, Terry Eagleton, David Carroll, Jonathan Loesberg, Frances Ferguson, J. M. Bernstein, and Christopher Norris, among others, have attempted to accommodate discussions of the aesthetic within the contemporary discourse of literary theory. It would seem that at the very moment when the study of the aesthetic is said to be on the verge of disappearing [. . .] it has reasserted itself more strongly than ever" (96).

My theoretical framework begins with an inquiry into Friedrich Schiller's definition of beauty, which he adapts and modifies from Immanuel Kant's proposal that the beautiful is characterized by the harmony of faculties of the *imagination* and *understanding* (Kant, "Critique" 137, 145, 155). In line with Kant, Schiller proposes from Letters XII to XV of his aesthetical and philosophical essays that beauty is "the common object" of both the "sensuous impulsion"/"sensuous instincts"/"imagination" and "the formal impulsion"/"formal instinct"/"intelligence." However, in "On the Sublime," Schiller goes further to suggest several times in that essay that "in the presence of beauty [. . .], the sensuous instincts are in harmony with the laws of reason." While Kant proposes that beauty "ought properly to be a question merely of the form"—in the "subjective agreement of the Imagination and Understanding" ("Critique" 137)—Schiller, in turn, characterizes beauty as being related not only to the imagination but also to reason. William F. Wertz Jr. thus points out that for Schiller, this formal drive is characterized by humankind's impulse "to impose a conceptual *and* moral order upon the sensuous world" (84; emphasis added)—that is, what Kant calls the *understanding* and *(practical) reason*, respectively.

However, the conceptual and the moral can be considered as two distinct systems of ordering. Kant himself differentiated between form and the moral, noting that "the feeling for the beautiful is specifically different from the moral feeling" ("Critique" 145). This persistent and complex interrelationship between aesthetics and ethics is rooted in early Greek tradition, whereby most ancient writers and thinkers "were neither able nor eager to detach the aesthetic quality" of works of art "from their intellectual, moral, religious and practical function or content" (Kristeller 7). Paul Oskar Kristeller notes that "when Plato discusses beauty," for instance, he is also speaking of "moral goodness" (4–7). Even among the ancients, however, some philosophers implicitly distinguished between several types of beauty. Plato's student Aristotle "refers to *beauty (kalos)* in terms of goodness, as found in ethical action" in *Rhetoric*, but also "refers to beauty (*kalos*) in an aesthetic fashion: [. . .] not associated with goodness, but with the perfection of a thing" in *Metaphysics* (Pontynen 59). This interrelationship also finds support in current understanding of neural structures: neuroscientists have found that both the default mode network and the orbitofrontal cortex are implicated in our ethical and aesthetic judgments, "supporting the existence of brain mechanisms shared between moral and aesthetic appreciation" (Cela-Conde et al. 10458; Wang et al. 7; Starr 23).

Rigorous distinctions between goodness/ethical/moral beauty and aesthetic beauty only began to properly emerge at the end of the seventeenth and start of the eighteenth centuries. Though philosophers such as the Third Earl of Shaftesbury (primarily influenced by Plato, Plotinus, and Cicero) "did not make a clear distinction between artistic and moral beauty," others such as his pupil Francis Hutcheson "distinguish[ed] between the moral sense and the sense of beauty"—a distinction subsequently adopted by David Hume and Kant, paving "the way for separation between ethics and aesthetics" (Kristeller 11). The recurrence of philosophers' and writers' emphasis on the moral impulse, however, suggests its importance and relevance to aesthetics, even if it is no longer viewed as necessarily *defining* art.[6] Contemporary aesthetics thus recognizes "a plurality of aesthetic values, of which the ethical values of artworks are but a single kind" (Gaut 589).

In setting up my revised system for understanding aesthetic impulses at work in post–world war fiction, I retain Kant's intellectual rigor in keeping form discrete from the moral, while retaining the latter category given its significance for twentieth- and twenty-first-century fiction. My revision and resynthesis of Kant and Schiller in this manner also allows for a more rigorous distinction between beauty and the sublime, without necessarily situating them in oppositional binaries. Neuroaesthetics research has shown that experiences of the beautiful and sublime reveal "distinctly different pattern[s] of brain activity" (Ishizu and Zeki 1), which suggests the theoretical efficacy of keeping the two concepts distinct—an issue I examine more closely in chapters 3 and 4.

I make heuristic use of Kant's and Schiller's aesthetic frameworks to propose that postwar fiction is dominantly concerned with the harmonies, engagements, and tensions between what I term the *form-drive*, *moral-drive*, and *sense-drive* in relation to readerly roles/responses. I regard all three drives as part of the reader's overarching "aesthetic relation" to the text—which Frederick Aldama situates "in the relationship between object and subject" (Aldama and Hogan 135)—and

---

6. For instance, Leo "Tolstoy rejected much of the celebrated art of his day because it did not fulfil his preferred criterion of communicating moral feeling between human beings" (Janaway 165).

in the following chapters, I explain how the three drives' functionalities are supported by studies in evolutionary psychology and neuroaesthetics. Briefly, I relate the sense-drive to the human impulse for seeking "information in an open-ended way" (Boyd 14), the form-drive to "encoding" and "pattern recognition" processes (Hogan, *Beauty* 159–60), and the moral-drive to deployments of what Jonathan Haidt terms our "hive switch" (223–33).

The *sense-drive* encompasses what Kant and Schiller have variously termed the "sensuous impulsion," "sensuous instincts," or "imagination." From an evolutionary perspective, Dutton suggests that "the ability to imagine scenarios and states of affairs not present to direct consciousness must have had adaptive power in human prehistory, as it does in today's world. [. . .] Imagination allows for the weighing of indirect evidence, making chains of inference for what might have been or what might come to be"—in what Brian Boyd identifies as the uniquely human ability to "seek, shape, and share information in an open-ended way" (Dutton 105; Boyd 14). Ellen Spolsky proposes that "narratives are themselves the processes that human beings have evolved to understand, express, and meet the need for revised and revisable behavior in an unstable world"; specifically, "the indirection of the way language means" underwrites such "open-endedness" and "generativity" (180, 196). Since the imagination's interest is "to emancipate itself from all laws, and to play its part freely," Schiller notes that "the sensuous impulsion desires change," such that "imagination, by its tyranny, ventures to destroy the order of the world" (*Aesthetical*, "The Pathetic"; "Letter XIII"; "Letter VI").

Such emancipatory tendencies likewise underpin Friedrich Nietzsche's notion of Dionysiac excess. Generally regarded as a "precursor to postmodernism," Nietzsche was influenced by Schiller's philosophical thought, identifying "the rapture of the Dionysian state with its annihilation of the ordinary bounds and limits of existence" (Aylesworth, "Postmodernism"; Nietzsche 225, 229–30). The sense-drive has taken on renewed importance in light of literary postmodernism, given that the postwar era we have been and are living through "has been singularly uncertain, insecure, self-questioning and culturally pluralistic" (Waugh 6). Jeanette Winterson notes that postmodernism foregrounded the notion that "reality is continuous, multiple, simultaneous, complex, abundant, and partly invisible," and that "the imagination alone can fathom this because [it . . .] is not limited by the world of sense experience" ("What" 185).

While the sense-drive seeks change, emancipation, indirection, open-endedness, and generativity, the form-drive and moral-drive—as systems of ordering—correspondingly tend toward unity/conformity, though in significantly different ways. The *form-drive* is concerned with unity, conformity, and order vis-à-vis "form-giving" characteristics such as shape, symmetry, pattern, grouping, orderliness ("visual repetition or rhythm"), and coherence, in the forms and structures of textual worlds (Dole, *Aesthetical*; Aldama and Hogan 116–18; Boyd 14; Ramachandran, *Brain* 199, 233; Chatterjee 302; Hogan, "Literary" 324; Sheridan and Gardner 281). Kant's notion of the *understanding* resonates distinctly with contemporary cognitive conceptions of the mind as craving formal qualities: for instance, his remark that our satisfaction in "geometrically regular figures" as being part of "common understanding" ("Critique" 137).

I further suggest that the form-drive works to determine relevance or what Hogan terms "encoding of target": a form of structuring which "recurs at various levels of processing," whereby "our mind selects elements of experience and structures them into relations with one another" (*Beauty* 75, 55; see also Chatterjee 301–2). Selection mechanisms (in the dorsolateral prefrontal cortex, for instance) are likely involved in such structuring processes, working to "stabilize the combinations of ideas that are most interesting, most useful, or sometimes merely most shocking or contagious" (Dehaene 322). Our brains are efficiently "geared to attach meaning to forms" (Shimamura 64), a process that in turn depends crucially on our ability to rapidly determine relevance.[7] Shimamura's explication of what medical science currently understands about agnosia (a visual disorder affecting object recognition) clarifies this relationship between form, relevance, and meaning-making: while "patients with visual agnosia have normal acuity and

---

7. Philipp Kanske, "Nicholas Frijda, Elizabeth Phelps, and others posit that emotions are 'relevance detectors,'" with neural bases in the amygdala, nucleus accumbens, and other cognitive architecture (Starr 21; Kanske 2). "David Rose, a prominent translator of theoretical neuroscience into applied educational technology," notes that the limbic region "helps us to prioritise and give value to whatever we read. On the basis of this affective contribution, our attention and comprehension processes become either stirred or inert" (Wolf 140–41).

can read text" or reproduce drawings, they are unable to "*recognize* what they have just drawn" and cannot "distinguish essential features from less relevant ones"—in other words, patients experience a loss in their "ability to assign meaning to visual forms" (64). I thus suggest that the form-drive is crucially involved in determining relevance and assigning meanings in our aesthetic appreciation of literary art.

It is important to note that form is subject to historical influences, particularly in tandem with artistic practices of its specific historical moment. While Impressionism was "scorned and ridiculed" by art critics of its time "as crude, unfinished, and lacking skill" or form, in the same paintings we now "see beauty, grace, and harmony" (Shimamura 1). Similarly, modern art, especially Cubism, was first charged with "formlessness" and then "criticized later from another point of view as excessively concerned with form" (Beckley and Shapiro 6). "The unstable, the fused, the scattered, [and] the broken, in composition" may thus "belong to a whole in which we can discern regularities if we are disposed to them by another aesthetic" (6). Jameson proposes that the postmodern period is characterized by a new "aesthetic model" in which "the postmodernist experience of form" is "no longer unified or organic, but now a virtual grab bag or lumber room of disjoined subsystems and raw materials and impulses of all kinds" (26, 31).

In response to Jameson, I draw on the cognitive sciences (and my own aesthetic experiences of reading postmodernist fiction) to suggest that a more productive way of understanding these discontinuous fragments lies in the tensions and complex harmonies of the form-, moral-, and sense-drives—an approach congruent with neuroscientist Jean-Pierre Changeux's understanding of "the essence of art" as "a harmonious synthesis between brain processors" (Dehaene 323). In so doing, I hope to offer a model for capturing the implicit cognitive processes at work in our enjoyment of postmodern and contemporary fiction.

The *moral-drive* is likewise concerned with unity and conformity vis-à-vis the vision of humankind's shared moral or ethical standards of beliefs and behaviors.[8] In making this statement, I do not mean that all human beings share identical ethical and/or moral judgments and standards—a patently impossible proposition which, in any case,

---

8. I use the word *vision* in the sense of an ideal: like the concept of infinity, we can keep working toward and approaching the vision without ever completely attaining it since human relations are complex and ever-changing.

would render the moral-drive pointless. Rather, I consider the moral in relation to John Rawls's notion of fairness as a "symmetry of everyone's relations to each other" (12) and suggest that the moral-drive is always working toward a greater congruence, unity, or conformity in a constructive, shared vision of how we are to live and act, especially with and toward others. As with the sense- and form-drives, I look to developments in the cognitive sciences to explicate the moral-drive's functionality. Drawing on studies in evolutionary adaptation (including the work of Tooby and Cosmides, Donald E. Brown, Stephen Pinker, and Joseph Carroll), Denis Dutton suggests that "an intuitive economics" involving "an associated sense of fairness and reciprocity" and "a sense of justice, including obligations, rights, revenge, and what is deserved," is an "innate, universal" feature and capability of the human mind (44).

Jonathan Haidt further observes that "there's more to morality than harm and fairness," associating humankind's innate capacity for moralization with our ultrasociality—a characteristic that drives our "cohesive and cooperative" behaviors in the evolutionary advantage it gives us over other species (xiii–xv, 206).[9] Haidt terms this cohesive adaptation the *"hive switch,"* identifying its neural bases in mirror neurons, neurotransmitters such as oxytocin, and brain structures such as the gustatory cortex (223, 235, 363, 60). There are many ways to trigger the hive switch: the experience of "awe in nature," for instance, can "shut down the self, making you feel that you are *simply a part of a whole*" (227–28)—an affective encounter that resonates with the aesthetic category of the sublime.

Drawing on experimental research in cognitive and moral psychology, Haidt notes that "moral intuitions" relating to care, fairness, liberty, loyalty, authority, and sanctity arise "almost instantaneously" and "drive our later reasoning" (xiv). If Haidt is right about the human tendency to engage in such "post hoc justification" (i.e., the use of rea-

---

9. Dutton makes a similar point when he notes that "stories provide regulation for social behavior" (110). Haidt argues specifically that "the social order is a moral order" (15), though human groups build such orders around the emphasis of different values. While individualistic morality privileges freedom and emphasizes distinctions "between moral rules preventing harm [and] social conventions regulating behaviors not linked directly to harm," sociocentric morality tends to emphasize their associations, especially social conventions that relate to disgust and/or disrespect (15, 19). Not only are human conceptions of morality about preventing harm, they are further driven by "emotional logic about avoiding disgust" (13).

soning to justify our emotional reactions to moral intuitions [325, 25]), readers' sustained affective engagements with innumerable fictional lives in literature have the potential to shape morality in two valuable ways.[10] First, reading fiction can actively stretch our capacities for flexibly considering the positions of those who adopt different moral foundations/matrices to our own, even and especially with those with whom we disagree. Second, literature can enlarge readers' repertoire of moral intuitions, triggering/eliciting/redirecting/challenging our initial moral judgments in ways that constructively offer a more inclusive shared vision of how we live and act, especially with and toward others.[11] Since evolutionary adaptations are intended "to maximize survival" rather than accuracy (Haidt 252), these exercises in flexibly enlarging our repertoire of moral intuitions when we read fiction are particularly valuable in advancing a vision of harmonious ultrasociality.

A ROADMAP TO THIS BOOK: NAVIGATING POSTWAR AESTHETIC FRAGMENTS

In this study of twentieth- and twenty-first-century literary aesthetics, I deal with texts from a variety of cultural and national traditions, including Irish, Scottish, British, Italian, Indian, US, and Latin American fiction. Amidst such heterogeneity, I identify three dominant aesthetic modes most pertinent to postwar fiction: an aesthetics of play, an aesthetics of literary sublime, and an aesthetics of muted beauty. Though the pleasure we derive from (literary) art is common to all

---

10. Joseph Paxton, Leo Ungar, and Joshua Greene found that people were more open to reasoned moral persuasion when given "increased deliberation time" (1). Fiction is thus uniquely well-positioned to modify our moral intuitions given the extensive time we typically have to devote to a novel. (Readers may alternately choose to abandon rather than work through a text that violates their sense of morality.) Our moral intuitions can thus "be shaped by reasoning," Haidt notes, "especially when the reasons are embedded in [. . .] an emotionally compelling novel, movie, or news story" (71).

11. Conversely, certain types of literature can shape our moral intuitions in ways that narrow rather than enlarge our regard for others. Hence, Haidt notes that our ultrasociality or "bee-like nature" is (paradoxically) able to facilitate "altruism, heroism, war, and genocide" (xv).

three modes, each engenders aesthetic pleasure of a different sort in its engagement with various drives; such distinctions are productive because different aesthetic designs foreground varying readerly tasks. In thus differentiating among kinds of textual designs, I hope to honor the phenomenology of reading and to defend the value of aesthetic experiences that other readers and I have derived from reading postmodern and contemporary fiction. Briefly, play has to do with the tension/conflict between the form- and sense-drives; the sublime relates to the sense-drive in increasing tension/conflict with the moral-drive, while beauty is characterized by the form-drive in complex harmonies with the sense- or moral-drive. I explicate aspects associated with each mode in relation to the three drives more fully in the chapters that follow.

Chapters 1 and 2 are devoted to the mode of play, which I propose is the dominant aesthetic energy characterizing postmodernist fiction. Play depends on a dynamic interaction of rules and freedom (Huizinga 3, 7–10; Caillois 27), which dovetails with my notion of postmodern fiction's tension between the form-drive's ordering impulses and the sense-drive's chaotic compulsions. In chapter 1, I use Jennifer Egan's *A Visit from the Goon Squad* and Italo Calvino's *The Castle of Crossed Destinies* to show how postmodern fiction's playful textual designs spur the form-drive into action. I explicate cognitive processes that are likely at work in imposing some form of (artificial and/or temporary) coherence, as a counter to postmodern fiction's Dionysiac energies. I extend this discussion of play in chapter 2 by moving from formal structures to world structures: using Flann O'Brien's *At Swim-Two-Birds* and Alasdair Gray's *Lanark: A Life in Four Books* as my case studies, I demonstrate how the possible-worlds approach to narrative fiction functions as a useful critical apparatus for capturing tensions between liberatory excesses of the sense-drive and recuperative processes of the form-drive. Chapter 2 deals in particular with readers' inhabitation and orientation of postmodern fiction's playful, ontologically complex worlds.

Chapters 3 and 4 focus on the postmodern literary sublime, where I streamline and revise existing theories by Longinus, Burke, Kant, Schiller, Hegel, and Lyotard to account for how postmodern and contemporary literature facilitates affective dimensions of the sublime in the reading experience. Like Kant and Schiller, I distinguish between two types of sublime experiences, but instead of binaries, I position them in relation to increasing degrees of conflict between the sense-drive and the moral-drive. Chapter 3 deals with the mode traditionally known as the *mathematical sublime,* where I use Flann O'Brien's *The Third Policeman* and Italo Calvino's *Invisible Cities* to explain how sublime moments in these texts relate to the sense-drive operating in minimal conflict with the moral-drive. Compared with the aesthetic mode of play which depends on tensions between the sense- and form-drives, I explain how the sublime is dominantly rooted in the sense-drive's inherent instability and demonstrate that versatile postmodern novelists like Calvino and O'Brien tend not to commit to single aesthetic modes/projects but their oeuvres often challenge and engage readers in dynamic ways.

In chapter 4, I address the category Kant terms the *dynamical sublime* (which I situate as being in continuum with the mathematical sublime), whereby the sense-drive comes into increasing degrees of conflict with the moral-drive. By attending to fragments of sublimity in Arundhati Roy's *The God of Small Things,* I explain how the moral-drive functions in relation to readers' experience of the sublime and show how texts that fall within this aesthetic mode imaginatively engage our "righteous minds" (Haidt xiii). Using Cormac McCarthy's *Blood Meridian* as my case study, I explicate the sublime's significance for postmodern and contemporary fiction and demonstrate how these texts in turn complicate traditional understandings of this aesthetic category.

Chapter 5 addresses the aesthetic category of beauty: following the postmodern period's radical skepticism in grand narratives (including those associated with beauty), a key issue in the (re)turn to fragmentary or incongruous beauty in late twentieth- and twenty-first-century fiction is how literature might reconcile beauty with the brokenness of human experience. I explicate my approach to literary beauty as a function of the form-drive in complex harmonies with the sense-drive/moral-drive. While Jeanette Winterson's *Written on the Body* deals with a more traditional conception of beauty (as conceived by Kant and Schiller) in the harmony of the form- and sense-drives, Kazuo Ishiguro's *Never Let Me Go* complicates this classical understanding of beauty by foregrounding the harmony *and* tension between the form- and moral-drives. I propose that much of contemporary fiction is strikingly beautiful in its muting of contexts, in what these texts leave unsaid and in the gaps that readers are thus called upon to fill.

In the coda, I turn my attention to the relationships among the three aesthetic categories and suggest how they can be viewed as junctures that offer an alternative trajectory for thinking about forms of literary practice in the post–world war era. The modes of play, sublime, and beauty do not exhaust the diverse aesthetics characterizing twentieth- and twenty-first-century fiction, but they do capture the period's dominant aesthetic energies. The three modes shade off into one another, with porous rather than rigid borders: the proliferation of worlds in radically playful texts, for instance, tends to verge on the sublime's postulation of infinite worlds, as I explicate in chapter 3. I propose that distinctions between modes involve considerations of what Adorno terms the "dynamic totality of the work of art" ("Concept" 80), and I use my analysis of Gabriel García Márquez's *One Hundred Years of Solitude* to discuss texts that straddle the borders of aesthetic modes.

Clive Bell notes that the "starting-point for all systems of aesthetics must be the personal experience" of an aesthetic emotion—what G. Gabrielle Starr terms its "hedonic signature"—a notion shared by philosophers including Kant, Nehamas, George Santayana, and Noël Carroll, among others (Bell, "Art" 262; Starr 14–15).[12] "A good critic may be able to make me see in a picture that had left me cold things that I had overlooked, till at last, receiving the aesthetic emotion, I recognise it as a work of art," but she can "affect my aesthetic theories only by affecting my aesthetic experience" (Bell, "Art" 262–63). Given the inevitable subjective dimension that underpins most, if not all, aesthetic analyses—particularly in the present study, where readerly roles and responses are a dominant feature of my proposed model—when I refer generically to the *reader's response,* I use the term as a heuristic construct for the real, flesh-and-blood reader's likely response, modeled after my personal experience of the text. I contend that these responses are not so idiosyncratic as to be mine alone, since they tend to be in line with at least some critics' general attitudes toward the chosen texts, even if we have chosen to highlight different aspects of the novels. My discussion encompasses readers' shifting positions of temporarily "treat[ing] the fictional action as real" (i.e., as part of the "*narrative*

---

12. See Nehamas 78–79; Santayana, *Sense* 31; Carroll 158.

audience"), even as we "operate[ ] with the tacit knowledge that the characters and events are synthetic constructs" (*"authorial audience"*) (Phelan, *Narrative* 218, 215). I refer to critics' readings and reviews to highlight our common aesthetic judgments of texts—which have, after all, an implied social dimension to them in the implicit expectation that others likely share these judgments.[13]

Christopher Beach observes that

> despite his much-quoted statement that it is no longer possible to write poetry after Auschwitz—no longer possible to engage in the same *kind* of aesthetic activity as before the war—Adorno believed that a continuing examination of all forms of cultural production, including the aesthetic dimension, was not only possible in the postwar environment, but more necessary than ever. (107)

If contemporary aesthetic theorists are correct in positing that our experiences of art are ultimately meant to give us a changed sense of the world (Starr 20) or help us build better-adapted neurocognitive systems for revising "behavior in an unstable world" (Spolsky 180–81), I suggest that exploring interactions between what James Phelan calls textual and readerly dynamics in the manner I propose in this book yields fruitful insight into authors' and readers' expectations of what art/fiction has to offer to a world that continues to be devastated by violence. By gathering these eternalized fragments of beauty, sublimity, and play scattered on the shores of postmodern and contemporary fiction, I work to explicate the truth of my sense that despite the aesthetics' stumble in time, our ongoing love affair with fiction is grounded in our cognitive engagements with the text's aesthetic dimensions. Bridging discussions of traditional aesthetics (as exemplified by Longinus, Kant, Schiller, and others) with contemporary neuroaesthetics and evolutionary psychology (including the work of Boyd, Dutton, Aldama, Hogan, Haidt, Dehaene, Shimamura, Ramachandran, and Stuart Brown), I explicate the significance of a cognitive approach to literary studies in the chapters that follow.

---

13. Nehamas proposes that our judgments of beauty offer the hope "of *establishing* a community that centers around it—a community, to be sure, whose boundaries are constantly shifting and whose edges are never stable" (82).

CHAPTER 1

Play (I)

Formal (Dis)Order, Sensory Chaos

FICTION READING involves an element of *pretense* that similarly defines *play*. Denis Dutton notes that "pretend play predictably occurs among children of all cultures at around eighteen months to two years—about the time that they begin to talk and engage socially" (108). Evolutionary psychology suggests that "humans have evolved specialized cognitive machinery that allows us to enter and participate in imagined worlds"—what Tooby and Cosmides term *decoupled cognition* ("Does" 9). We tap upon this capacity for pretend play when we read fiction, drawing on subtle "mechanisms to decouple the play world from the real world" (Dutton 106). When readers inhabit fictional worlds like Yoknapatawpha County and Middle-earth, adopting "a belief in the reality of the characters and events" as we become emotionally invested in their fates and outcomes, we take on the role of what Peter Rabinowitz calls the *narrative audience* (Phelan, "Rhetorical" 503).

My discussion of play as an aesthetic category begins with reviewing aspects of play theory that resonate with postmodern and contemporary fiction. I focus on what John Huizinga terms play's "profoundly aesthetic quality," particularly its potential for creating order (2, 10), and explicate its relation to my conception of the form-drive. "Never imposed by physical necessity or moral duty," Huizinga notes, play is "an interlude in our daily lives" that carves out its own time and space, since it can be freely "deferred or suspended" (8–9). Its "quality of freedom" resonates with what Immanuel Kant postulates as critical to aesthetic judgment—the "feeling of freedom in the play of our cognitive faculties"—and it is perhaps for this reason that Huizinga detects deep affinities between play and aesthetics (Huizinga 7, 2, 10; Kant, "Critique" 150). Though "rules are inseparable from play," Roger Caillois posits that "a basic freedom is central to play in order to stimulate distraction and fantasy" (Huizinga 3, 10; Caillois 27). This tension between freedom and rules simulates the dynamic interactions of the sense-drive's chaotic compulsions and the form-drive's ordering impulses that I detect at work in postmodern fiction.

The freedom to play—especially the refusal to do so—is most evident in the figure of the spoilsport: Huizinga notes that "the cheat and the hypocrite have always had an easier time of it than the spoilsports," because "the spoil-sport shatters the play-world itself. By withdrawing from the game he reveals the relativity and fragility of the play-world" and "robs play of its *illusion*" (11–12). Stuart Brown and Christopher Vaughan further suggest that "bending rules and pushing through limits" as the cheats do "aren't the dark side of play—they are the essence of play" and "should happen within the realm of play" (193). Postmodern novelists were happy to comply with their dazzling arrays of kaleidoscopic worlds that transgress boundaries and challenge readers, pushing our cognitive abilities to their limits.

A critical quality of play—which relates to the difficulty scholars have had with pinning it down within a theoretical framework[1]— is that, like the aesthetic, play is "intensely pleasurable" (Brown and Vaughan 56; Huizinga 1; Kant, "Critique" 131; Ryan, "Narrative" 354). Its central emotional quality, "the experience of fun and enjoyment," resists analysis; though contemporary neuroscience has equipped us

---

1. Huizinga explains from the outset that his objective was to understand play as a "cultural phenomenon": "to ascertain how far culture itself bears the character of play" (ix). It is thus perhaps unsurprising that later theorists find Huizinga's theory to be "so broad that it is indistinct," since the scope of his model "incorporates nearly every human behavior into a broad definition of Play," rendering it "almost useless" for a direct "application to a literary-theoretical mode" (Bohman-Kalaja 15–16; Detweiler 57).

with tools to explain the value of play as "a profound biological process," it remains difficult to define "the *fun* of playing" (Huizinga 1–3; Brown and Vaughan 56). Huizinga's characterization has been crucial in shaping other scholars' engagements with play theory; his conception of play (now more than a half-century old) has aged surprisingly well. Consider its correspondence with medical doctor Stuart Brown's definition: play is "voluntary," "done for its own sake," enjoys "freedom from time," and is inherently appealing in the "psychological arousal" it excites (Brown and Vaughan 17). Brown likewise notes that its affective dimensions are crucial to any understanding of play: "what years of academic and clinical research has taught me about the power of play" is that it is most obviously "intensely pleasurable" and "there is no way to really understand play without also remembering the feeling of play" (4, 20).

Like Huizinga, Brown and Vaughan concur that play is vital to the essence of life and the basis of "what we think of as civilization" (11).

> Neuroscientists, developmental biologists, psychologists, social scientists, and researchers from every point of the scientific compass now know that play is a profound biological process. [. . .] In higher animals, it fosters empathy and makes possible complex social groups. [. . .] We are built to play and built through play. When we play, we are engaged in the purest expression of our humanity, the truest expression of our individuality. (5)

It is for these reasons that Brown and Vaughan also see play as "the basis of all art" (11). Though I agree with their contention that the spirit of play underlies all art, I add that play takes on varying degrees of dominance depending on the kind of artistic practice, its specific genre, and the particular aims of individual works of art. As compared to novels examined in later chapters, I propose that play is the dominant aesthetic mode of texts discussed in this chapter and the next, positing that their textual designs explicitly invite the reader to play along. The works of Flann O'Brien, Georges Perec, Samuel Beckett, Italo Calvino, Vladimir Nabokov, Umberto Eco, Albertine Sarrazin, André Breton, Harry Mathews, Witold Gombrowicz, René Belletto, and Alina Reyes are examples of "playtexts" which "allow themselves to be played again and again" in their adoption of "game structures"

(Motte, *Playtexts*; Bohman-Kalaja 38). Marjorie Perloff recognizes similar energies at work in the OuLiPo project, calling its device "game-playing," and notes that Perec himself saw "writing as practice, as work, as play" (140).

Drawing on the work of John Byers, who studies the evolution of animal play behavior, Brown and Vaughan observe that the extent to which human beings engage in play is "correlated to the development of the brain's frontal cortex" (which relates to cognitive processing) and "tied to the rate and size of growth of the cerebellum" (which is "responsible for key cognitive functions such as attention [and] language processing"); in short, "play activity is actually helping to sculpt the brain" (33–35). "The brain is making sense of itself through simulation and testing" when we play, and "play's most valuable benefit" for humans may be in creating such simulations through "storytelling, art," and other sorts of play activity (35).

Game theorists have proposed a variety of models for studying play categories: Robin Humicke, Marc LeBlanc, and Robert Zubek's MDA framework (Mechanics → Dynamics → Aesthetics) attempts to account for how a game's system and rules work to foster the "fun" element in games, while Brian Sutton-Smith strives to capture play's diversity of forms and experiences using his nine categories of "play phenomena" (LeBlanc 440–41; Sutton-Smith 299–301). Caillois's model, however, is the most productive for describing the nature of gameplay in postmodern fiction, particularly for my purpose of foregrounding the affective disorientation that readers are likely to experience when encountering these chaotic textual worlds. Caillois identifies four types of games: *agôn* (foregrounding the competitive dimension of games), *alea* (highlighting the role of chance), *mimicry* (emphasizing the dimension of pretense, which I associate with shifts between positions of the narrative and authorial audience), and *ilinx*—derived from the Greek words for *whirlpool* and *vertigo* (14–26). (I focus only on *mimicry* and *ilinx*, given their relevance to Egan, Calvino, O'Brien, and Gray's textual designs.)

Marie-Laure Ryan identifies Caillois's category of *ilinx* with Mikhail Bakhtin's notion of the *carnivalesque*: as characterized by "chaotic structures, creative anarchy, parody, absurdity, heteroglossia," "transgression of ontological boundaries," and "treatment of identity as a plural, changeable image—in short, the destabilization of all structures"

(Ryan, *Narrative* 186). Caillois defines *ilinx* as games which are "based on the pursuit of vertigo and which consist of an attempt to *momentarily* destroy the stability of perception and inflict a kind of *voluptuous panic* upon an otherwise lucid mind. [. . .] The *disturbance* that provokes vertigo is commonly *sought for its own sake*" (23; emphases added). Examples of such games include roller-coaster rides and bungee jumping. Within the realm of fiction, Ryan observes that "*ilinx* expresses the aesthetics, sensibility, and conception of language of the postmodern age" (*Narrative* 186). Caillois's concept of *ilinx* is invaluable to my study not only because of its relevance for postmodern aesthetics and sensibilities, but more important is its emphasis on the affective dimensions of vertigo: the sensation of "voluptuous panic" in the chaotic yet simultaneously pleasurable disorientation that many readers tend to experience in our encounters with postmodern textual worlds.

I suggest that such cognitive disorientation spurs the form-drive or "formal instinct" into action as readers attempt to comprehend the text by imposing some form of (artificial and/or temporary) "global coherence" in order to restore stability of perception (Schiller, *Aesthetical*, "Letter XII"; Ryan, *Narrative* 223). While classical aesthetics dominantly locates such harmonizing tendencies in the artifact's formal design—as a product of the artist's efforts—postmodern literature modifies or redefines our understanding of contemporary aesthetics by partially displacing the latent energies of coherence, order, and harmony from the artifact/artist to the reader/audience/participant/player. This shift in or shared onus of formal coherence resonates with Roland Barthes's notion of the *writerly*, which likewise promotes the "active and playful participation of the reader in the act of writing" (Ryan, *Narrative* 195–96). Order and coherence are no longer readily perceptible characteristics of the artifact but are in part relocated to readers' consciousness. Postmodern fiction's playful textual designs thus foreground functions of the form-drive in readers' cognitive attempts to manage the complexities of its disorienting worlds.

While the "jarring fragmentation and incoherencies" of postmodern playworlds have their own "stimulating aesthetic (and cognitive) effect," Richard Shusterman points out that the "human need to perceive and experience satisfying unities in the disordered flux of experience" also "motivates our interest in art" (75–77). Italo Calvino's *The*

Castle of Crossed Destinies (1969/1977) plays explicitly with this tension in the patterned sequences of tarot cards that its characters mutely use in attempts to impose a semblance of order on their terrifying encounters. Jennifer Egan's *A Visit from the Goon Squad* (2010; hereafter *Visit*) in turn implicitly invites readers to cohere the polyphony of its thirteen chapters by reassembling the timeline and webs of character relations. Readers vividly experience the novel's form in the same way that Alex experiences its narrative world: as one in which "every intersection brings up another familiar face, old friends and friends of friends, acquaintances, and people who just look familiar" (*Visit* 337). Since *ilinx* is characterized by the pleasurable, *momentary* destruction of stable perceptions, the implication is that coherence-restoring cognitive processes in readers' reconstructions of chronology, relationships, interpretations, and meaning assignments complement the disorienting effects of play.

I now turn my attention to explicating such dynamic interplays between the form- and sense-drives in Egan's and Calvino's work.

A VISIT FROM THE GOON SQUAD

Egan's novel teases the sense-drive in the plurality of narrative styles, focalizations, forms, and tense choice that constitutes its thirteen chapters. Though the first two chapters begin in the past tense with a heterodiegetic narrator, chapter 3 unfolds in the present tense narrated by Rhea—a homodiegetic narrator whose identity remains uncertain to the reader until the fifth paragraph. The jarring shift from past to present tense feels particularly counterintuitive since events in chapter 3 take place almost thirty years *earlier* in relation to the preceding chapters. Time—the *goon squad* to which the novel's title alludes—becomes the central sensuous impulsion for readers and characters alike: Ted and Susan Hollander, for instance, "felt the passage of time [. . .] in the leaping brown water, the scudding boats and wind—motion, chaos everywhere" (*Visit* 240). This sense of chaos that likewise characterizes the sense-drive—which seeks change, destabilization, and open-endedness—is palpable in the novel's dynamic juggling of chronology.

The chronological chaos we encounter in *Visit* arises not simply because of differences between story and discourse—the Genettean distinction between the order in which events occur versus the order in which they are narrated—but is exacerbated by glaringly uneven gaps of time lapses between chapters and by the inconsistent direction of time's arrow. The first four chapters move backward in time—with gaps of one, twenty-seven, and six years between chapters—before leaping forward in chapter 5 and reversing yet again in chapter 6. Readers must rely on limited clues to reconstruct chronology because dates (when they are offered) are given in a circuitous fashion: we infer the first two chapters as being set sometime after 2001, given Sasha's references to the absent Twin Towers (12, 38); we learn that "nineteen eighty is almost here" in chapter 3 (42); and finally we figure out that it is 1973 in chapter 4 when we are told "thirty-five years from now, [it will be the year] 2008" (65).

Time's sensuous impulsions prompt the search for an alternate cognitive anchor in the character relations Egan carefully threads throughout the novel: notwithstanding the chronological chaos of the narrative discourse, readers likely experience a sense of the chapters being in lockstep even as each chapter moves in a new direction. Chapter 10, for instance, assembles characters fleetingly mentioned in preceding chapters, even as it prefigures events to come in the two chapters that follow. Sasha is an NYU college freshman at this point, whose circle of friends includes Rob (chapter 10's narrator who, readers are told early on, drowns in college [15]), Lizzie (from whom Sasha once stole bath salts and years later becomes estranged, as we learn in chapter 1 [17]), and Drew (the boyfriend with whom Sasha will lose touch for a time before eventually marrying him, as we later learn in chapters 11 and 12 [241, 280–81]). Sasha meets Bennie Salazar at a Conduits gig in Pyramid Club (an event referenced in chapter 2 [29] and again later in chapter 12 as a photograph [266]), where the lead guitarist Bosco "fling[s] himself around like a berserk scarecrow" (204)—a description that invokes Bennie's (ex-)wife Stephanie's memory of him as a "demented scarecrow performer" in chapter 7 (138). (See table 1 at the end of this chapter for a summary of such cross-chapter narrative threads.)

Countering the novel's sensuous impulsions via the recourse of ordering story time and character relations in this piecemeal fashion becomes a key game task in which readers engage, as evident from the reviews and critical essays responding to these aspects of Egan's novel. Jessica Jernigan, for instance, notes that we are continually required to revise our notions of characters given the novel's shifting viewpoints: "it's something of a shock—possibly even a gentle rebuke—when a real person emerges" in chapter 7 "to replace the cartoon ex sketched by Bennie" in chapter 2, and to "wonder what it means that awkward social encounters continue to torture him decades after they occurred, yet the various ways in which he betrayed his wife do not figure prominently in his mental universe" (5). Wolfgang Funk similarly remarks that "the reader must piece together the succession of events" and characters' life-stories from such "interconnections" and "hints," since Egan relinquishes "authorial control over the fragmented text in favor of stimulating its readers to (re)create story and plot from the novel's *récit*" (Funk, Gross, and Huber 48, 16).

Olivia Laing observes that although "these sorts of links were rarely visible in real life" before Facebook, "even in our digitally connected age they still have the power to evoke the same half-disturbing gasps of pleasure Egan elicits here" (48). The affective pleasure readers derive from our implicit cognitive reconstructions of *Visit* relates to the form-drive's interest in patterns and structures: neuroscientist V. S. Ramachandran notes that art can "make something more attractive by making it less visible," since keeping these links and relationships between characters and events implicit "leaves something to the imagination" (227). Boyd makes a similar point when he notes that "before a pattern can be desired by the brain, that pattern must play hard to get" (90)—a coyness evident in the circuitous routes readers must take in order to (re)assemble these fragments of information in Egan's novel.

Ramachandran explains that "we prefer this sort of concealment because we are hardwired to love solving puzzles," "resolving ambiguities, testing hypotheses, searching for patterns, and comparing current information with memories and expectations," such that "each time a partial fit is discovered, a small 'Aha!' is generated in your brain. This signal is sent to limbic reward structures, which in turn prompt the search for additional, bigger 'Ahas!,' until the final object or scene crystallizes" (228–29). The novel's gamelike design thus invites readers to participate in a "mode of clairvoyance [that] is not accessible to the characters, who blunder on, preoccupied and baffled, without ever quite realizing the *marvellous patterning* of their lives" (Laing 49; emphasis added). To paraphrase Hogan, it is the reader/participant/

player who derives aesthetic pleasure from such "retrospective pattern recognition" ("Literary" 324), which is palpable in our vivid sense of the chapters being in lockstep despite the novel's sensory chaos—a testament to the sophisticated artistry that underpins Egan's writing.

The novel's Dionysiac energies in its rendering of time may be discerned both in the playful juggling of chronology across chapters and within each individual chapter. It is strongly implied in chapter 4's final subsection, for instance, that eleven-year-old Rolph's seemingly innocuous account of his father's girlfriend Mindy's "rudeness" to their safari guide Albert irrevocably changes the course of the characters' lives. It is initially assumed that Mindy and Lou's "temporary" relationship is "an interlude" (*Visit* 72). In the wake of Rolph's disclosure, however, his sister Charlie/Charlene revises her initial assessment that their father "is tired of Mindy" and remarks, "I think he's going to marry Mindy," when she observes the possessive change in their father's behavior (80, 84). Unlike the youthful Rolph, Lou and the reader recognize Mindy's rudeness as thinly veiled sexual attraction toward Albert and her sudden increase in sexual appetite for Lou as an outlet for that attraction; since "Lou is a man who cannot tolerate defeat [. . .] he'll marry Mindy because that's what winning means" (83–85).

Rolph experiences an intuitive uneasiness at his revelation's yet unseen butterfly effect—"he senses the story landing heavily, in a way he doesn't understand" (82)—which finds confirmation in the narrative prolepsis toward the end of the chapter. As Lou and Mindy dance together that night,

> Mindy is thinking of Albert, as she will periodically after marrying Lou and having two daughters [. . .] in quick succession, as if sprinting against the inevitable drift of his attention. [. . .] For a time her life will be joyless; the girls will seem to cry too much, and she'll think longingly of this trip to Africa as the last happy moment of her life, when she still had a choice, when she was free and unencumbered. She'll dream senselessly, futilely, of Albert, wondering [. . .] how her life would have turned out if she'd run away with him as he'd suggested, half joking, when she visited him in room number three. Later, of course, she'll recognize "Albert" as nothing more than a focus of regret for her own immaturity and disastrous choices. When both her children are in high school, she'll finally resume her

studies, complete her PhD at UCLA, and begin an academic career at forty-five, spending long periods of the next thirty years doing social structures fieldwork in the Brazilian rain forest. (85–86)

In a single paragraph, the story spans sixty years of Mindy's life across three continents: first propelling from the narrative present of twenty-four-year-old Mindy dancing with Lou in Africa, to several years later as a young mother in the US, before cycling back to several days before the narrative present as Mindy recalls her rendezvous with Albert. Mark Currie notes that "the narration of a memory is not quite the same thing as the narration of the past in the sense that it is not the past itself [. . .] but the subjective act of recall" which is the object of narration; however, "the effect is anachronous because of the complex temporal structure of the events being narrated" (36). The narration foregrounds the sensuous impulsions of time, skillfully creating the simultaneous effect of meandering to the past, darting in rapid excursion to an alternate possible future as we imagine how Mindy's life might have turned out had she made different choices, even as time plows forward several decades to forty-five-year-old Mindy working in Brazil till she is eighty-five, before returning to the narrative present of 1973 in Africa.

A more tragic proleptic excursion awaits the reader still as Charlie/Charlene and Rolph dance together this same night, a memory "she'll return to again and again, for the rest of her life, long after Rolph has shot himself in the head in their father's house at twenty-eight" (*Visit* 87). By situating readers at the very moment where things could have spun out differently, the "teleological retrospect" (Currie 33) created by the prolepsis invests everyday events—such as an apparently innocuous conversation between a father and son—with the potential to become life-changing moments. The effect of these proleptic "excursion[s] into a future which is already in place" (33) intensifies our affective sense of the tragedy toward which the characters are inevitably headed, unbeknownst to themselves.

Effects on the sense-drive are also discernible in the dynamic plurality of forms that constitute *Visit*. Its amalgamation of narrative styles includes first-person narration by different characters in chapters 3, 5, and 6; second-person narration in chapter 10, emphasizing the suicidal character-narrator Rob's acute sense of dissociation; and third-person narration in the remaining chapters. Each of the thirteen chapters is dominantly focalized through a different character, which undermines novelistic convention of a protagonist serving as a story's center (see table 1 at the end of this chapter). Such destabilizations make it difficult to determine a character's or an event's initial relevance, since the targets to encode are ever-shifting.

Once readers cognize the pattern of shifting story anchors from chapter to chapter, the authorial audience attends more closely to the text by working against the habituation of reading norms (such as encoding certain characters as being more important than others), since unexpected focalizers may return to surprise us and we can connect these threads only if we recall their initial appearance. As earlier pointed out by Jernigan, Stephanie's appearance in chapter 7 "replace[s] the cartoon ex sketched by Bennie" (5) in chapter 2. Alex's return in the final chapter, after he has completely faded out of sight at the end of chapter 1—likely leading many readers to write him off as Sasha's one-night-stand—produces "aesthetic pleasure" associated with "retrospective pattern recognition" that we derive from such instances of "partial unexpectedness" (Hogan, "Literary" 324). While Sasha and Bennie anchor the novel's ensemble of characters, their identities as protagonists are decentered by Egan's polyphonic narrative style.

Like Sasha's collages, Egan's novel as a whole is assembled out of heterogeneous forms. Chapter 8 incorporates newspaper headlines to gauge the success of a public relations campaign for a genocidal dictator, while chapter 9 employs an extensively annotated and highly self-reflexive celebrity interview to frame the interviewer's attempted rape of a starlet. Chapter 12 is rendered in seventy-six PowerPoint slides, including diagrams, dialogue, and graphs, while chapter 13 incorporates textspeak/textese in the form of T messages and T poems, characterized by dropped vowels, abbreviated text, and so on. "The variety of form," Funk astutely observes, is "representative of Egan's (authentic) narrative approach, i.e. to present human existence as a 'heap of broken stories'" (Funk, Gross, and Huber 49).

Jernigan rightly observes that while PowerPoint has been "much maligned for the way it compels users to reduce complex information to a facile series of sentence fragments," Egan makes the form "sing": "the elisions necessitated by the form become poignant, as these silences echo the inability to communicate that infects the relationships limned in this chapter" (5). For instance, the slide titled "Lincoln Wants to Say/Ends Up Saying" details a seven-step process of association leading from Linc's desire to say "I love you, Dad" to the onrush of analyzing a partial silence at the end of the song, "Fly Like an Eagle" (*Visit* 283). Lincoln's inhibited emotional expression is poignantly rendered as Alison transfigures his enthusiasm for musical pauses into a hidden language of love—one that is bittersweet in his younger sister's ability to clearly discern it but also in their father's inability to decode it. The distance in understanding between Lincoln and Drew is glaringly illustrated in the pointed contrasts between Linc's enthusiastic analyses that crowd entire slides (252, 257, 284, 286) versus Drew's sparing, single-sentence response given in a separate slide framed by volumes of empty space (258, 287)—vividly rendering Drew's sense of helplessness in his inability to connect with his son.

PowerPoint is used with great dynamism in the sensuous impulsions created by the ambiguities of meaning: Martin Moling notes that "the slides allow for multiple readings [since] the bubbles featured on some of them can be read either horizontally or diagonally" (65). Since our brains are efficiently "geared to attach meaning to forms" (Shimamura 64), Alison/Ally's use of framing and visual arrangement allows us to read her candid report of facts in nuanced ways. Using simple shapes of a triangle (as a pivot), a long rectangle (as a beam), and nine text-boxes, her slide "Ways It Can Be When Dad Comes Back" offers an achingly poignant family portrait that reverberates with all that is left unsaid. Four neatly stacked, light-colored text-boxes ("Kissing Mom," "Telling Stories," "Laughing," and "Wine Cork Popping") are outweighed by five dark-colored text-boxes ("Sits in Car before Coming In," "Hugging Mom," "Silent," "Angry," "Gin Pouring"—the first two teetering unsteadily atop the stack). The somber mood created by the dark-colored blocks weighing heavily against the joviality depicted in the light-colored blocks not only reflects the family dynamics but offers readers insight into the unease that twelve-year-old Ally experiences but does not articulate. The distillation of affect created by reducing narration into these fragments invites readers to share more vividly in Ally's emotional life, as the form-drive leads us to explicate structures of affect encoded in her slide journal. Egan's playful textual design continually fosters this dynamic interaction between the form- and sense-drives as readers participate in its covert gameplay.

THE CASTLE OF CROSSED DESTINIES

The Castle of Crossed Destinies, in turn, functions as an overt "game" or "puzzle": Warren Motte describes the novel as "a studied gesture of ludic interchange," where Calvino "exposes his game and invites the reader to play along with him" (Calvino, *Castle* 127; Motte 144–45). Unlike *Visit*, where characters never "quite realiz[e] the marvellous patterning of their lives" (Laing 49), *The Castle of Crossed Destinies* (hereafter *Castle*) visually foregrounds such patterning explicitly in its mapping of the tarot cards illustrated alongside the textual narrative (40, 98).[2] Marilyn Schneider describes "the slim volume [as] a tapestry of European literature" that Calvino has "craftily and ironically snipped and pieced together again with all the seams dazzlingly displayed" (73–74).

Notwithstanding critics' admiration for the originality, beauty, and craft of Calvino's writing, some remain perturbed by aspects of his work which they deem too "brittle," "artificial," "self-absorbed," and perhaps "lacking in human warmth" (Hume, "Calvino's" 71, 80). Constance Markey notes, "Important as the novel was once to its author, *Castle* is not Calvino's most popular novel, and no wonder. Perched combatively on the edge of the metaphysical abyss," "Calvino's darkest novel" is a work "intended to affront reader sensibilities" (105–6). More pointedly, Beno Weiss suggests that "in all frankness Calvino reaches a point of exhaustion with his belabored combinatorial game which borders on self-parody with such an intense virtuoso performance. He overdoes his own card tricks and thereby loses the reader, the ostensible master of this game, whose deciphering codes have been disrupted by a short circuit caused by an excessive surge of energy" (145). Weiss further questions, "Does Calvino succeed with *The Castle of Crossed Destinies*? As a theorist, unequivocally yes; as an artist, alas no" (144).

In the analysis that follows, I suggest that the "game" and "deciphering codes" are a veneer for a different concern underlying Calvino's "card tricks": in the dynamic interplay of energies between the sense- and form-drives, *Castle* offers alternate modes for understand-

---

2. Emma Kafalenos notes that by including the tarot card illustrations alongside the narrator's "ekphrastic responses," readers "recognize the degree to which the narrator supplies the interpretations he offers" and the polysemy of meanings thus constructed (27, 55).

ing art and the world and the way we narrativize those understandings. Despite the novel's "hallucinatory" quality and the "ghostly figures" that haunt its pages (Schneider 73–74), an unexpectedly pedestrian aspect of the human condition underpins characters' muteness and their limited means of using available tarot cards to explain their stories: the notion that narratives of the self are invariably restricted by imperfect communication tools and interpretive subjects, and thus constantly subject to negotiation by others and to (implied) collective narrativization. The homodiegetic narrator's extensive use of the first-person plural pronoun—references to "all of us," "some of us surely thought," and "we sighed in relief at the news given us" (*Castle* 9)—implies or assumes characters' and the narrative audience's shared impressions and/or emotional experience.

Schneider notes that *Castle*'s "many intersecting dramas" featuring "personified abstractions such as *Justice, Fortune,* and *Death* [. . .] are drawn from conventional plots and personae, which Calvino drives to their extremities by extravagant amplification of the raw material" (73). The "psychedelic" effect thus achieved—what Weiss terms *Castle*'s "excessive surge of energy"—is a central quality of *ilinx*, in its momentary disruption of stability and the "voluptuous panic" fostered (Schneider 73; Weiss 145; Caillois 23). In *The Uses of Literature*, Calvino reflects on writing as his process of counteracting an inconstant and ever-changing world: "Faced with the *vertigo* of what is countless, unclassifiable, in a state of flux, I feel reassured by what is finite, 'discrete,' and reduced to a system" (17; emphasis added). Such dynamic interactions of the sense- and form-drives characterizing Calvino's writerly experience of the world are channeled into *Castle*, even as the novel highlights "the unresolved tension [. . .] between the attraction of latent ordering structures and the acknowledgement of the ephemerality and propensity for self-disintegration of any ostensibly stable system" (Cavallaro 102).

Castle's narration gains a dynamic sense of present-ness not only from the homodiegetic narrator's use of the present tense and second-person address, but also from his constant amendments to his own interpretations, drawing readers' attention to the tentative nature of his tales. The narrator notes in "The Surviving Warrior's Tale" that "if you look carefully at that portrait [the Knight of Clubs], you see it also contains elements that correspond to [the warrior's] present appearance: white hair, raving eye, the lance broken, reduced to a stub. Unless it is not a lance stump (especially since he was holding it in his left hand) but a rolled up sheet of parchment" (*Castle* 71–72). Sensuous impulses are engendered by the provisional and plural ways in which tarot cards can be read or understood—an open-endedness facilitated by the narrator's overt admissions to the interpretive and metafictional nature of his tales. In "Two Tales of Seeking and Losing," not only do Faust's and Parsifal's "stories constantly risk stumbling over each other," but the Faustian tale further becomes "mingled with that of Don Juan Tenorio" and "also with that of King Midas" (91–95). Shakespearean tragedies are shuffled with ease in "Three Tales of Madness and Destruction," as Prince Hamlet, Lady Macbeth, and King Lear jointly begin their tales in the tarot card of The Tower and then diverging and meeting again in the cards Hermit, The Stars, and The Chariot, before eventually ending similarly in Death (113–20). *Castle*'s self-reflexive references to its own narrative adulterations foreground the fluidity with which cards, stories, characters, and lives can be shuffled.

The novel posits the notion that chance and design, chaos and order—dynamic tensions between the sense- and form-drives—are merely two sides of the same coin. The narrator notes that "the more the stories become confused and disjointed, the more the scattered cards find their place in an orderly mosaic. Is this pattern only the result of chance, or is one of us patiently putting it together?" (89). Pluralism is *Castle*'s default mode, as the narrator experiences "two contradictory impressions [that] could nevertheless refer to a single object: whether the castle [. . .] had gradually degenerated into an inn [. . .]; or whether a tavern, such as one often sees in the vicinity of castles," had "invaded" a long-abandoned castle (3–4) are presented as equally plausible. In "The Tale of the Ingrate and His Punishment," the Knight of Swords is read "either [as] a mounted messenger" who interrupts the wedding feast, "or the groom himself had abandoned the wedding banquet to hasten, armed, into the woods at some mysterious summons, *or perhaps both things at once*" (10; emphasis added).

Such sensuous possibilities are further played out in the novel's form, which constitutes two sections named "The Castle of Crossed

Destinies" and "The Tavern of Crossed Destinies," though their interrelationship remains unexplained—including details such as whether it is the same Faust we encounter across both sections (17, 91) or the same homodiegetic narrator/writer who reports/interprets tales in both sections. Tarot cards are arranged in fairly linear sequences in "Castle," but such visual patterns are disrupted in "Tavern," which likewise attempts but ultimately fails to adhere to a coherent order as characters "snatch the cards away from one another," "scatter[ing] them over the table" (53; see table 2 at the end of this chapter for a cross-comparison). Even within the orderly progression of tales in "Castle," Calvino continually varies patterns established: the grave robber, for example, does "not simply confine himself to adding one tarot to another"—as the ingrate and alchemist do in their tales preceding his—but proceeds instead "with pairs of flanking cards, in a double horizontal row" (26). Such pattern disruptions and repatternings tease the form-drive by playing with readerly expectations, which (to paraphrase Boyd) are just as easily satisfied, overturned, or revised in subsequent tales.

Sensuous impulsions are exacerbated by textual contradictions that are presented as non-mutually exclusive: readers learn in chapter 8 that "as Astolpho began to recount his adventure," Helen of Troy "was already placing at his path's destination *The Hermit* [. . .] because that is precisely how her story began" (41). However, this contradicts the account in the previous chapter, where we are told that, having been charged with the difficult task of restoring Roland's reason, "What was Astolpho to do? He had a good card up his sleeve, the Arcanum known as *The Hermit*" (37). The apparent order painstakingly established in the preceding chapters is thus rendered moot, as we learn midway into the novel that stories proceed simultaneously and such logical inconsistencies are a default mode of *Castle*'s storyworld.

The sense-drive's impulse to imaginatively "seek, shape, and share information" (Boyd 14) in open-ended ways underpins *Castle*, where

> each story runs into another story, and as one guest is advancing his strip, another, from the other end, advances in the opposite direction, because the stories told from left to right or from bottom to top can also be read from right to left or from top to bottom, and vice versa, bearing in mind that the same cards, presented in a different

order, often change their meaning, and the same tarot is used at the same time by narrators who set forth from the four cardinal points. (*Castle* 41)[3]

The novel thus enacts a consistent ambiguity in its sequential fluidity, plurality of interpretations, and interchangeability of its characters' stories. Neurobiologist Semir Zeki posits that ambiguity—which I associate with workings of the sense-drive—has neural and evolutionary bases.

Using the optical illusion of the Kanizsa cube to illustrate his point, Zeki notes that "what appears to be the front (i.e. towards the observer) can spontaneously change position and occupy a rear position away from the observer, and vice versa. Here, then, is an example of a lability or instability in the brain's response to a physically unchanging stimulus," where the brain "project[s] its own apparently unstable operation onto the stable physical stimulus" (*Splendors* 61).[4] Crucially, Zeki points out that "the brain does not have much choice in the multi-interpretations that its organization makes possible. *The ambiguity, in other words, is stable*" and, "in a sense, an inherited brain concept" (85). This "neurological definition of ambiguity [...] differ[s] from common dictionary definitions" in that "it is not vagueness or uncertainty, but rather certainty, the certainty of different scenarios" with "equal validity" (88), which Calvino renders artistically in *Castle*. By playing with the tensions between patterned forms and textual features emphasizing sensuous fluidity and multiplicity, Calvino offers this stable ambigu-

---

3. Even at the level of individual tales, each time Faust and Parsifal "retrac[e] their routes, card after card, on the table of the tavern [...], their story reads another way, undergoes corrections, variants, affected by the moods of the day and the train of thoughts" (*Castle* 96–97).

4. Zeki notes that "stimuli that are capable of being interpreted by the brain in more than one way" tend to "engage higher cortical areas in the frontal and parietal lobes of the brain" (*Splendors* 62). "Why the brain should have developed such a system [to project its own unstable operation onto stable stimuli] is not immediately clear but is very likely to be due to the fact that some, indeed many, stimuli in the world can be deceptive in the sense that they can be given more than one interpretation. If the brain did not have the capacity to project more than one interpretation onto the stimulus, it may find itself in a dangerous situation. [...] Better for the brain to entertain several possibilities and thus protect itself" (61).

ity—rather than absoluteness—as a (default) mode for understanding the/our world.

While *Visit* challenges readers to accurately encode targets in its dynamic amalgamation of shifting focalizers and narrative styles, *Castle* figuratively illustrates neural mechanisms of target-encoding by foregrounding the narrator's processes of selecting, structuring, and assigning meaning to the tarot cards. Calvino explains in *Castle*'s endnote that "this book is made first of pictures—the tarot playing cards—and secondly of written words. Through the sequence of the pictures stories are told, which the written word tries to reconstruct and interpret" (123). Visually representing these cards alongside the text not only challenges readers to the game task of assessing the narrator's reconstructions—in terms of their plausibility, aesthetic merit, and so on—but also invites us to come to our own interpretations,[5] which may contradict, resist, or subvert the accompanying textual narrative.

The sensuous impulsions of indirection, open-endedness, and generativity that characterize *Castle* are thus emblematic of the process by which we experience art: "In and through art, we readily turn the actual around within the much larger space of the possible, the conditional, and the impossible" (Boyd 124). Contrary to Weiss's assessment that Calvino succeeds as a theorist but fails as an artist with *Castle* because he "loses the reader, the ostensible master of this game, whose deciphering codes" are disrupted by the novel's "excessive surge of energy" (144), I argue that these energies work precisely to destabilize the very notion that there can be a master of the game and Calvino succeeds as an artist precisely by giving us a storyworld that channels his idiosyncratic vision of how provisional our understandings are for navigating the world which is constantly in flux. Notwithstanding the imperfect and limited tools with which we communicate and reach out to one another, our intersecting stories are the rich fabric from which the tapestries of human lives are fashioned. To paraphrase Boyd, "Art

---

5. JoAnn Cannon makes a similar point with recourse to Jonathan Culler, noting that "interpretation is not a matter of recovering some meaning which lies behind the work and serves as a centre governing its structure; it is rather an attempt to participate in and observe the play of possible meanings to which the text gives access" (Culler, *Structuralist Poetics* 247; qtd. in Cannon 90). Gretchen Busl remarks that "no text can ever completely be exhausted of meaning because it will always have new eyes to read it. Calvino places the responsibility of assigning meaning on the reader" (811).

develops us in [such] habits of imaginative exploration, so that we take the world as not closed and given" in the physically unchanging stimuli of the tarot cards, "but open and to be shaped on our own terms" (124) in the interpretive multiplicity of stories that emerge from them.

TRANSITIONS: BETWEEN MODES OF PLAY

Theorists posit that contemporary play culture "demand[s] the critic who will function as *magister ludi*" (Detweiler 62; see also Weiss 145). However, I argue that postmodernism's spirit of plurality decries the very notion of a singular or absolute master of the game; rather, the fragmented storyworlds that characterize postmodern fiction resist mastery in favor of offering imaginative explorations in cognitive play. The next chapter continues to explore such issues of literary play through the lens of possible worlds theory; like *Castle* and *Visit*, the case studies in chapter 2 fall within the aesthetic category of play but emphasize instead "the notion of world as a source of aesthetic experience in narrative texts" (Bell and Ryan, *Possible Worlds*). Since postmodern fiction's tangled textual worlds tend not to be given but are gradually uncovered during the process of reading/play, "by fostering our inclination to think about possible worlds, art allows us to see the actual world from new vantage points" in its playful "creation of other symbolic worlds" (Boyd 124; Waugh 34). How we navigate these worlds and their ontological challenges is the issue to which I now turn.

TABLE 1. Cross-chapter relations in *A Visit from the Goon Squad*

SECTION/ CHAPTER	NARRATIVE PRESENT	FOCALIZER	NARRATIVE THREADS
A1	2007	Sasha	Chapter 1 prefigures "The Gold Cure" of chapter 2, where readers learn that Bennie "sprinkled gold flakes into his coffee" and "sprayed pesticide in his armpits" (Egan 5)—the reasons for which are explicated in chapter 2.
A2	2006	Bennie	Chapter 2 notes "the rapturous surges of sixteen-year-old-ness" that punk rock induces in Bennie, reminding him of "his high school gang—Scotty and Alice, Jocelyn and Rhea" (24), whom we meet in chapter 3.
A3	1979	Rhea	Chapter 3 references Jocelyn and Rhea poring over a picture of Lou's children, Charlie and Rolph. They listen to his account of "being on a train in Africa that didn't completely stop at the stations" (53), which we learn in chapter 4 was on its way to Mombasa.
A4	1973	Rolph	Chapter 4 ends with eleven-year-old Rolph dancing with Charlie and the proleptic image of Rolph shooting "himself in the head in their father's house at twenty-eight" (87)—the same house in which chapter 5 begins.
A5	2005	Jocelyn	Chapter 5 weaves together characters from the two preceding chapters and picks up sometime after the end of chapter 3 to explicate Jocelyn and Rolph's relationship.
A6	1997	Scotty	Chapter 6 picks up on threads left trailing in earlier chapters, detailing the "disturbing encounter" (24) between Scotty and Bennie referenced in chapter 2 and explicating how Scotty and Alice's relationship from chapter 3 eventually ends in a failed four-year marriage (60, 107).
B7	2003–2004	Stephanie	Chapter 7 explicates the events leading from Bennie and Stephanie's marriage with a newborn son in chapter 6 to the cause of their divorce referenced in chapter 2. Stephanie's relationships with her boss and her brother prefigure chapters 8 and 9.
B8	2008	Dolly	Chapter 8 explicates an event fleetingly mentioned in chapter 2—La Doll/Dolly's party, which turned into a debacle, landing her in jail (23, 149–51)—leading to her present desperate circumstances, working as a publicist for a genocidal dictator. We meet Dolly's nine-year-old daughter Lulu and the "washed-up female star" Kitty Jackson—whom Dolly hires for her PR stint (152).

B9	1999	Jules	Chapter 9 details Stephanie's brother Jules's attempted rape of Kitty, mentioned in chapters 7 and 8.
B10	1993	Rob	Chapter 10 depicts Sasha's circle of friends, including Rob and Lizzie (mentioned in chapter 1) and Drew (who reappears in chapter 12). Sasha meets Bennie at an event referenced in chapters 2 and 12, where the lead guitarist Bosco is described as "a berserk scarecrow" (204)—invoking Stephanie's memory of him as a "demented scarecrow performer" in chapter 7 (138).
B11	1991	Ted	Chapter 11 explicates Sasha's father's disappearance (noted in chapter 1 [9]) and her time as a runaway in Naples (noted in chapter 10 [199–200]). It also prefigures chapter 12, where she lives in "the California desert" more than twenty years later, after "reconnect[ing] on Facebook with her college boyfriend" (whom we learn in the next chapter is Drew from chapter 10), with whom she has two kids, "one of whom was slightly autistic" (241).
B12	202–	Alison	Chapter 12 picks up the prolepsis from the end of chapter 11 and partially resolves questions left hanging in chapters 7 and 10: Jules, who is given exclusive rights to cover Bosco's suicide tour (137–38) returns to writing, and Bosco does not die but "ends up recovering and owning a dairy farm" (265). Rob's drowning in chapter 10 spurs Drew to become a doctor (280).
B13	2022	Alex	Chapter 13 is partly driven by Bennie and Scotty's musical collaboration once more, following their fallout in chapter 3 and brief reunion in chapter 6. Nine-year-old Lulu in chapter 8 is identified with Lulu in her twenties here when she mentions her parentage (325, 329). Lulu's fiancé Joe's appearance (346) connects them to the brief proleptic mention in chapter 4: "He and Lulu will buy a loft in Tribeca," where the warrior for whom Charlie once danced in Africa—Joe's grandfather—will have his hunting dagger displayed in their home (65). Sasha, as the indirect link between Alex and Bennie in the first chapter, is foregrounded by her absence, where her prophetic sense of someday becoming "a glint in [Alex's] hazy memories" (14, 318–49) comes to pass.

TABLE 2. Visual cross-comparison of the order in which tarot cards are placed in the first tale from "The Castle of Crossed Destinies" (left) versus "The Tavern of Crossed Destinies" (right)

CASTLE OF CROSSED DESTINIES		TAVERN OF CROSSED DESTINIES			
01 Knight of Cups					
11 Empress	02 King of Coins				
12 Eight of Cups	03 Ten of Coins	1.01 Knight of Cups	1.02 Ten of Clubs	1.03 Eight of Cups	
13 Knight of Swords	04 Nine of Clubs			1.04 Love/Lover(s)	1.05 The Chariot
14 The Sun	05 Strength/Force		1.29 Nine of Coins	1.18 Five of Cups	
15 Justice	06 Hanged Man	1.27 Six of Swords	1.31 Knight of Coins	1.19 The Stars	1.20 The Moon
16 Two of Swords	07 Temperance				
17 Popess	08 Ace of Cups		1.26 Judgment		
18 Eight of Swords	09 Two of Cups				
	10 Seven of Clubs		1.28 Seven of Cups		

TAVERN OF CROSSED DESTINIES (CONTINUED)

1.07 Page of Coins	1.08 Ace of Coins	1.15 Justice	1.17 Queen of Cups		
1.06 Two of Clubs	1.10 Ace of Clubs		1.14 Two of Cups		
1.12 Ace of Cups	1.11 The Sun	1.13 Empress	1.16 Queen of Swords	1.30 Six of Clubs	
	1.24 The World	1.23 Hanged Man			
1.25 The Wheel	1.22 The Devil	1.09 Five of Clubs			
1.21 The Tower					

CHAPTER 2

Play (II)

Postmodern Play with Possible Worlds

POSTMODERN FICTION typically instantiates an aesthetics of play in which ontological questions about the sorts of worlds characters inhabit, and the ways in which readers orient to these worlds constitute a central readerly concern. Brian McHale notes that unlike modernist fiction's preoccupation with epistemological issues, "the dominant of postmodernist fiction is *ontological*" whereby questions such as "What is a world?" "What kinds of worlds are there, how are they constituted, and how do they differ?" are brought to the fore (*Postmodernist* 10). I contend that the cognitive disorientation readers tend to experience in our encounters with postmodern textual worlds spurs the form-drive into action, in our attempts to facilitate textual comprehension by imposing some form of (artificial and/or temporary) coherence. While classical aesthetics dominantly locates such harmonizing tendencies in the artifact's formal design—as a product of the artist's efforts—postmodern literature modifies our understanding of

---

A portion of this chapter was previously published in Wang (2019), "Postmodern Play with Worlds: The Case of *At Swim-Two-Birds*," in Alice Bell and Marie-Laure Ryan (eds.), *Possible Worlds Theory and Contemporary Narratology* (pp. 132–56), University of Nebraska Press.

contemporary aesthetics by partially displacing the latent energies of coherence, order, and harmony from the artifact/artist to the reader/perceiver/participant/player.

In this chapter, I use Flann O'Brien's *At Swim-Two-Birds* (hereafter *Two-Birds*) and Alasdair Gray's *Lanark: A Life in Four Books* (hereafter *Lanark*) as case studies to explain how the possible worlds approach serves as a useful apparatus for capturing readers' cognitive attempts at managing the complexities of postmodern fiction's disorienting textual worlds. Just as the human auditory cortex uses "its short-term memory for sound (in the left posterior hemisphere) to uncover patterns" and "extract *order*" when noise exceeds our processing abilities (Lehrer 130), I posit that the form-drive's impulse toward order and pattern discernment is likely to have similar neural bases in readers' processing of chaotic postmodern fictional worlds. By explicating the dynamic tensions at play between the form- and sense-drives in both novels, I suggest that navigating their labyrinthine landscapes—as readers attempt to disentangle and make cognitive sense of their fictional worlds in order to deal with the ontological challenges they pose—is part of the gameplay that postmodern novelists implicitly invite us to participate in. My adoption of the possible worlds and other narratological models is thus subsumed under my larger project of explaining the aesthetics of play that characterizes much of postmodern and contemporary fiction.

POSSIBLE WORLDS THEORY

Marie-Laure Ryan's account of possible worlds theory designates *reality* as a universe that is "the sum of the imaginable," with the *actual world* (AW) at the center of its system ("Possible" 446). Theorists like David Lewis and Nicholas Rescher have further debated and finessed the concept, but for my purpose, the AW simply refers to the world we live in, inhabited by real authors and real readers, including the late Brian O'Nolan (better known by his pseudonym, Flann O'Brien), Alasdair Gray, and readers of *Two-Birds* and *Lanark*. All other satellite worlds are "the product of a mental activity, such as dreaming, imagining, foretelling, promising, or storytelling" (Ryan, "Possible" 446–47). Ryan explains that "there is only one *actually* actual world [AW], but there is an infinity of potentially *pretended* actual worlds" (*Possible* 24). Known as the *textual actual world* (TAW), fictional texts determine their "own horizons of possibilities" by giving "imaginative existence to worlds, objects, and states of affairs" ("Possible" 447). Through the process of fictional recentering, readers "become *in make-believe* temporary members of the recentered system"—that is, part of the narrative audience—as we shift our attention from the AW to the TAW (*Possible* 26; emphasis added).

My use of Ryan's possible worlds model entails a crucial revision to its default reliance on "the principle of minimal departure," which states that "when readers construct fictional worlds, they fill in the gaps in the text by assuming the similarity of the fictional world to their own experiential reality. This model can only be overruled by the text itself" (*Possible* 51; "Possible" 447).[1] Scholars who dispute aspects of the minimal departure principle include Lubomír Doležel, who argues that the principle's assumption of "ontologically complete" fictional worlds is problematic, because "incompleteness [is] the distinctive feature of fictional existence. He argues that by filling the gaps, the reader would reduce the ontological diversity found in fictional worlds to a uniform structure" ("Possible" 447). The other objection comes from Thomas Pavel, who suggests that when "confronted with radical oddities," readers are likely instead to anticipate "'maximal departure' from the real world" (93)—in other words, we expect the emancipatory energies of the sense-drive to be at full play. If minimal departure relies on a default assumption of the fictional world's similarity to our own experiential reality, I propose that maximal departure proceeds from readerly expectations that such real-world frames are repurposed, reconfigured, and retooled as building blocks of the fictional universe. Under the principle of maximal departure, the fantastic, strange, and nonsensical (to borrow from J. R. R. Tolkien) are not anomalous, but default modes of the fictional world.

---

1. Experiential reality refers not only to readers' first-hand knowledge and experience of the actual world (AW), but also to various forms of textual knowledge—fictional or otherwise—that we use as frames of reference in the AW (Ryan, *Possible* 54). Thus, depending on each individual's experience, knowledge, and "literary competence" (Culler 101), readers' sense of what departs from experiential reality will vary.

To address these challenges raised by Doležel and Pavel, I propose two revisions to the possible worlds model that are designed to accommodate the ontological difficulties posed by postmodern and contemporary fiction. First, I suggest that three factors mediate accessibility relations that readers use to determine the shape and nature of these postmodern textual worlds. Second, I posit that when readers are faced with ambiguous (and therefore multiple) ways of regarding the configuration of particular textual worlds, they tend to approximate the TAW and its satellite worlds in ways that "enhance the reading experience," thereby maximizing the work's interpretive power (Phelan, "Implausibilities" 175). I use these analytic frameworks to help explain the functional purpose of some of postmodern fiction's difficulties—in terms of their effects on the experience of reading as a form of participatory gameplay—and to explore possible strategies that readers intuit or undertake in coping with the challenges posed by such texts.

My revision to Ryan's model proposes that three types of textual cues mediate our beliefs/knowledge about the distance/proximity between the *actual world* (AW) and the *textual actual world* (TAW), and of the TAW from its *textual alternate possible worlds* (TAPWs):

1. At which point or how far into the narrative do departures take place?
2. How frequently do we encounter departures?
3. What is the qualitative nature of these departures?

I use the word *departures* in reference to Ryan's "accessibility relations"—qualities we use to determine the relevance of assuming that principles operating in the AW will continue to operate in the TAW (*Possible* 32). The criteria of comparison in "decreasing order of stringency" include (1) "identity of properties," (2) "identity of inventory," (3) "compatibility of inventory," (4) "chronological compatibility," (5) "physical compatibility," (6) "taxonomic compatibility," (7) "logical compatibility," (8) "analytical compatibility," and (9) "linguistic compatibility" (Ryan, *Possible* 32–33). The qualitative nature of departures relates both to how explicitly such departures are signaled in the text and to the perceived degree of estrangement: the lower its position on Ryan's list of accessibility relations, the more readers are likely to regard such deviations as radical.

I propose that the position, frequency, and nature of the textual universe's departures from the AW determine whether readers are likely to adopt the principle of minimal or maximal departure. In general, readers likely assume *minimal* departure the *later* a deviation occurs, the *fewer* the number of departures, the more *implicit* authors are about them (such that readers likely fail to observe their occurrence), and/or the *less radical* the nature of these departures. Conversely, readers likely assume *maximal* departure the *sooner* we notice deviations from the AW, the more *frequently* we observe them, the more *explicitly* authors signal them, and/or the more *radical* the nature of these departures. Furthermore, indeterminacy or "undecidable relations"—such as "when epistemic access to these facts is denied" (39)—is also likely to facilitate the principle of maximal departure. I suggest that readers remain engaged in discerning accessibility relations even in textual worlds that cue maximal departure, since it is a pertinent cognitive act that gives us traction for gaining a foothold (however slippery and tentative) in these fictional worlds.

Kendall Walton likens "fiction to a game of make-believe," whereby readers "participate in fictional happenings by projecting a fictional ego who attends the imaginary events" (Ryan, *Possible* 23; Pavel 85)—that is, by becoming part of the narrative audience. Having sent their fictional egos out to inhabit these worlds for a time, readers may come to hope that playing in or with these textual worlds will somehow help enrich our lives. As Pavel puts it, "Schiller's hopes for a betterment of humanity through aesthetic education" were "based on the presumption that after their return from travel in the realms of art, fictional egos would effectively melt back into the actual egos, sharing with them their fictional growth" (85). Richard Gerrig's model of "transportation" (as outlined in his *Experiencing Narrative Worlds*) makes a similar point about being transformed by the experience of engaging with fictional narratives.

Though critics like Suzanne Keen rightly caution against making overreaching claims for fiction's efficacy in transforming behavior—given that "scant evidence" exists for making active connections between reading and real-world altruistic action—Keen nonetheless points affirmatively to fiction's *potential* for such transformations (4, 146–47). My revisions to Ryan's model ultimately work to incorporate this dimension of the fictional ego's potentially transformational experience: first, by positing the reader as co-constructor of textual worlds engaged in literary gameplay, and second, by showing how textual cues such as position, frequency, and the qualitative nature of departures mediate readers' sense of the distance/proximity of these worlds from our own.

AT SWIM-TWO-BIRDS

Though the "Irish comic tradition" has been well established since "approximately the ninth century down to the present day" (Mercier vii), its associated quality of play is a distinct historical and aesthetic project of twentieth-century postmodern fiction—a project in which O'Brien was perhaps a little too far ahead of the curve. The first edition of *Two-Birds* (1939), O'Brien's first novel, "sold only 244 copies before Longmans' London warehouse was destroyed" during World War II, following which the novel "sank into obscurity for over twenty years" (Murphy and Hopper 10). However, this also meant that *Two-Birds* was a perfect fit with the moment of its re-issue and the new edition met with "critical acclaim" in 1960 (Donohue xxx), as experimental postmodern writing was gaining momentum in Europe and the Americas.[2]

Consider the amount of critical effort that has been expended in attempts to offer a comprehensible structure of the novel. Thomas Shea observes, "From the beginning, we assume that [the characters] Finn, Furriskey, and The Pooka exist adjacent to one another [. . .]. Not until the fifth autobiographical reminiscence do we find that Finn has been 'demoted' a level, serving as a character of Dermot Trellis who is himself a character of the undergraduate. Once we think we have it settled, however, our quandary begins anew" (58). David Herman describes the novel as a "baroquely hypodiegetic narrative," with characters like Orlick Trellis, whose "diegetically unstable status" allows him to "metaleptically migrate to a frame positioned somewhere between O'Brien's narrator and Dermot Trellis" (136–39). Shea notes that "critics often

---

2. The publication history of O'Brien's *The Third Policeman* was similarly circuitous, when the author "pretended to have lost the manuscript" after its initial rejection by his publishers in 1940 and the novel "remained unpublished until 1967, a year after his death" (Murphy and Hopper 11)—emerging at the height of postmodernism, more than two decades after it was written.

struggle to impose thematic shape onto *At Swim*" (74), and the very tentativeness of the language used (e.g., "struggle," "quandary," and "somewhere between") evinces the difficulties scholars and readers have faced in navigating the text's ontological challenges.

My adaptation of the possible worlds approach makes it possible to untangle some of these navigational nightmares, giving us a sense of how readers possibly handle *Two-Birds*'s ontological challenges. With reference to table 3 at the end of this chapter, the *textual actual world* (TAW) is inhabited by the student-narrator and his family and friends. TAPW 1 refers to the dominant *textual alternate possible world* inhabited by Dermot Trellis and his fellow authors, as well as their created and hired characters. Embedded within TAPW 1 are at least two *textual alternate possible subworlds,* TAPsW 1.1 (characterized by Finn Mac-Cool's imaginings) and TAPsW 1.2 (characterized by events that occur in Orlick Trellis's manuscript). TAPW 2 refers to a minor *textual alternate possible world* as characterized by the events of William Falconer's epic poem, "The Shipwreck." By explicating the configuration of textual worlds in *Two-Birds* with reference to the position, frequency, and nature of their departures from the AW, I focus on moments that cue fictional recentering to show how a possible worlds approach allows us to account for some of the novel's difficulties in terms of their effects on the reading experience.

Readers are cued to approach the TAW using the principle of minimal departure, since it is characterized by few departures from the AW, none of which is radical, such that readers can readily adopt the belief that the homodiegetic student-narrator plausibly lived in Dublin, Ireland, of the AW at some point, without any great leaps of imagination.[3] TAPW 1, on the other hand, is characterized by frequent and radical departures from the AW and TAW: readers learn early on that Dermot Trellis—a product of the TAW student-narrator's story and hence of TAPW 1—buys "a ream of ruled foolscap and is starting on his story. He is compelling all his characters to live with him in the Red Swan Hotel so that he can keep an eye on them" (O'Brien, *Two-Birds* 31). Readers are thus directed to approach TAPW 1 using the principle of maximal departure, since we are explicitly cued early on to make a rad-

---

3. I focus on explicating the relationships between worlds in this chapter; for a comprehensive discussion of *Two-Birds*'s textual universe, see my chapter in Bell and Ryan's (eds.) *Possible Worlds Theory and Contemporary Narratology.*

ical break with the AW. Furthermore, the comic intent of such radical departures—of a dictatorial author sharing his characters' physical space for surveillance purposes—prompts readers to take a playful attitude towards TAPW 1.

Such logical incompatibilities (in relation to the AW and TAW) are ad hoc features of TAPW 1 that are continually foregrounded: Dermot, for instance, sexually assaults his fictional creation, who later gives birth to a son, Orlick Trellis (58, 142–43). Furthermore, like the character John Furriskey, Orlick is born into TAPW 1 as a fully grown man rather than a baby, through the process of "aestho-autogamy" (36–37, 142–43). To compound the challenges readers face in cognitively processing TAPW 1, its inhabitants are not fully fleshed out early in the narrative discourse: consider the Good Fairy, who enters only midway through the novel, significantly modifying our existing mental model of TAPW 1, which has thus far largely been confined to the Red Swan Hotel and its inhabitants. The possible worlds approach allows readers to trace patterns in the novel's configuration of narrative worlds, where part of the reader's game task is to figure out who belongs (and how) to which world—an issue to which I return shortly.

The effect of creating a TAW that is very similar to readers' sense of AW reality (i.e., as a buffer between the AW and TAPW 1) is that it prevents us from simplistically reading—or, worse still, dismissing—*Two-Birds* as pure fantasy. By juxtaposing these worlds that operate on different principles within the same textual universe, O'Brien foregrounds issues of metafictionality by preserving the strange and wonderful texture of TAPW 1 (operating on maximal departure) alongside overt confrontations about the nature of fiction writing thus raised in the TAW (operating on minimal departure). O'Brien further problematizes the very idea of a fictional "center" by displacing its centrality altogether; most of the novel's action, so to speak, occurs not in the TAW, but in TAPW 1 and TAPsW 1.2.

TAPW 1's inhabitants include author figures (Dermot Trellis, William Tracy, Henderson, the poet Jem Casey, and an unnamed "Belgian author" [99]), created characters (Trellis creates Furriskey, Peggy, Sheila Lamont, and the Pooka, while Tracy creates Shanahan, Slug, Shorty, and the Red Indians—some of whom Trellis borrows), "hired" characters (Antony Lamont of unknown origin and Finn MacCool from Celtic mythology [57–58]), at least one begotten character (Orlick

Trellis), familiar figures from Celtic folk and fairy lore (the Good Fairy and Sweeny), and Teresa of the Red Swan Hotel.

This eclectic configuration of characters that constitute TAPW 1 comically stages O'Brien's "irritation" with Ireland's intellectual environment of his time (Taaffe 27–28). Published in 1939, *Two-Birds* was composed during a period of volatile cultural and political change, as an increasingly independent Ireland moved from the formation of the Irish Free State to the establishment of its own Constitution in 1937. Carol Taaffe notes that though O'Brien was "disdainful of modernism's elitism, he was also nevertheless ambivalent in his attitude to the populism extolled by Gaelic Revivalists and other cultural nationalists" (3). This "impatience with all forms of literary pomposity" (31) is playfully invoked in *Two-Birds* when Finn MacCool's recitations of Celtic lays and ballads are constantly interrupted by Shanahan's complaints ("bloody blather" being one of his choice responses) that the old Irish lays fail to account for "the man in the street" like himself (9–16, 69–82).

O'Brien's response was finally to playfully parody all of these attitudes, by situating this diverse "rag-bag" of characters and "incongruous styles" (Taaffe 40) in TAPW 1—a world operating on the principle of maximal departure, characterized by frequent and radical departures from the AW he was irreverently responding to. O'Brien's decision to situate these characters and their corresponding voices—a parody of the inherent conflict that characterized Ireland's intellectual environment at the time—in a textual world twice-removed from AW reality implies how far removed such polemical attitudes were to the fruitful development of a rich, independent Irish culture.

Though I situate Finn MacCool in TAPW 1, what we are to make of the character remains critically disputed. Readers are explicitly told from the beginning that "Finn MacCool was a legendary hero of old Ireland," who was subsequently "hired by Trellis [. . .] to act as [Peggy's] father" (*Two-Birds* 5, 57). Finn, however, turns out to be an abusive cad of an adoptive father, since Peggy's "virtue has already been assailed" by him a quarter way into the novel (57). Some critics are inclined to delineate two different Finns in *Two-Birds*: one being the cadlike adoptive father and the other being the legendary Irish giant who recites Celtic lays and ballads. However, using my revision of the possible worlds model based on mediated accessibility relations, I suggest that we are dealing with the same Finn in both cases (excepting the judge/jury member "F. MacCool" [193], who indeed belongs to a different textual world—a point to which I will return). Debates as to whether the tale about Finn MacCool is "part of the Trellis book" or "a 'book' in its own right" (Imhof 168) remain unresolved in critical scholarship. Compounding the confusion is the fact that the Finn mythology exists in the AW—and, by the principle of minimal departure, we take it to exist in the TAW as well—leading readers to wonder if Finn's narrative possibly warrants a new TAPW of its own, like the narrated events from William Falconer's poem, "The Shipwreck."[4]

The difficulties entailed in delineating TAPW 1 from its subworlds are thus aggravated by the readerly confusion perpetuated in O'Brien's play with *homonymy* ("a proper name borne by two different characters") and *transworld identity* (a character's "identity across possible worlds") (Ryan, *Narrative* 232; Ryan, *Possible* 52; Bell and Alber 171; Mackie and Jago, "Transworld Identity"). O'Brien's playful use of naming functions facilitates a chaotic sensory overdrive, which readers in turn respond to by establishing some form of provisional order so as to keep pace with the onrush of narrative developments. Akin to the way human minds respond to "the onrush of noise"—where our inability to "decipher all the different sound waves" leads the brain to "stop[ ] trying to understand the individual notes and seek[ ] instead to understand the relationships *between* the notes" (Lehrer 130)—our order-obsessed brains likely sort through the chaos of O'Brien's novel by discerning relationships between worlds and characters. The Pooka's account of "one of the old Irish sagas" (*Two-Birds* 138) ultimately allows readers to pin Finn to TAPW 1.

As the Pooka and other characters await the birth of Orlick Trellis at the Red Swan Hotel, the Pooka relates having "played a small part" in "the old story about Dermot and Granya" a "long time ago" (138–42). The old story to which the Pooka refers—"The Pursuit of Diarmuid and Gráinne" (original Celtic forms of the anglicized names Dermot and Granya)—is a well-known tale from the Fenian cycle of Celtic mythology, a series of narratives centered on Finn MacCool, wherein

---

4. Readers are cued to consider narrated events from Falconer's poem as a satellite world of the TAW (rather than of TAPW 1), because we are explicitly told that this is a poem that the student-narrator peruses in "a volume [he took] from the mantelpiece" (*Two-Birds* 207, 209–10).

Granya rejects her betrothal to the aged Finn and elopes with one of his warriors named Dermot. In *Two-Birds*, the Pooka relates meeting Dermot and Granya during their time on the run; readers are thus cued to treat the Finn narrative as events that happened at an earlier time in TAPW 1, such that AW myth is transposed into TAPW 1 history.[5] When the mythological in the AW is made historical in TAPW 1, readers are correspondingly prompted to consider the potentially "mythic" dimensions of historical accounts rendered in our own AW— not in order to negate the existence/reality of events that did occur in the AW past, to paraphrase Waugh, but to foreground the difficulties of comprehensively rendering accurate accounts of those events, or what we call "history." To simply treat the Finn narrative as a separate TAPW would be to miss such nuances.

Two-Birds features at least two subworlds that are satellites of TAPW 1. Though the mythologies Finn narrates (first his own and later Sweeny's) belong to the "historical fabric" of TAPW 1, I suggest that the companions who prompt Finn to relate his story at the beginning of *Two-Birds* belong to the subworld TAPsW 1.1—which I identify as part of Finn's imaginings. Finn's recitation begins and then stalls repeatedly, even as Conán, Diarmuid Donn, Caolcrodha Mac Morna, Liagan Luaimneach O Luachair Dheaghaidh, and Gearr mac Aonchearda in turn urge him on (9–16). Like Finn, all five characters are adapted from the Fenian cycle of Celtic mythology, but several textual cues suggest that Finn's interactions with these characters exist only in his own mind. For instance, Adrian Oțoiu notes that Finn "seems to have [. . .] lost his eye-sight, or to be sitting in complete darkness," as he addresses his "invisible" companions (295–96). Furthermore, Conán, who initially instigates Finn to tell these stories, is later revealed as "hidden Conán" (*Two-Birds* 12, 60).

We encounter Conán once more when Finn, Furriskey, Lamont, and Shanahan are gathered in a room after Dermot has fallen asleep: "Relate,

---

5. Crucially, the figure of Finn MacCool has repeatedly weaved back and forth between the pages of AW Celtic myth and history: "originally a mythological figure [. . .] confined in the learned lore of the eighth, ninth and tenth centuries," Finn was then believed to be a historical figure by eleventh-century chroniclers, only to be displaced yet again "to the realm of mythology" by later historians (Ó Háinle 15; Oțoiu 302). O'Brien reverses this displacement in *Two-Birds* by transposing myth into (fictional) history once more, insistently exposing the porous frontiers between both genres.

said hidden Conán, the tale of the Feasting of Dún na nGedh. Finn *in his mind* was nestling with his people" (60; emphasis added). Even though Conán's remarks are interspersed with Furriskey's, Lamont's, and Shanahan's comments, Conán remains ontologically distinct from TAPW 1 and likely exists only in Finn's mind since the other three characters do not react or respond to Conán's remarks. I thus suggest that the interactions between Finn and Conán (and likely their other "invisible" contemporaries mentioned earlier) exist only in Finn's mind, TAPsW 1.1—though the stories he tells are part of his memories and belong to the historical fabric of TAPW 1. The shift between worlds here is relatively covert and infrequently encountered since it happens only twice, making it easy for the reader to misread these moments as belonging to TAPW 1. O'Brien's textual worlds thus constantly threaten to collapse or blend into one another, if our attention lapses even momentarily. Readers have to constantly shift gears as we traverse worlds in order to make sense of the chaotic, gamelike structures that characterize *Two-Birds*'s textual universe. Using possible worlds theory to delineate such ontological shifts suggests how readers gain a tentative interpretive foothold in O'Brien's complex, disorienting layering of worlds.

Orlick Trellis, Shanahan, Furriskey, and Lamont are members of TAPW 1 who fantasize about wreaking vengeance on Dermot Trellis, whereby Orlick records these imaginings in his manuscript— the events of which constitute TAPsW 1.2. Inhabitants of TAPsW 1.2 include Shanahan, Furriskey, Lamont, other jurors/judges/witnesses (including Sweeny, F. MacCool, and a talking short-horn cow), the Pooka, a Sweeny-like Dermot Trellis, and other characters adapted from the Sweeny/*Suibhne* legend (including Moling and an unnamed cleric likely to be Ronan). Dermot is recast as the protagonist of Orlick's rescrambled *Suibhne* tale in TAPsW 1.2, but continual interruptions from characters in TAPW 1 cause the events of TAPsW 1.2 to be restarted several times (163, 168, 170)—yet another gamelike quality of O'Brien's postmodern fictional worlds. With reference to table 3 at the end of this chapter, the novel's impish spirit is evident in the explicit overlapping taxonomy of character names between TAPW 1 and TAPsW 1.2, heightening the affective disorientation readers experience in their attempts to make sense of its tangled textual worlds.

Toward the end of *Two-Birds*, while TAPsW 1.2 Dermot is on trial for his life and about to be put to death, Teresa finds "to her surprise" in TAPW 1 that Dermot's room is empty—an unusual occurrence since we learn early on that he rarely leaves his bed and spends his days mostly in a drugged coma (214). It is only when, by "a curious coincidence," she accidentally burns "the pages which made and sustained the existence of Furriskey and his true friends" in TAPW 1 that "just at that moment, Teresa heard a knock at the hall-door," and it turns out to be Dermot (215). The "curious coincidence" of TAPW 1 Dermot's reappearance immediately after Teresa burns the pages containing TAPsW 1.2 strongly suggests that intrauniverse relations between the two worlds have been deliberately muddied, as O'Brien coyly implies the confluence of Dermots from TAPW 1 and TAPsW 1.2. Dermot's identity comes into question since "taxonomic compatibility" between the two worlds becomes an "undecidable relation" (Ryan, *Possible* 33, 39): is this an instance of transworld identity or of homonymy? Leaving this accessibility relation indeterminate leaves room for readers' playful imaginations to fill these gaps as we will, reinforcing the fluid shapes of worlds operating according to the principle of maximal departure.

LANARK: A LIFE IN FOUR BOOKS

Notwithstanding the confusion engendered by *Two-Birds*'s entangled satellite worlds, critics and readers generally agree on the stability of the student-narrator's world—that is, the TAW encountered on the first page—which loosely anchors the rest of the novel. In Alasdair Gray's *Lanark: A Life in Four Books* (1981), however, even the TAW is subject to indeterminacy. *Lanark*'s TAW may be characterized in multiple ways depending on readers' conceptions of the interrelations between the "four books." The table of contents informs us that *Lanark* begins with Book Three, followed by a Prologue, Book One, an Interlude, Book Two, and Book Four—which is in turn interrupted by an annotated Epilogue four chapters before the novel ends (*Lanark* v–vii). Critics and readers thus have to contend with the jumbled order or chronological discontinuities of these "books" or this "life," which reads like the lives of two protagonists: Duncan Thaw's in the "realist" section (Books One and Two) and Lanark's in the "fantastic" section (Books Three and Four). These challenges are part of numerous play-oriented mechanics characterizing *Lanark,* which I argue spur readers' form-drive into action.

Such mechanics include the novel's play with both distance and proximity between the AW and uneven TAW, its self-reflexive Epilogue, and indeterminacies between the text's "realistic" and "fantastic" sections (and how they complicate readers' sense of the TAW). I examine five different ways critics have conceived of the relationship between *Lanark*'s four books and unfold the implications of each hypothesis for our understandings of the novel's global design. I argue that the readerly impulse to reduce indeterminacy vis-à-vis a working hypothesis is congruent with postmodern texts exemplifying an aesthetics of play, because it is precisely such tensions between the sense- and form-drives, between indeterminacy and interpretation, that propel play's dialectical energies.

Lanark's Uneven TAW

I posit that *Lanark*'s TAW spans all four books and encompasses Glasgow (Prologue, Books One and Two), the Institute (Prologue, Interlude, Books Three and Four), Unthank (Books Three and Four), and Provan (Book Four, including the Epilogue)—though readers are cued to shift between principles of minimal and maximal departure, approaching distinct locations within this same TAW differently, in a process I term *departure switching.* Unlike other locations in the TAW, for instance, *Lanark*'s Glasgow contains few departures from the AW and is recognizably meant to represent AW Scotland circa the 1940s and '50s, with references to AW locations such as Riddrie, Alexandra Park, and Sauchiehall Street (*Lanark* 217; Bernstein 36; Falconer 172). Departure switching in *Lanark* tends to be explicitly marked and dominantly occurs from section to section, book to book, or even chapter to chapter (e.g., "Chapter 7: The Institute"; "Interlude" between Books One and Two [*Lanark* v–vi]). Departure switching is also cued in characters' direct speech, such as the Oracle's announcement at the end of Book Three that he is about to begin narrating Duncan Thaw's life in Glasgow, which spans the subsequent Books One and Two (219).

Lanark opens with Book Three, at the Elite Café in Unthank. While there appears to be some "identity of inventory"[6] between readers' AW and the TAW—there is a café, cinema, Social Security office, and so on (3, 19)—the opening chapter contains multiple textual cues signaling that readers should proceed from a maximal rather than minimal departure framework. Lanark's extraordinary remark about "looking for daylight" and Sludden's disdainful emphasis on the question "How do you spend your . . . *days*?" (4–5) implies chronological disjunctures between the TAW and readers' AW understanding of time. Readers also suspect "taxonomic compatibility"[7] has been violated when we learn of Lanark's "dragonhide" relatively early on in chapter three. These suspicions are confirmed when the dragonhide keeps growing over the next three chapters, eventually turning his entire arm into a dark green limb with a "glossy cold hide" and "curving steel-blade claws" (40–41). To draw on Ryan's terms, repeated emphases on such chronological, taxonomic, and physical incompatibilities between the AW and TAW early on in the narrative cue readers to adopt the principle of maximal departure.[8]

The departure switching that occurs as a result of our varying sense of deviations between the AW and these different TAW locations thus creates a radically uneven sense of *Lanark*'s TAW, aggravating our sense of readerly disorientation. This fragmented textual design can be understood as Gray's implicit metaphor for Scotland, a country which is "fragmented, cut to pieces by historical circumstances," with geographical "differences between Highland and Lowland, east and west coast," and linguistic differences in a "three way split between English, Scots and Gaelic" (Bold 2; de Juan 33–34, 39). Like the uneven yet contiguous TAW, Cairns Craig situates Scottish identity in this "intersec-

---

6. "Identity of inventory" is established when "TAW and AW are furnished by the same objects" (Ryan, *Possible* 32).

7. "Taxonomic compatibility" between AW and TAW is established only "if both worlds contain the same species, and the species are characterized by the same properties" (Ryan, *Possible* 32).

8. Other TAW locations characterized by radical deviations include the intercalendrical zone, where the eponymous protagonist Lanark learns that "all sizes and distances are deceptive [here]. Even the gravity varies" (*Lanark* 374). The subterranean Institute—in which people's diseases can turn them into dragons and "existence is helical" (60–61), such that death is a process of "creating" people anew as they are flung "back into a second-class railway carriage" (219)—also prompts readers' reliance on the maximal departure principle.

tion of diverse but contiguous narratives" (*Out* 223). Alluding to the moment of *Lanark*'s composition, Rachel Falconer observes that "1970s [AW] Glasgow was a victim of global capitalism and its consequences. The damage to the environment represented in the fantasy section of *Lanark* also reflects what was happening to Scottish natural resources at the time" (172). Only when readers treat the "apocalyptic fires and floods that threaten to overwhelm Unthank at the end of *Lanark*" (173) not as a separate textual possible world but as part of the same uneven TAW can we appreciate how Gray effectively brings AW Scotland's sociohistorical and sociopolitical concerns to the fore through a hellish transfiguration of Glasgow.

Readers are also cued to treat Provan—and the dizzying twenty-one-page Epilogue embedded therein—as operating on the principle of maximal departure. The Epilogue, inserted four chapters before the novel ends, has a playful nature that is discernible in the very position it occupies in *Lanark*. Described as a chamber behind "a white panel without hinges or handle" in a four-storied building overlooking a stadium in Provan, the "epilogue room" has a mise-en-abyme structure that bears "no architectural similarity" to other parts of the edifice:

> The rest of the room was hidden by easels holding large paintings of the room. The pictures seemed brighter and cleaner than the reality and a tall beautiful girl with long blond hair reclined in them, sometimes nude and sometimes clothed. The girl herself, more worried and untidy than her portraits, stood near the door wearing a paint-stained butcher's apron. (*Lanark* 480)

Glyn White observes that page 479, which bears the single word EPILOGUE on an otherwise blank page, operates in "two distinct ways": "as a door" for Lanark and the narrative audience, and "as a title" (or section of the novel) for the authorial audience (57). This so-called section, however, is likewise problematized; while the Prologue and Interlude are distinct sections that buffer separate books, the Epilogue is inserted two-thirds of the way into Book Four, such that it functions like an independent section but is by the same token a *non*-section integrated with Book Four. The metafictional Epilogue thus functions as an "inside out" space that works to account for the novel's dynamics from one of the most embedded geographical locations within *Lanark*'s textual universe.

Lanark's posited author, Nastler, who resides in the epilogue room, self-reflexively gestures to its existence and construction in response to Lanark's (and readers' implicit) observation: "'I thought epilogues came after the end.' 'Usually, but mine is too important to go there'" (*Lanark* 483). Like Dermot Trellis in *Two-Birds*—an intertext explicitly acknowledged in the Epilogue's "Index of Plagiarisms" (481–90)—Nastler is also an author whose powers of creation enable him to coexist alongside his characters. White observes that the Epilogue is full of "textual furniture which defies convention," such as "descriptive running headers" that add "a second active voice to the page," the Index of Plagiarisms that provides a third, while the annotated footnotes supply a fourth—culminating in a complex polyphony of voices intent on satirizing the act of literary criticism (58). To add to such giddying confusion, the Index of Plagiarisms includes entries that endlessly loop back unto each other (see "BLACK ANGUS," "MacNEACAIL, AONGHAS," and "NICOLSON, ANGUS") and entries that refer to nonexistent chapters (*Lanark* 486–99; see also White 59; de Juan 314–15). Furthermore, what might be considered Gray's Acknowledgments page has been displaced from its customary position at the novel's beginning/end and stuffed into footnote 13, with references to AW entities and persons such as Tennessee's Kingsport Press and Stephanie Wolfe Murray (misspelled[?] as "Wolf Murray"), the owner of Scotland's Canongate Press which published *Lanark* (*Lanark* 499, xi).

Such playful features elicit the reader's form-drive in managing the text's vertiginous, sensuous impulses. Given our "human need to perceive and experience satisfying unities in the disordered flux of experience" (Shusterman 76), the disorientation perpetuated by *Lanark*'s mise-en-abyme structures and polyphonic voices foregrounds readers' impulse for order, coherence, and meaning. The "mental gymnastics" readers engage in as we maneuver such gamelike textual designs stretches our imaginations and sharpens our "aesthetic perceptions" by honing "the agility and adaptability one gains in being *playful*" (Bohman-Kalaja 234). Using the possible worlds model as a tool to demonstrate the cognitive challenges readers face when they encounter such playful fictional worlds, I suggest that postmodern fiction does not evacuate but rather modifies aesthetic experience in the twentieth century by honing such readerly dexterity.

Though *Lanark* also contains textual alternate possible worlds (TAPWs), including Duncan Thaw's imaginings in Books One and

Two (for example, 157–59, 233–34, 288–89, etc.) and Lanark's dreams in Books Three and Four (see 512–17),[9] these satellite worlds generally do not feature heavily in my analysis since such departures tend to be relatively explicitly marked and are less functionally related to the aesthetics of play I am interested in exploring. Several notable exceptions are instances of "undecidable relations," such as "whether Thaw [is] a murderer, whether he committed suicide or even whether he died at sea," since the "ambiguous or inconclusive" textual cues make it impossible to determine if these events did indeed occur in the TAW (Ryan, *Possible* 39; Falconer 189). Even the certitude of Books One and Two are subject to indeterminacy, since they are conveyed entirely through the Oracle's voice.

How readers conceive of *Lanark*'s TAW tends to hinge on two factors: the way we interpret the relationship between Thaw and Lanark, and what we make of the Oracle's existence—particularly given the comment at the end of Book Two: "I'm only able to tell the story as he saw it" (*Lanark* 350). Since the Oracle's comments are visually or typographically given as part of the narration without quotation marks, this "he" could refer to either Thaw or Lanark. The Oracle's revelation that Books One and Two have been wholly subjective in nature—knowledge that has been withheld from readers for effectively most of the Glasgow narrative—comes somewhat as a surprise (de Juan 112), since we are likely to assume some degree of objectivity given the Oracle's extradiegetic position or nonparticipation in Thaw's life. Even this aspect of the novel, however, cannot ultimately be counted upon.

What these indeterminacies imply for readerly experience of *Lanark* is the unshakeable sense that we *do* rely on a particular working interpretation of the TAW, notwithstanding the value of ambiguity. "Despite the widely accepted view that a rich multiplicity is characteristic of literary meaning," as Ralph Rader puts it, it is difficult to fight the sense that "to have too many meanings is too much like having no meaning" (31). Critics have made convincing arguments to champion the value of indeterminacy in *Lanark,* which is in line with post-

---

9. In Book Two, for instance, Thaw "invented a maggot called the Flealouse. It was white and featureless [. . .]. While elaborating this fantasy he fell asleep several times" (*Lanark* 233). Words such as "invented," "fantasy," and "fell asleep" are explicit textual cues that direct the reader to regard such moments as a recentering from the TAW to a TAPW.

modernist aesthetic sensibilities that advocate "maintaining free play is superior to achieving meaning" (Ryan, *Narrative* 183). I believe Gray to be wholly committed to the value of such indeterminacies, but I also suggest that particular interpretations tend to be privileged over others as readers take up one position or another in the reading experience—and that the process of weighing out these interpretive possibilities is part of the cognitive pleasure we derive from reading *Lanark* and other postmodernist texts.

Readers embrace the value of uncertainty in postmodern fiction as part of the authorial audience, appreciating the dynamics at work in the novel's global textual design and its overall aesthetic project. But our role as members of the authorial audience is also contingent on joining the narrative audience, which depends crucially on responding to a particular interpretation of the textual world. Given that readers cannot simultaneously inhabit more than one position as a member of the narrative audience without losing the affective sense of immersion (Ryan, *Narrative* 199), I posit that we are inclined to adopt one of the multiple possible working interpretations, even as we remain cognizant of other available options and their functional value from the position of the authorial audience. How each reader determines the criterion for a compelling interpretation is the issue to which I now turn.

"Story-over-Discourse Meta-Rule": Maximizing Interpretive and Affective Pleasure

Given the multiple "critically defensible" interpretations of *Lanark*'s textual worlds (Falconer 188), an important way the form-drive "projects imaginary order" (Boyd 90) to counter the sense-drive's emancipatory impulses—perpetuated by the text's undecidable relations, its self-reflexive Epilogue, and other play mechanisms—is to determine how its uneven narrative spaces relate to each other. Especially when the textual design promotes ambiguity, uncertainty, or indeterminacies, I concur with rhetorical narrative theorists that readers tend to favor the interpretation that offers the greatest payoff and/or maximizes the work's interpretive power by approximating the textual world in ways that enhance our pleasure of the text.

James Phelan's "Story-over-Discourse Meta-Rule" usefully explicates how readers likely decide on a particular interpretive hypothesis as their working model or understanding of the textual world: "once fictional narratives establish their commitment to providing readers that 'focal illusion of characters acting autonomously as if in the world of real experience,' readers privilege—and seek to preserve—their mimetic interests in those characters and that storyworld" ("Implausibilities" 175).[10] Phelan's meta-rule reflects the notion that as a species, humans are highly motivated to share in the "emotions, attention, intentions, and information" (Boyd 53) offered by fictional minds and that this mimetic interest forms an important aspect of our engagements with narrative fiction.

Since Phelan's story-over-discourse meta-rule was formulated in relation to texts that foreground the mimetic, the meta-rule becomes significantly complicated by *Lanark*'s uneven TAW, which foregrounds different readerly treatments of or attitudes toward the text at different points in the narrative. Ryan uses the metaphors of text-as-world and text-as-game to characterize two distinct readerly attitudes: "the aesthetics of immersion" is concerned with readerly tasks such as imaginative and "emotional participation" in the textual world, while "the aesthetics of interactivity presents the text as a game, language as a plaything, and the reader as the player" (*Narrative* 175, 16, 94–95). In general, I posit that when readers' investment in the text's immersive dimensions reaps greater payoff (in terms of affective, mimetic, and/or thematic interests) than our investment in its interactive dimensions—that is, treating text-as-world rather than text-as-game—our role as members of the narrative audience is foregrounded and the story-over-discourse meta-rule applies. Conversely, when readers' investment in the text's interactive dimensions reaps greater payoff, our role as members of the authorial audience is foregrounded and the meta-rule fails to apply.

The Glasgow section of Books One and Two, for instance, emphasizes *Lanark*'s text-as-world dimensions: via our immersive participation in Thaw's world as members of the narrative audience, readers gain a clearer sense of the circumstances that led to his eventual suicide at the end of Book Two, having been privy to his struggles as an unsuccessful artist. Other sections such as the Epilogue emphasize *Lanark*'s

---

10. "Mimetic interests arise when the narrative represents characters, places, and events as like those we encounter in the extratextual world"—that is, the AW (Phelan, "Implausibilities" 171).

text-as-game dimensions, requiring readers to distance themselves from their role as members of the narrative audience—and the corresponding limitations of perspective, for example—in order to appreciate the playful exchange between Nastler and Lanark, which causes some distress to both parties but keeps the reader enormously tickled. Readers are likewise more invested in *Two-Birds*'s text-as-game dimensions as Dermot Trellis undergoes the fantastic torture his characters have devised for him, distancing ourselves from the position of the narrative audience, of treating Dermot as an embodied human.[11]

To demonstrate readers'/critics' implicit reliance on Phelan's meta-rule of readerly engagement, I recast existing interpretations of Gray's novel in terms of the possible worlds approach and explain how my working interpretation of the TAW (which is in line with that of many commentators) maximizes interpretive and affective pleasure, given its implications for *Lanark*'s larger aesthetic project. The first and perhaps most contested interpretation suggested by Douglas Gifford posits Books One and Two as the TAW and Books Three and Four as one or multiple TAPWs, such that fantastic sections of the novel are interpreted as "Thaw's mental breakdown" during his hospitalizations in the text's realist sections (112). Lanark is thus treated as a hallucinatory alter ego that Thaw imagines into being and, by implication, characters like the Oracle, Nastler, Rima, and even his son, Alexander, are mere figments of Thaw's tortured imagination. While Gifford recognizes the interpretive limitations of his proposition—noting that "if the only viable way to read *Lanark* is to see it as happening inside the head of a disintegrating social failure, how can we trust the assessments of society that are implicit in that trapped account?"—he maintains that it is "the only consistent way to read the novel" (111–13). Gifford's remarks reveal an impulse that I suggest many readers likely experience: it is precisely in light of the novel's disorienting tendencies that we feel the urgent need to "'hold' the entire novel together in our mind" (113).

However, interpretation (1) neglects some of *Lanark*'s most important textual dynamics. Despite its dystopic tendencies, Falconer rightly observes that "the novel as a whole is richly affirmative of ordinary virtues and pleasures: individual autonomy, breathable air, the affec-

---

11. Readers become more invested in their position as members of the narrative audience when they experience the immersive pull of the textual world and react to fictional characters "as if they were embodied humans" (Ryan, *Narrative* 112).

tion between a father and son, light and architectural grace," and, more broadly, of "the transformative possibilities of the journey through Hell" (172). Interpretation (1) transforms the genuine possibility of redemption offered in the novel's conclusion into an extended hallucination, diminishing the value of *Lanark*'s affective, thematic, and mimetic (text-as-world) dimensions, while failing to satisfactorily account for the functions/purposes of its synthetic (text-as-game) dimensions. This interpretation also likely leads readers to negative aesthetic judgments of Gray's textual design, since synthetic elements such as the Epilogue's complex mix of voices seem digressive, adding unnecessary complexity without explicable justification or relation to the thematic concerns or affective registers of Books One and Two. This relatively impoverished reading goes against what Phelan calls "the logic of readerly response" ("Implausibilities" 169), such that most readers are unlikely to consider it a satisfactory interpretation.

Interpretation (2) posits an inverse hypothesis, whereby Books Three and Four constitute the TAW, while Books One and Two are a TAPW that constitutes Lanark's imaginary longings. This reading gains textual support from the novel's problematization of "Lanark's access to his own past by underlining the composition, the linguistic nature, of the Oracle's report" (de Juan 225), especially in passages such as, "The oracle began speaking. His voice sounded so far inside the head that the story seemed less narrated than remembered. It was not delayed by eating, or going to the lavatory, or sleeping: at night Lanark dreamed what he could not hear and woke with no sense of interruption" (*Lanark* 117). Such textual evidence may thus "be interpreted as pointing towards a voyage into Lanark's unconscious" (de Juan 121), supporting the hypothesis that Thaw simply exists as part of Lanark's ardent desire for a past.

Interpretation (2) is also partly motivated by Rima's objection: "In the first place that oracle was a woman, not a man. In the second place her story was about me. You were so bored that you fell asleep and obviously dreamed something else" (*Lanark* 357). The radical subjectivity of perspective, where the narration is almost exclusively focalized through the protagonist's mind, makes the exact nature of Lanark's past an undecidable relation. However, there are distinct overlaps between Lanark's and Rima's versions of the Oracle's story: for one, they certainly do seem to have known each other in their lives prior to Unthank and were engaged in a troubled courtship that eventually ended in her marriage to someone else (357). Though both characters implicitly endorse that life before Unthank, interpretation (2) leaves the exact nature of the events that constitute that life and whether it was indeed Glasgow indeterminate.

Perhaps more significantly, since Nastler validates the existence of the Glasgow books—"I worked poor Thaw to death, quite cold-bloodedly [. . .], his death gave me a chance to shift him into a wider social context. You are Thaw with the neurotic imagination trimmed off and built into the furniture of the world you occupy" (493)—interpretation (2) also necessitates readers' treatment of the Epilogue as part of Lanark's hallucinations, even when there seems to be little textual justification for doing so. If we take the world of Books Three and Four to be the TAW, whereby the Epilogue is part of Book Four, the evidence to justify that the Epilogue constitutes only Lanark's imagination and is thus a TAPW seems a little thin at best, considering that "the Red Girl" and the unnamed "morose" man Lanark meets in Provan (i.e., characters deemed to exist in the TAW) validate Nastler's existence (478). This is an instance where the story-over-discourse meta-rule fails to apply, since preserving its text-as-world dimensions—that is, treating Lanark as embodied being instead of as Nastler's creation—at the expense of its text-as-game dimensions contradicts *Lanark*'s textual design.

Apart from the way it contradicts readerly logic, the reason interpretation (2) ultimately remains unpersuasive to me has to do with Gray's purpose of creating "an epic" (492) to animate Glasgow, as the conversation between McAlpin and Thaw illustrates:

> "Glasgow is a magnificent city," said McAlpin. "Why do we hardly ever notice that?" "Because nobody imagines living here," said Thaw. [. . .] "Then think of Florence, Paris, London, New York. Nobody visiting them for the first time is a stranger because he's already visited them in paintings, novels, history books and films. But if a city hasn't been used by an artist not even the inhabitants live there imaginatively. What is Glasgow to most of us? A house, the place we work, a football park or golf course, some pubs and connecting streets. That's all. [. . .] Imaginatively Glasgow exists as a music-hall song and a few bad novels. That's all we've given to the world outside. It's all we've given to ourselves." (243)

The textual reality of an explicitly recognizable Glasgow *and* its purgatorial counterpart is imperative to Gray's artistic purpose and to *Lanark*'s global textual design—in imaginatively illuminating and transfiguring existing literary representations of AW Glasgow. I am thus inclined to regard both the realist and fantastic sections of *Lanark* as jointly constituting the TAW—their joint textual reality maximizes the interpretive pleasure we derive from Gray's text and is integral to exercising readers' imaginary inhabitations of Scotland.

Interpretations (3), (4), and (5) consider both the novel's realist and fantastic sections as bases for constituting *Lanark*'s TAW, treating Thaw and Lanark as a single entity and accepting the Oracle's existence as a given. However, each interpretation configures the relations between books a little differently. The third interpretation posits that Book Four is a TAPW to the TAW of the first three books, taking Book Four's events to be a prophecy made by the Oracle of events that have not yet come to pass. Gavin Miller explains that the "narratorial voice of *Lanark* is explicitly the voice of an 'oracle'—it also narrates predictively. Unless we arbitrarily posit two narrators for *Lanark*, then we must recognise that the oracle continues to speak" (320). Miller contends that *Lanark* "ends not with the protagonist's rather lonely death, but with the ending addressed to Lanark, who is still in the Institute, and who is still in a position to forestall the events of the fourth book" (320)—an interpretation that captures the way the Oracle's "words could never be printed between quotation marks" (*Lanark* 104), thus giving rise to the ambiguity of whether her/his/its narration ends at the end of Book Two or Book Four (de Juan 246, 256).

While Miller's proposition opens up fascinating possibilities, his notion that *Lanark* has only one narrator (the Oracle) would also mean that the first eleven chapters of Book Three, prior to the Oracle's pleas of "Help, help, can nobody hear me? [. . .] It said I am glad you called" (*Lanark* 104) are likewise part of her/his/its narration, when there is little textual evidence to support such a reading. Further, to read the final book as prophecy reduces the significance of powerfully affective moments in Book Four, which depend on the momentum gained in the first three books. These include Lanark's experience of plenitude in the novel's conclusion, even as Unthank collapses around him in the possibility of a phoenix-like rebirth, and the excruciating "withdrawal of paradise" (Hobsbaum 154) in his interaction with his son at the end of chapter 41, when Lanark's joyful epiphany that even when the "world has lapsed into black nothing, it will have made sense because Sandy once enjoyed it in the sunlight" is exposed as a cruel dream, leaving him with "a feeling of terrible loss" (*Lanark* 515, 519).[12]

Notwithstanding its postmodernist tendencies that work to expose Lanark's identity as fictional construction, the novel as a whole is invested in the reader's imaginative and emotional participation with its characters' inner struggles and challenges, in the immersive pull of its textual world, and in our affective engagements as members of the narrative audience. As compared to *Two-Birds,* where the novel's text-as-game dimensions dominate, readers are more invested in *Lanark*'s text-as-world dimensions for much of the 573-page novel, even as we are cued to engage in departure switching while navigating its uneven TAW. The story-over-discourse meta-rule applies at many points of Gray's novel as "readers privilege—and seek to preserve—[our] mimetic interests" in these characters and the storyworld (Phelan, "Implausibilities" 175). By positing the cumulative momentum of Book Four's events as prophetic rather than as part of *Lanark*'s textual reality, interpretation (3) diminishes the powerful affective pleasure—and part of its corresponding mimetic and thematic significance—by rendering them all hypothetical, including Lanark's reunion with Sandy, his eventual realization that Rima did love him, and the equanimity with which he is prepared to face his/the end (*Lanark* 558–60).

Most critics, including myself, fall somewhere between a combination of interpretations (4) and (5), which postulate, respectively, that Thaw is Lanark's younger self who has passed from life in Glasgow to a sort of hellish afterlife, and/or that the disjunctures between the realist and fantastic sections represent a shift in perspective on micro and macro versions of the same reality (Craig, "Going" 20; Duncan

---

12. As Philip Hobsbaum observes, this scene where Lanark and Sandy bury the dead seagull together is made extremely "poignant by the sense of loss that inevitably" ensues: "Alasdair Gray has many themes. But this one, the withdrawal of paradise, is what renders him highly distinctive. It is this that causes the hills and valleys, the variegations of intensity, the quirks and the depressions of his prose. There is something of torment in his effort to establish happiness in action only to use even greater technique for the purpose of taking it away. The loss of Eden becomes more poignant than Eden itself. No writer can simulate happiness more convincingly than Alasdair Gray. His prose burgeons with joy, with discovery [. . .]. But this is the fiery surface that is an exhalation over the fathomless depths of despair" (151, 154).

43; Bernstein 32; Smethurst 131; O'Gallagher 546; Falconer 188–89). This dominant critical/readerly approach treats all four books as forming what Thomas G. Pavel terms a "'dual' or 'layered' ontology," which posits death as the implicit, ambiguous transition that splits the TAW into "sharply distinct domains obeying different laws," whereby each domain is not a separate TAPW "but complementary territories" within the same TAW (Pavel 57–58; Ryan, *Possible* 40). By elucidating the shortcomings in the earlier interpretations, I hope to have shown how this dominant paradigm for understanding *Lanark*'s TAW ultimately offers a more powerful interpretive hypothesis.

CONCLUSION: POSSIBILITIES OF PLAY

Boyd notes that as human minds develop and mature, "the right hemispheres of our brains seek explanation at a deeper level and coherence on both a local and a larger scale" (151). Nobel Laureate and neural scientist Gerald Edelman theorizes that human beings integrate new information by coding experience "within the brain in scattered 'maps'" via "complex network[s] of interconnected neurons," and the "vitality of these maps depends on the active and incessant orchestration of countless details" (Brown and Vaughan 35–36). Such orchestration likely "happens most fully through play" vis-à-vis our engagements in storytelling, art, and other forms of play activities (35–36). If Edelman, Boyd, Brown and Vaughan, and others are right in positing that art in general is "a kind of cognitive *play*" designed to appeal to the brain's preference for "inferentially rich," "patterned information," the readerly onus of projecting order in our co-construction or co-orchestration of postmodernist fictional worlds certainly seems to be an important way by which we "extend and refine [such] cognitive competences" (Boyd 85, 190).

Patricia Waugh observes that

> "playfulness" within the novel is certainly not confined merely to literary form but is part of a broader development in culture which is registered acutely in all postmodernist art. [. . .] In its awareness of the serious possibility of play, it in fact echoes some of the major concerns of twentieth-century thought: Piaget's work on the educational

value of play; Wittgenstein's view of language as a set of games; the existential notion of reality as a game of being [and so on]. (41–42)

Some postmodern texts like O'Brien's *At Swim-Two-Birds* and Calvino's *The Castle of Crossed Destinies* dominantly emphasize the text-as-game metaphor, where readerly pleasure is largely driven by the play with "informational chaos" (Ryan, *Narrative* 240) and its engagement of readers' cognitive capacities: a large part of the fun *is* the difficult process of form-giving or our co-constructions of textual worlds. Other postmodern narratives like Gray's *Lanark* and Egan's *A Visit from the Goon Squad* emphasize both dimensions of "game" and "world," where our appreciation of the texts' interactive dynamics of play entails our immersive treatment of its characters as embodied beings whose fates we become invested in over the course of the novel (i.e., readers' roles as members of both the authorial *and* narrative audience).

One possible objection that may be raised against my use of possible worlds theory to interpret texts like *Lanark* and *Two-Birds* is that the approach too "cleanly" delineates worlds in ways that violate the fundamental purposeful entropy that animates their spirit of chaotic play. I suggest that many postmodern fictional worlds are designed to *simulate* pandemonium, forcing the form-drive to kick into play as readers attempt to dispel the feeling of vertigo and to restore stability of perception in order to apprehend the novels' larger concerns, such as issues of metafictionality and historiography in *Two-Birds* or the fragmentary sense of Scottish identity and imaginative transfigurations of Glasgow in *Lanark*. Rather than defend the possible worlds approach as a critical framework that offers an absolute or authoritative interpretation that "explains away" the text, I suggest that the model offers one way of accounting for how readers cognitively deal with postmodern fiction's textual mayhem. Furthermore, as I pointed out in my analyses, there are certain characteristics of O'Brien's and Gray's textual universes that remain indeterminate or undecidable. Thus, I do not see my approach as one that violates postmodern fiction's purposeful chaos and ambiguity; the possible worlds lens merely works as a tool to explicate some implicit readerly tasks we likely engage in when encountering such anarchic texts.

Gray explicitly makes form-giving part of the reader's game task, asserting that only the flow of "readers' enjoyment" over *Lanark* "can unify" the novel's seemingly disparate sections (Axelrod 109).[13] In line with Hogan, I argue that crucial aspects of such enjoyment pertain to readers' abilities to detect "pattern in story structure" amidst the welter which dominantly characterizes postmodern fiction and that we experience "aesthetic delight" (*Beauty* 13) in such pattern recognitions. Through our participation in their puzzle- or gamelike structures, postmodern texts partly shift the onus of creating narrative form onto readers. In this way, postmodern literature redefines aesthetic experience by bilocating the form-impulse, so to speak: both as part of the author's textual design and in his invitation for the reader to enjoy the difficult yet pleasurable task or process of co-constructing the textual worlds.

Foregrounding multiplicity, ambiguity, disorientation, and "free play,"[14] postmodernist fiction is characterized by plenty of sensuous change that entertains, pleases, and tantalizes the sense-drive—correspondingly sending readers' form-instinct into overdrive as they attempt to gain an interpretive foothold amidst such chaos. These dynamic tensions between the form- and sense-drives underpinning the aesthetic category of play highlight the fact that readers "are not passive receptacles but highly active reconstructors" (Boyd 173). Schiller notes that an "equilibrium" between the formal and sensuous impulsions "remains always an idea that reality can never completely reach. In reality, there will always remain a preponderance of one of these elements over the other, and the highest point to which experience can reach will consist in an oscillation between two principles" (*Aesthetical*, "Letter XVI"). What the authors of postmodernist fiction have done is to destabilize the text as the site of this aesthetic equilibrium and to foreground readers' roles in simulating fictional order, inviting us to participate in a more active and self-aware mode of reading.

---

13. In response to a question about how he harmonized "the artificially constructed life of the novel," Gray explains: "I felt no need to harmonize them. I yoked the bits together and expected the reader's interest to flow over all, as my imagination had done. [. . .] The only thing that can unify it is the readers' enjoyment" (Axelrod 107–9).

14. "In literature, *ilinx* and its free play are represented by what Bakhtin calls the carnivalesque" or "the destabilization of all structures, including those created by the text itself" (Ryan, *Narrative* 186).

TABLE 3. Possible worlds model of *At Swim-Two-Birds*

TEXTUAL WORLDS	INHABITANTS
Textual actual world (TAW)	Student-narrator
	Brinsley
	Byrne
	Cryan
	Kerrigan
	Kelly
	Verney Wright
	Student-narrator's uncle
	Mr. Connors
	Mr. Fogarty
	Mr. Corcoran
	Mr. Hickey
	William Falconer
Textual alternate possible world 1 (TAPW 1): characters in the student-narrator's manuscript	Dermot Trellis
	Orlick Trellis
	Sheila Lamont
	Antony Lamont
	John Furriskey
	Peggy
	William Tracy
	Paul Shanahan
	Slug Willard
	Peter (Shorty) Andrews
	Red Indians
	Henderson
	Red Kiersay
	Unnamed Belgian author
	Timothy Danaos
	Dona Ferentes
	Good Fairy
	Pooka (Fergus MacPhellimey)
	Finn MacCool
	Dermot
	Granya
	Sweeny
	Jem Casey
	Detective-Officer Snodgrass
	Superintendent Clohessy
	Judge Lamphall
	Teresa
Textual alternate possible subworld 1 (TAPsW 1.1): characters in Finn MacCool's imaginings (Correspondingly, also characters in the student-narrator's manuscript)	Conán
	Diarmuid Donn
	Caolcrodha Mac Morna
	Liagan Luaimneach O Luachair Dheaghaidh
	Gearr mac Aonchearda

(continued)

TABLE 3. Possible worlds model of *At Swim-Two-Birds* (con't)

TEXTUAL WORLDS	INHABITANTS
Textual alternate possible subworld 2 (TAPsW 1.2): characters in Orlick Trellis's manuscript (Correspondingly, also characters in the student-narrator's manuscript)	Dermot Trellis (accused) Paul Shanahan John Furriskey Antony Lamont Samuel (Slug) Willard William James Tracy S. Andrews Sweeny J. Casey R. Kiersay Lamphall F. MacCool Supt. Clohessy Pooka (F. MacPhellimey) Good Fairy Moling Unnamed cleric Short-horn cow
Textual alternate possible world 2 (TAPW 2): characters in William Falconer's "The Shipwreck"	Master Albert Rodmond Arion Palemon Anna

CHAPTER 3

Literary Sublime (I)

Imagination Reigns

IN OFFERING an alternate strategy for framing twentieth- and twenty-first-century literary studies—one that downplays chronology in favor of foregrounding aesthetic energies—this book strives to reflect the period's diverse aesthetic ambitions, even within a single author's oeuvre. To distinguish between aesthetic categories of play and the sublime, I return in this chapter to works by Calvino and O'Brien (authors discussed in chapters 1 and 2) to demonstrate that though *Invisible Cities* and *The Third Policeman* likewise present disorienting worlds, navigating their textual universe tends to be subsumed under the dominant readerly task of negotiating the sublime's conflicting affective states.

In my conceptualization of a distinctly postmodern literary sublime, I synthesize various traditions to offer an overview of key characteristics that artists and authors use to explicate the aesthetic mode. By extending and revising existing theories, I work to develop the category of the literary sublime in a way that is faithful to its "plurality, richness and complexity" (Zuckert 65), explaining its integral relevance to the experience of reading postmodern and contemporary fiction—and how these works in turn complicate traditional understandings of the sublime. Like Longinus, Kant, Schiller, and others, I distinguish between two types of sublime, positioning them not as binaries but along a continuum, in relation to increasing degrees of conflict between the sense- and moral-drives. In this first of two chapters addressing the literary sublime, I focus on novels that dominantly engage the sense-drive and minimally engage the moral-drive; in the next chapter, I turn my attention to works that illustrate the two drives operating at maximal conflict.

THEORIZING THE SUBLIME

The earliest known treatise on the sublime dates back to Longinus, a Greek rhetorician who lived sometime between the first and third centuries, who observed that "sublimity flashing forth at the right moment scatters everything before it like a thunderbolt"; in other words, the sublime is primarily "recognized by its effect," which is why Longinus preferred "the illustrative example" as his expository device (Longinus, "Sublime" 77; Heath 12, 14). Longinus "does not define the sublime" and in fact "goes out of his way to avoid a stable terminology," drawing instead on Homer, Demosthenes, and other examples from ancient Greek and Latin literatures, to distinguish between a "sudden and abrupt" mode versus a "diffusive" mode of the sublime (Heath 14; Longinus, *Sublime* §12)—a point I elucidate more fully later in this chapter. The sublime's affiliations with the moral- and sense-drives can also be traced to Longinus, who emphasizes the moral character of the speaker (one "whose spirit is generous and aspiring," and capable of "grandeur of thought") and "a certain disorder of language, imitating the agitation and commotion of the soul" (*Sublime* §9, §8, §20).[1]

Following Longinus, the sublime received its first extensive treatment as an explicitly literary phenomenon from the mid-eighteenth- to the early nineteenth-century. This included the British Romantic and Gothic traditions, comprising figures such as Irish philosopher Edmund Burke and English poets William Wordsworth and Samuel Taylor Coleridge; the German Romantic tradition, best exemplified by Caspar David Friedrich's landscape paintings; the American tradi-

---

1. Longinus proposes five sources of the sublime: "grandeur of thought," "vigorous and spirited treatment of the passions," "figures of thoughts and figures of speech," "dignified expression" in diction and use of metaphor, and, most importantly, "majesty and elevation of structure" in all of the above (§12).

tion of landscape painting, as represented by the work of Thomas Cole, Fredric Edwin Church, Fitz Hugh Lane, and others; as well as Kantian and Nietzschean philosophical traditions. The sublime's emergence "reflected a new cultural awareness of the profoundly limited nature of the self," which led artists, writers, and philosophers "to draw attention to intense experiences which lay beyond conscious control" (Morley 14-15). The British Romantic movement's emphasis on a "sublime of transcendence"—invoked through the concept of the *infinite*—eventually became "subservient to the *moral sublime*" (Potkay 204-7). Robert Rosenblum notes that the sublime thus "provided a flexible semantic container for the murky new Romantic experiences of awe, terror, boundlessness and divinity that began to rupture the decorous confines of earlier aesthetic systems," by paralyzing "the spectator's traditional habits of seeing and thinking" (109).

Critical theorizations of the sublime regained momentum in the early twentieth century through the work of poets such as W. B. Yeats[2] and the art movement eventually known as the *abstract sublime*. Doreet Harten identifies Russian painter Kazimir Malevich as the "founding father" of twentieth-century "art of the sublime," and she credits Malevich, Wassily Kandinsky, Piet Mondrian, Barnett Newman, and Mark Rothko with developing the notion of the abstract sublime (73; see also David B. Johnson, "Postmodern" 122).[3] Other critics discuss the importance of works by Newman, Rothko, Clyfford Still, and Jackson Pollock, characterizing their paintings through terms such as the infinite, indeterminacy, ambiguity, and challenges to "the continuity and wholeness of spatial experience" (van de Vall 72-73). Rosenblum suggests that the "new kind of space created" by these "masters of the Abstract Sublime" in their use of "flattened, spreading expanses of light, colour and plane" was a response not only to "formal needs" but also to "emotional ones that, in the anxieties of the atomic age, suddenly seem to correspond with a Romantic tradition of the irrational and the awesome as well as with a Romantic vocabulary of boundless energies and limitless spaces"

---

2. See R. Jahan Ramazani's "Yeats: Tragic Joy and the Sublime."

3. In particular, Barnett Newman has invited special attention from critics given that his magnum opus, *Vir Heroicus Sublimis,* explicitly invites viewers and critics to associate his work with the sublime tradition. Philip Shaw writes that in Newman's paintings, "a yearning for transcendence is pitted against an open acknowledgement of the impossibility of this desire" (7).

(112). Unlike the Romantics, however, Philip Shaw notes that postmodernists "no longer seek[ ] to temper this feeling through reference to a higher faculty," foregrounding instead "the inability of art or reason to bring the vast and the unlimited to account" in their emphases on "the paradoxical, unfulfilled, or self-baffling" (115, 7–8). By putting forward "the unpresentable in presentation itself," postmodernism "searches for new presentations, not in order to enjoy them but in order to impart a stronger sense of the unpresentable" (Lyotard, *Postmodern* 81; Philip Shaw, *Sublime* 116).

A main characteristic of the postmodern literary sublime relates to this "unresolvable tension between representation and [the] unrepresentable" (Hooker 48). For the postmodernists, Amy Elias notes that history "is perceived as a sublime and decentered Absence, in all of its terrifying, chaotic and humbling incomprehensibility" (56). Joseph Tabbi in turn locates this sense of the incomprehensible or unpresentable in Thomas Pynchon's novels, pointing not only to "the powerfully significant failure to signify [that] has always characterized the rhetoric of the sublime," but also to Pynchon's impulse for meaning-making "at the point where categories break down"—in its "intersecting worlds, absent centers, and dissolving categories" (13–14). Whether it is Tabbi's postmodern sublime, Elias's historical sublime, or "Jameson's geopolitical or paranoid sublime," Sianne Ngai notes that in each case, "the sublime refers to what is finally or properly unrepresentable" (22; see also Lyotard, *Sublime* 69; David B. Johnson, "Postmodern" 118–19).

The urgency with which artists and writers attempt to impart this sense of the unpresentable is in part conditioned by the traumas of the twentieth and twenty-first centuries. Andrew Slade suggests that interest in the sublime is "grounded in violent historical experience" ("Violence" 87). "How, for example, should we speak of the terrors of recent history, of Auschwitz, Hiroshima, Cambodia, Rwanda, and 9/11? How could these events be described as evidence of human progress, still less as objects of sublime delight?" (Philip Shaw, *Sublime* 127). Philip Shaw observes that these events can only be "'known' by refusing to phrase [them] in terms of a judgment of understanding; for what the Holocaust [and other horrors of the contemporary age] signifies is nothing less than the impossibility of such knowledge" (128). Artists such as Joseph Beuys, Anselm Kiefer, Doris Salcedo, and others likewise address "the sublime's connection to traumatic historical events" (Morley 13).

The relationship between trauma and history is further rendered in what Gilbert-Rolfe terms the "techno-sublime," where "many thinkers of the early and mid twentieth century" regard "daily life within modern technological society" as a "continuous and disturbingly uncanny or sublime experience, causing what the German writer Walter Benjamin termed a disorienting psychic condition of traumatic 'shock'" (Gilbert-Rolfe, *Beauty* 135, 80; Morley 17). Jameson, for instance, emphasizes the "'derealizing' effect of postmodern representations," where the world threatens to become "a stereoscopic illusion" (Jameson 34, 37, 77; Redfield 152). Tabbi notes that "the sublime persists as a powerful emotive force in postmodern writing," especially in "works that regard reality as something newly mediated, predominantly by science and technology" (ix). These mediated realities tend to be characterized by "extreme space-time compressions," leading "to a perception of the everyday as fundamentally destabilizing and excessive" (Morley 12)—what I term impulses of the sense-drive, discernible in the works of O'Brien, Pynchon, and William Gibson, among others. In *The Third Policeman*, O'Brien's unnamed narrator's encounters with the policemen's contraptions—which turn sound into light and light into heat, magnify objects "to invisibility," and split not only a smell "into its sub- and inter-smells," but taste and touch into their respective sub- and inter-states (110, 136, 139)—facilitate such traumatic shock associated with the techno-sublime of hell and its eternity.

A key idea that theorists of the sublime return to repeatedly is Kant's notion of boundlessness or the limitless and the interrelated concept of "the infinite" ("From" 394).[4] An illustrative example is Newman's use of indeterminacy in his paintings, which Gilbert-Rolfe argues is "clearly involved with the idea of limitlessness" and "the possibility of formlessness" (*Beauty* 51). Though discussions of the sublime tend to focus on visual art or natural "phenomena whose intuition brings with it the idea of its infinity," Burke, Lyotard, and others have argued that as compared with other aesthetic materials, words have "the privilege of engendering a limitlessness" (Kant, "From" 394; Lyotard, *Sublime* 66–67, 55; see also Gilbert-Rolfe, *Beauty* 68; Philip Shaw, *Sublime* 49, 52). I suggest that postmodern literature's persistent engagements with the limitless, boundless, and infinite in the works of O'Brien, Calvino,

---

4. See Hazard Adams, *Critical* 378; Rosenblum 112; Crowther 7; David B. Johnson, "Postmodern" 122; Burke 118; van de Vall 72; Merritt 39; Etlin 233, 230.

Jorge Luis Borges, José Saramago, and others offer a valuable opportunity for more extensive explorations of the sublime in the domain of literary art.

Frequently described as "exceed[ing] what imaginative thought can grasp at once in a form" or as "an overabundance of stimulation," writers remain divided on the question of whether to locate the sublime in "features of the objects (such as magnitude, height, and elevation)" and/or in "the affective states (such as transcendence, awe, fear, and terror) they produce" (Lyotard, *Sublime* 53–54; Weiskel 105; Costelloe 7, 2).[5] Though Lyotard remarks that "there are no sublime objects but only sublime feelings" (*Sublime* 182), philosophers vary widely on what these "sublime feelings" might entail. While Edmund Burke believed that the sublime "rises from the power of terror," his Scottish contemporaries Alexander Gerard, Henry Home, Archibald Alison, and Dugald Stewart suggest "terror is not the definitive moment"; instead, they locate the "central, defining characteristic of the sublime" in its etymological root *sublīmis* or "elevation" (Burke 117; Zuckert 66).

Recent developments in neuroaesthetics offer productive interventions on such debates. Based on experiments in functional magnetic resonance imaging (fMRI), neuroscientists Tomohiro Ishizu and Semir Zeki found that the amygdala and the insula (i.e., portions of the brain typically "associated with the experience of fear and threat") remain deactivated during participants' exposure to the sublime in visual art—findings that weaken the popular Burkean notion of terror as a source of the sublime (Ishizu and Zeki 7; Burke 114). Neuroaesthetics also refines our understanding of *awe*—likewise crucially linked to the sublime—as "a major driver of aesthetic response"; though awe is traditionally linked to concepts of "fear" and "dread," its effects have been observed "in the pontine reticular formation (part of the midbrain)" rather than the amygdala or insula (*Oxford English Dictionary*; Starr 57).

G. Gabrielle Starr further links the notion of *transport*—"the term commonly employed to describe the peculiar feeling of intense aesthetic involvement," which Longinus also identifies as the sublime's key effect—with functions of the brain's default mode network (Starr 63;

---

5. See also Potkay 204–7; Philip Shaw, *Sublime* 7. Kant, in particular, emphasizes the cognitive dimension of the sublime, remarking that "true sublimity" does not reside in the object which occasions this state, but "only in the mind of the subject judging" ("From" 393–94).

Longinus 77). Comprising "an interlinked set of brain regions" which include the posterior cingulate cortex (linked to "episodic memory and forward planning") and the anterior medial prefrontal cortex (which is "sensitive to negative emotions"), Starr observes that "the default mode network shares a good deal of its architecture with the systems that enable mental imagery" (62–63, 41–42, 24–25). Given "its ability to mediate the interconnectivity of the internal and external worlds, an interconnectivity lit up by pleasures and reward" (63), the default mode network likely enables the sense of absorption and transport we experience when reading works of sublime literary art.

If our response to the sublime is not driven by fear/terror, yet continues to engage neuroanatomy that is "sensitive to negative emotions" (Starr 42), I posit that it may be possible to attribute this phenomenon to the *resistance* or *conflicting affective states* that characterize the sublime. Most philosophers regard sublime experience as a "negative pleasure" that alternates between attraction and repulsion, "two contradictory perceptions in a single feeling" produced by "a momentary checking of the vital powers and a consequent stronger outflow of them" (Kant, "From" 391; Schiller 182–83; Ramazani 164).[6] The conflict underpinning the sublime is perhaps best illustrated in twentieth-century Surrealist writing and iconography, given their "preoccupation with incongruity and contradiction" in the juxtapositions of "beauty and monstrosity" and "horror and delight" (Dickson and Romanets 22). "The ascendancy of the sublime" in the twentieth century, Adorno notes, "is one with art's compulsion that fundamental contradictions not be covered up but fought through in themselves" (*Aesthetic* 197).

For Kant, Schiller, Lyotard, and others who follow in the tradition of the Kantian sublime, "the struggle is between the evidence of the senses [. . .] and the supersensible power of reason" (i.e., the conflict between "imagination and reason"), "and it is precisely this contradiction between the two which makes the charm of the sublime" (Philip Shaw, *Sublime* 6; Schiller 182, 71).[7] Though Lyotard, Derrida, and others suggest that sublime feeling ultimately lies with *reason*,[8] I modify this position in my account to align the sublime principally with Dionysian

---

6. See also Lyotard, *Sublime* 67, 109; Derrida 42; Merritt 40; Philip Shaw, *Sublime* 7; Slade, *Lyotard* 85.

7. See Kant, "From" 393; Lyotard, *Sublime* 109, 125; Prager 115.

8. See Lyotard, *Sublime* 58; Gilbert-Rolfe, *Beauty* 63; Derrida 43.

energies of the sense-drive—which seeks to rupture ordering systems, including that of reason—given my revised emphasis on the sublime's *imaginative* dimensions of limitlessness, infinitude, awe, transport, and negative pleasure.

Philosophers traditionally position the sublime as a dual mode, a distinction that can be traced to Longinus, who notes that the "vehement and inspired passion" characterizing the sublime takes two forms: the first is comparable "to a thunderbolt, or flash of lightning," in its "speed, power and intensity"; the second, "after the manner of a widespread conflagration, rolls on with all-devouring flames, [. . .] fed by an unceasing succession" (Hazard Adams, *Critical* 76; Longinus, "Sublime" 85). The sublime can thus be experienced in a given instant or as a successive buildup across the text. Alexander Gerard's *Essay on Taste* (1759), Kant's *Critique of Aesthetic Judgement* (1790), and Schiller's *On the Aesthetic Education of Man* (1794) also distinguish between two types of sublime; unlike Longinus, however, they identify this distinction as a difference in kind rather than duration. Paul Guyer contends that Gerard's distinction between "the quantitative magnitude of natural objects" and "the qualitative magnitude of human moral dispositions" paved the way for Kant's distinction between the "mathematical" and "dynamical" sublime (104).[9] Channeling Kant's discussion of the sublime from a response to nature into a response to art and literature, Schiller renames the two modes "the sublime of knowledge and the sublime of force" (Schiller 133; Guyer 106).

Drawing on Derrida's notion that the sublime presupposes violence done to the senses by the imagination (43), I reposition the sublime's dual modes on a continuum that is principally concerned with the sense-drive/*imagination* in increasing degrees of conflict with the moral-drive/*reason*, as we move from the mathematical to the dynamical end of the sublime. This chapter focuses on the mathematical sublime, where I use O'Brien's *The Third Policeman* and Calvino's *Invisible Cities* to explain how the texts' engagements with the infinite, limitlessness, and tensions between representation and the unpresentable facilitate the imagination's assault on readers' senses.

---

9. For a comprehensive discussion of the mathematical and dynamical sublime, see Kant, *Critique,* part I, §I, book II, subsections 25–28; Guyer 104; Merritt 39–42.

THE THIRD POLICEMAN

As with *At Swim-Two-Birds* and *Lanark,* O'Brien's *The Third Policeman* (1939–40/1967) features a disorienting textual universe, where the unnamed character-narrator undergoes a series of bizarre encounters in a world partly governed by de Selbian eccentricities (Hopper 195, 220). Unlike novels that fall within the aesthetic mode of play, however, the reader's central difficulty here is not an attempt to orient to the storyworld; the eventual realization that the narrator is in (a version of) hell provides only a frame for understanding *The Third Policeman* (hereafter *Policeman*) without resolving or alleviating most of the cognitive and existential challenges it presents in moments that facilitate the experience of the mathematical sublime. It is only when readers begin to appreciate the increasing distance between positions of the narrative audience and authorial audience—when we detach from realist frames, delighting in the policemen's absurd theories in all the glory of their pseudological trappings—that an important renegotiation of affect takes place.

Best-known as an exemplary instance of "postmodernist fiction," Keith Hopper notes that *Policeman* is an extremely sophisticated example of the genre, wherein typical postmodern literary devices such as metalepsis "operate more organically" than mechanically (McHale, *Postmodernist* 191–92; Hopper 136; see also Murphy 37–38; Hopper 195; Robin 37). Variously interpreted through the lens of "nonsense writing"[10] and as a uniquely Irish form of speculative writing, *Policeman* may be read as an instance of the techno-sublime. As "a locus of collision between Ireland's rich fantasy tradition and the twentieth century's idiom of science and technology," Val Nolan observes that O'Brien uses the fictional philosopher de Selby to satirize "the rampant, destructive pace of change and progress" in the wake of mass industrialization after the First World War (178–79).

Terence Dewsnap, Todd Comer, Thierry Robin, and Carol Taaffe in turn read the novel through the lens of (Anglo-)Irish politics, focusing on themes such as dispossession, power and agency, and the cultural dynamics of postindependence Ireland. Hopper remarks that

---

10. "Nonsense writing" stretches "logic to its illogical ends" in ways that expose "the irrationality of rational thinking" (Taaffe 69).

Policeman is an allegorical "microcosm of the Irish Free State and the tragedy of Irish male attitudes to sexuality," detecting "a certain Irish tradition of cruel humour" in O'Brien's use of the macabre and the grotesque (62, 84). Like Hopper, M. Keith Booker has examined the novel's engagements with Menippean satire and carnivalesque ambivalence, while Anthony Adams and Mary O'Toole interpret the novel through Alfred Jarry's pataphysics and J. W. Dunne's theories of time and serialism. Such vibrant and diverse critical scholarship attests to the novel's protean nature and its enormous imaginative capacities, which I argue are inextricably linked to *Policeman*'s engagements with the sublime.

Representation and the Unpresentable: Struggling with Language

Tension between representation and the unpresentable is vividly evoked in the narrator's recurring, excessive verbosity, as he struggles with language's inadequacy for verbalizing his sublime experiences:

> *I cannot hope to describe* what it was but it had frightened me very long before I had understood it even slightly. It was *some* change which came upon me or upon the room, *indescribably subtle, yet momentous, ineffable.* It was as if the daylight had changed with unnatural suddenness, as if the temperature of the evening had altered greatly in an instant or as if the air had become twice as rare or twice as dense as it had been in the winking of an eye; *perhaps* all of these and other things happened together for all my senses were bewildered all at once and could give me no explanation. [. . .] I heard a cough behind me, [which. . .] seemed to bring with it some more awful alteration in everything, just as if it had held the universe stand-still for an instant, suspending the planets in their courses, halting the sun and holding in mid-air any falling thing the earth was pulling towards it. [. . .] *It is hard to write of such a scene or to convey with known words* the feelings which came knocking at my numbed mind. [. . .] *I will not try to tell of* the space of time which followed. (O'Brien, *Policeman* 23–25; emphases added)

This lengthy quotation demonstrates the narrator's difficulties in articulating (what readers later learn is) his unconscious passage from life into the afterlife. Such arduous wordiness, however, seems to forestall affect typically associated with the sublime—such as terror, elevation, awe, rapture, wonder—by redirecting readers' attention to the inadequacy of words. To paraphrase Richard Hooker's critique of Caspar David Friedrich's paintings, O'Brien likewise represents a situation in which "we might experience the sublime *if we were there*"; Hooker insists that while it is possible to make claims about art's ability to "represent situations which might evoke a feeling of the sublime," it "cannot evoke in us the *experience* of the sublime" (47; emphases added). It is thus implied that though sublime experience is (theoretically) possible at the level of taking up position with the narrative audience, its affective dimensions ultimately elude the authorial audience.

I suggest that for *Policeman*'s authorial audience, the sublime functions (as Longinus describes it) in a successive buildup "after the manner of a widespread conflagration" rather than the instantaneity of a lightning bolt ("Sublime" 85). Instead of cuing readers to approach the novel using the principle of maximal departure from the outset, O'Brien "uses the type of illusion associated with realism, slowly stretch[ing] the reader's suspension of disbelief as the situations grow more bizarre" (Baines 81). The sense-drive's propensity for defying order in favor of imaginative potentialities is discernible in the narrator's difficulty of accounting for the "indescribable" objects that fall through the chute in Eternity, which cannot be described in any known color and lack "an essential property of all known objects" (*Policeman* 135).[11] In another instance, the narrator's terrifying experience of attempting to discover the source of an inexplicable burning light that spans seven pages of discourse ultimately turns out to be from Policeman Fox's barracks situated *within the walls* of Mathers's house (175–82).

---

11. "But what can I say about them? In colour they were not white or black and certainly bore no intermediate colour; they were far from dark and anything but bright. But strange to say it was not their unprecedented hue that took most of my attention. They had another quality that made me watch them wild-eyed, drythroated and with no breathing. I can make no attempt to describe this quality. It took me hours of thought long afterwards to realise why these articles were astonishing. *They lacked an essential property of all known objects*. I cannot call it shape or configuration since shapelessness is not what I refer to at all. I can only say that those objects, not one of which resembled the other, were of no known dimensions. They

Notwithstanding the narrator's admission to being a murderer in the novel's opening line, Anne Clissmann rightly observes that most readers are likely (at least initially) to identify with the narrator's "fear and bewilderment" (156) from the position of the narrative audience, since the knowledge of his death and of the fact that the Parish is literally hell is withheld from both the narrator and readers alike until the novel's conclusion.[12] The narrator's encounters in the Parish and Eternity confound and bewilder precisely because, like the narrator, we as readers struggle to make sense of the textual world using real-world cognitive frames of physics or philosophy—a method largely prompted by O'Brien's textual design, whereby characters like Sergeant Pluck espouse Atomic Theory and Martin Finnucane reflects on the meaning(lessness) of life (*Policeman* 85–91, 47). Adapting what Hooker terms "sublimity as process" (48) for my own purpose,[13] I suggest that as readers gradually detach themselves from the narrator's (and their own) logic-driven, realist frames of seeing and understanding the textual world, the narrator's excessive verbosity and bewildered sense of the world becomes uproariously funny and dark instead of tediously illogical.

Consider, for instance, Sergeant Pluck's explication of Atomic Theory, where people "get their personalities mixed up with the personalities of their bicycle as a result of the interchanging of the atoms of each of them and you would be surprised at the number of people in these parts who nearly are half people and half bicycles"—a revelation that causes the narrator to let forth "a gasp of astonishment that made a sound in the air like a bad puncture" (*Policeman* 85). The comic implications of Pluck's theory include both unorthodox fornications

---

were not square or rectangular or circular or simply irregularly shaped nor could it be said that their endless variety was due to dimensional dissimilarities. Simply their appearance, if even that word is not inadmissible, was not understood by the eye and was in any event indescribable. That is enough to say" (*Policeman* 135).

12. "For O'Brien's purpose," Clissmann observes, "it is important that the reader should not know that this is a hell earned for the crime until the end, for this would make the story a fantasy rather than what seems to be, as it is read, a picture of dislocated reality. O'Brien goes to considerable lengths to make the reality seem convincing, though he does give many clues as to the true state of affairs [. . .]. The choice of a first-person narrator serves to make the reader identify with the fear and bewilderment of the narrator as he goes through his strange experience" (156).

13. Hooker does not use the term in the way I set out here, but his phraseology inspired my thought processes here.

between Gilhaney's blackguard bicycle and a blameless lady teacher, and hungry bicycles too clever to be caught stealing food (89). The tension between such de Selbian frames of understanding that tease the sense-drive unceasingly and the narrator's (and readers') realist frames and trappings of scientific knowledge facilitates our sublime experience of the text. It is only when readers break with such realist frames of acquiring knowledge about the textual world—that is, move from the position of narrative to authorial audience—that we begin to enjoy the infinitely dizzying storyworld which attests to the strength of O'Brien's lively imagination.

This affective about-turn facilitated by the aesthetic mode of the sublime is congruent with *Policeman*'s thematic emphasis that the quest for absolute knowledge or understanding is impossible, futile, and/or destined to fail. Robin notes that O'Brien's postmodern awareness of the limits of language is evident in "the hollowness of all attempts" at depicting reality in *Policeman*, "be [they] performed at a scientific, literary, social, historical or purely linguistic level" (33). Booker likewise observes that "O'Brien's central theme" of "the futile efforts of science and philosophy to describe the world through epistemological inquiry" in *Policeman* is as much a comment on "the futility of all human endeavors in the modern world" as it is "a parody of such commentaries" (6–7). The aesthetic project at stake here is thus significantly different from the one in *Two-Birds*, since the readerly task of orienting the chaotic textual world prompted by play mechanisms is doomed to futility here; what we *can* do is choose to enjoy the mad ride that is the afterlife.

"Hell goes round and round": Gestures toward Infinity, Eternity, and Beyond

The non-orientable surface of *Policeman*'s Möbius strip–like world loops around when the unnamed character-narrator learns the truth about his posthumous status on the novel's antepenultimate page— winding back to the moment 150 pages earlier, when he first(?) encounters the policemen's barracks, ominously implying the infinitely recurring and interminable circularity of his futile quest. Numerous critics find it disquieting that *Policeman*'s "afterworld differs so little from everyday life in Ireland," since the novel "implies that something approximating rural Ireland is in itself sufficient punishment for all eternity" (Booker 148; Taaffe 82, 78; O'Connell 234–35; Robin 42). Booker adds that the motif of failure that informs postmodern Irish writing—in the work of O'Brien, Beckett, and others—"goes beyond mere artistic mask or fashionable twentieth-century pessimism and speaks directly to political realities in Ireland, a country whose history is fundamentally informed by futility" (13).

O'Brien's response to such futility, however, is far from pessimistic. His parody of rural Ireland, of scientific method and philosophical inquiry, and of other things besides, illustrates what Clissmann calls a quintessentially "Irish humour which depends for its effect on a close connection between the sublime and the ridiculous" (164). Philip Shaw suggests that "the sublime does indeed verge on the ridiculous" in that it continually gestures toward the "infinite when all the time it is drawing us closer to our actual material limits: [. . .] the encounter with lack, an encounter that is painful, cruel, and some would say comic" (*Sublime* 10). Consider MacCruiskeen's painstaking process with his nested chests:

> He took a something from his pocket that was too small for me to see and started working with the tiny black thing on the table beside the bigger thing which was itself too small to be described.
>
> At this point I became afraid. What he was doing was no longer wonderful but terrible. [. . .] When I saw the table it was bare only for the twenty-nine chest articles but through the agency of the glass I was in a position to report that he had two more out beside the last ones, the smallest of all being nearly half a size smaller than ordinary invisibility. [. . .]
>
> "Six years ago they began to get invisible [. . .]. Nobody has ever seen the last five I made because no glass is strong enough to make them big enough to be regarded truly as the smallest things ever made. Nobody can see me making them because my little tools are invisible into the same bargain. The one I am making now is nearly as small as nothing. [. . .] The dear knows where it will stop and terminate." (*Policeman* 70–74)

Not content merely to devise a world that stretches our imagination with its insistence on absurd precision—where objects can be "nearly half a size smaller than ordinary invisibility" and silence has degrees of loudness and softness[14]—its "illusion of wonder" is "exploded, with a classic move of Flannian absurdity, in the comic scene where the tiniest (and microscopic) chest is knocked to the floor" (Anthony Adams, "Butter-Spades" 115). Genuine alarm and amusement attend our reading of the text as MacCruiskeen's ominous rage hovers over the narrator and Gilhaney, who crawl "feebly about the floor, peering and feeling for something that could not be felt or seen and that was really too small to be lost at all" (*Policeman* 113).

Kant's mathematical sublime, Paul Crowther notes, references that which "overwhelms our perceptual and imaginative capacities. [. . .] Indeed, our very inability to wholly assimilate it at the sensory level, makes the fact that we can thus assimilate it in rational terms all the more vivid. We come to *feel* the scope and superiority of our rational being" (11). O'Brien's novel challenges readers' perceptual and imaginative capacities through its use of mise-en-abyme: with images of chests within chests, mirrors within mirrors, houses within houses, bodies within bodies, eyes within eyes, and so on (*Policeman* 70–74, 64–65, 182, 118, 24–25; see also Hopper 79, 100, 213, 220–21; Booker 16; O'Toole 225). Hopper notes that "the stark implication of the motif of infinite regress" finally begins to dawn on the narrator in chapter 8, when he questions, "Was I in turn merely a link in a vast sequence of imponderable beings [. . .]? Who or what was the core and what monster in what world was the final uncontained colossus? God? Nothing?" (Hopper 115; *Policeman* 118). By refusing solace in the knowledge of "the scope and superiority of our rational being," the sublime experience facilitated by postmodern fiction thus denies readers the transcendent knowledge espoused by the Romantics; only cognizance of the infinite, unknowable deferral of self remains finally available to readers.

This unknowable instability of self extends to the fabric of *Policeman*'s storyworld, which is underpinned by a distinctly Schopenhauerian understanding of reality, whereby the (after)world—as the narrator experiences it—is "the mere appearance of an underlying

---

14. MacCruiskeen's music box "made sounds too esoterically rarefied to be audible to anybody but himself. [. . .] The silence in the room was so unusually quiet that the beginning of it seemed rather loud when the utter stillness of the end of it had been encountered. How long this eeriness lasted or how long we were listening intently to nothing is unknown" (*Policeman* 105–6).

reality, structured by the subjectively valid forms of space, time, and causality" (Guyer 112). The narrator's encounters gradually stretch and ultimately destroy his subjectively held forms of knowing the world through such spatiotemporal parameters: eternity, for instance, "has no size at all" and can be reached by going through a countryside "where it was always five o'clock in the afternoon" (*Policeman* 133, 96). The narrator's failure to discern this disconnect between appearance—that is, his (and readers') subjective sense of how the world works—and the underlying reality that hell and its eternity will not conform to these epistemological parameters ultimately becomes the narrator's undoing.

When the truth about *Policeman*'s underlying reality is revealed—that the narrator has been "dead for sixteen years" and these sublime experiences are part of his afterlife odyssey—he is once again condemned to forgetting: "My mind became quite empty, light, and felt as if it were very white in colour. [. . .] I did not recall who I was, where I was or what my business was upon earth" (197–98). In line with the narrator's punishment of being denied structures of meaning, understanding, and knowledge throughout *Policeman*, this realization of his posthumous state on the novel's antepenultimate page is likewise rescinded or wrested from him, as he resumes his terrifying, eternally repetitive quest of futility.

R. Jahan Ramazani suggests that Nietzsche's "notion of eternal recurrence is a covert version of the mathematical sublime, though [Nietzsche] would never admit such a debt to Kant": for both Nietzsche and Kant, "the failure to constellate reality into higher and higher aggregates" is "an intuition not subject to empirical tests; and it is a revelation of the infinite that is at once empowering and terrifying" (168). This sublime revelation of the infinite offered to the reader ultimately remains unavailable to the narrator, who embodies George Santayana's sobering maxim that "those who cannot remember the past are condemned to repeat it" (*Life* 172). Though *Policeman* loops back unto itself as the narrator is once again terrified by the "extraordinary spectacle" that is the constabulary (198–99, 52–53), in a postmodern subversion of the mathematical sublime, O'Brien slyly refuses readers the security of transcendent knowledge—of understanding exactly how eternal recurrence will play out—by adding Divney to the journey this time around.

As the narrator wanders blankly out of Divney's house upon learning of his own death, he goes "to get [his] bicycle. It was gone" (197; strictly speaking, it is Sergeant Pluck's bicycle, with which the narrator eloped). The narrator's mind eventually goes void as he reembarks on the "rough cheerless road" to the constabulary (197). Joined by Divney, the narrator reenters the barracks where he is once again greeted by Sergeant Pluck's terrifying mantra in the novel's final line: "'Is it about a bicycle?' he asked." While the question—first encountered on page 54 of the novel—reflects Sergeant Pluck's morbid obsession with bicycles, its repetition at the very end is disconcerting since (unbeknownst to the narrator, whose brain is already void) a lost bicycle has indeed precipitated the journey. Throwing the missing bicycle into the mix thus gives readers pause since we are suddenly less certain of how accurate our previous narrative judgments of Sergeant Pluck have been, for his repeated question in the final line of the novel now ambiguously implies a (previously absent) transcendent knowledge of events. Unlike the narrator condemned to forgetting, readers have the framing knowledge this time around that this is some sort of afterlife, hell, or eternity that we are dealing with in the textual world; but much remains uncertain and eludes our complete understanding, as O'Brien implies it well should.

INVISIBLE CITIES

Like O'Brien, I argue that Calvino is yet another postmodernist writer who is committed to diverse aesthetic ambitions when we examine the oeuvre of his work. Published just three years after *The Castle of Crossed Destinies*, *Invisible Cities* (1972/74) remains similarly invested in issues such as multiplicity, ambiguity, and form—though Calvino addresses them here in distinctly different ways. Stefano Bartezzaghi observes that the novel's ingenious formal structure produces

> a design in which 55 cities will appear (as in Thomas More's *Utopia*), plus another nine frame chapters (the dialogues between Marco Polo and Kublai Khan) to produce a total of 64 texts (thus implicitly alluding to the number of squares on a chess-board). [. . .] The state of repose suggested by the initial symmetry (eleven rubrics each

containing five cities) is disrupted by the ladder-like structure: like a progressive attack on the chess-board, or a flight of birds in the sky, the arrow of the diagram wedges itself into the shape and dynamizes it into life. (134)

Upon closer inspection, however, Kathryn Hume points out that the novel's "overt orderliness is deceptive," since the arrangement of its "elaborately patterned" textual world "proves arbitrary" (*Calvino's* 135). Without reference to the table of contents, for instance, it is difficult to tell if "Euphemia, the city where memory is traded at every solstice and at every equinox," belongs under the rubric of "Cities & Memory," "Trading Cities," or "Cities & the Sky" (Calvino, *Invisible Cities* 37; hereafter *Cities*). I propose that cities fit comfortably within different rubrics precisely because Calvino works to negate the limits of formal order by pointing instead to the cities' fluidity and generativity. This is not to say that formal order has no utility; rather, its value lies in its multiplicity, as the sense-drive takes precedence over the form-drive.

Cities renders a sublime textual universe that exposes the limits of form, knowledge, and other ordering systems in favor of the sense-drive's engagement with imaginative potentialities and ontological ambiguities. The novel opens with Kublai Khan's rumination on "the desperate moment" in which emperors discover that their empire, which had seemed to them "the sum of all wonders, is an endless, formless ruin" (5). Kublai's sublime realization that he "shall soon give up any thought of knowing and understanding" the "boundless extension" of territories conquered precipitates "a dizziness that makes rivers and mountains tremble on the fallow curves of the planispheres where they are portrayed" (5). It is an affective moment of cosmic magnitude, in which the empire's very rivers and mountains seem to reverberate with Kublai's despair, with references to the "boundless," "endless," and "formless" invoking the sublime mode. Marco Polo's evocative vignettes of the cities that constitute the empire thus become the means by which Kublai alleviates or stays this moment of desperation, in "the traces of happiness still to be glimpsed" as "faint lights in the distance" (59).

As with *Policeman*, *Cities* continually foregrounds the difficulties of representation and communication—and, in so doing, facilitates an implicit indictment of empire as an inadequate form of political order, where Kublai's alienation is manifest in the communication breakdowns with his envoys: "the emperor is he who is a foreigner to each of his subjects [. . .]. In languages incomprehensible to the Khan, the envoys related information heard in languages incomprehensible to them"; only "revenues received by the imperial treasury" emerged "from this opaque, dense stridor" (21). Such communication failures, however, correspondingly offer imaginative opportunities for dynamic engagements between Kublai and Marco.

Unschooled in Kublai's language, Marco initially relies on objects from his travels to relate his experiences, wherein "connections between one element of the story and another were not always obvious to the emperor" because "the objects could have various meanings: a quiver filled with arrows could indicate the approach of war, or an abundance of game, or else an armorer's shop [. . .]. But what enhanced for Kublai every event or piece of news reported by his inarticulate informer was the space that remained around it, a void not filled by words" (38). Such multiplicity of meanings and this space/void are crucial to Calvino's sense of the *imagination*, which, he writes, "must have the benefit of areas in flux" and be "open to interpretations that leave some margin for the creativity of the interpreter" (Calvino, *Uses* 247; cf. Modena 117). For Calvino, then, literary art that trades on the imagination is an act of co-construction between author and reader, teller and interpreter.

Upon learning Kublai's language, Marco paradoxically discovers that "words failed him, and little by little, he went back to relying on gestures, grimaces and glances," discarding the "closed, stable" system of language for "a new kind of dialogue" and understanding (*Cities* 39)—one that depends on the sense-drive's dynamism and fluidity for its effectiveness. In the city of Hypatia, for instance, Marco learns to discard learned systems of signification in order to "succeed in understanding the language of Hypatia": music is to be found in cemeteries where "musicians hide in the tombs" rather than concert halls, and in order to leave the city, "one must not go down to the harbor then, but climb to the citadel's highest pinnacle and wait for a ship to go by up there. But will it ever go by?" Polo wonders (48). Even when the traveler appears to have unearthed the city's underlying system, Calvino reveals the limiting nature of such ordering structures, opting instead for open-endedness, indeterminacy, and incertitude as ways of exceeding those limits.

The imaginative power of *Cities* springs in part from the space of void that hums with the possibilities of all that could happen. In Chloe, for instance, strangers

> imagine a thousand things about one another; meetings which could take place between them, conversations, surprises, bites. But no one greets anyone; eyes lock for a second, then dart away, seeking other eyes, never stopping [. . .]. A voluptuous vibration constantly stirs Chloe, the most chaste of cities. If men and women began to live their ephemeral dreams, every phantom would become a person with whom to begin a story of pursuits, pretenses, misunderstandings, clashes, oppressions, and the carousel of fantasies would stop. (51–52)

Taking the estrangement of modern cities as his backdrop, Calvino excavates imaginative possibilities from the malaise of alienation that grips many of our own cities today, suggesting that there is something far from aloof about them in the "voluptuous vibration[s]" of their inhabitants' "carousel of fantasies" and "ephemeral dreams."

The reader's sense-drive is continually engaged with potentialities of change in *Cities*: as Marco enters a city, "he sees someone in a square living a life or an instant that could be his," had he taken one road instead of another at crossroads encountered long ago (29). Yet he is now excluded "from that real or hypothetical past" and "must go on to another city, where another of his pasts awaits him, or something perhaps that had been a possible future of his and is now someone else's present. [. . .] 'Elsewhere is a negative mirror. The traveler recognizes the little that is his, discovering the much he has not had and will never have'" (29). The novel thus emphasizes ways of knowing that bend or challenge spatiotemporal order: the present can be understood only in light of pasts that could have been and futures that could be, exposing the infidelity of linear time for representing the flux of human experience.

The sense that linear structures of time and space are limiting holds true not only for individual experience but also at the level of cities' ontological structures. In Fedora, a building "with a crystal globe in every room" houses a "model of a different Fedora," created by someone in a different age who "imagined a way of making it the ideal city, but while he constructed his miniature model, Fedora was already no longer the same as before, and what had been until yesterday a possible future became only a toy in a glass globe" (32). The limits of representation are repeatedly foregrounded, since cities are never static but continuously shifting from moment to moment, and it is the energy of this dynamic change that Calvino seeks to capture in his writing using the aesthetic mode of the sublime.

Kublai remains preoccupied by issues of epistemology and representation throughout *Cities,* likening the empire at one point to "a zodiac of the mind's phantasms," "reflected in a desert of labile and interchangeable data, like grains of sand" (22). Though the novel was published in 1972, parts of the text illustrate workings of the mind that resonate strikingly with what we currently understand about contemporary neurobiology. Drawing on Zeki's explication of ambiguity's neural bases, I suggest that the simultaneous desert and port city of Despina, for instance, instantiates a "stable ambiguity" in the multi-interpretations that our brain's "organization makes possible" (*Splendors* 61; "Neurology" 187; see chapter 1 of this book).

Readers learn that "Despina can be reached in two ways: by ship or by camel," displaying "one face to the traveler arriving overland and a different one to him who arrives by sea" (*Cities* 17). Like a Kanisza cube where front and rear appear to "spontaneously change position" (Zeki, *Splendors* 61), the city's extraordinary quality lies in its camel-ship[15] optical illusion: "In the coastline's haze, the sailor discerns the form of a camel's withers" in Despina's outline, seeing himself "at the head of a long caravan taking him away from the desert of the sea, toward oases of fresh water"; the camel driver, in turn, perceives the city as a ship "that will take him away from the desert," its flapping windsocks and smoking chimneys imaginatively transfigured into swelling sails and steamboat smokestacks (*Cities* 17). Just as "the brain is only interested in [. . .] constant, essential and non-changing properties" in the task of object recognition (Zeki, *Splendors* 61), Calvino takes two apparently very different situations—that of being surrounded by water at sea versus the arid barrenness of the desert—and highlights the sailor's

---

15. I coin this term after its better-known predecessor, the rabbit-duck illusion.

and camel driver's common experience, in their mirage-like recognitions of Despina, reinforcing the stable ambiguity that characterizes the novel's cities.

Like Kublai, who wonders if his empire "is nothing but a zodiac of the mind's phantasms," Calvino proffers the possibility that our knowledge of the world (particularly through sensory perception) is a construction of the mind/imagination, simultaneously real and a mirage—and that this imaginative sense crucially enriches rather than impoverishes our ways of knowing. To paraphrase Zeki, akin to the concept of color as "a construction of the brain" (i.e., "the tagging of a visual language" to the "constant property of reflectance"), Calvino's cities foreground the notion that "the brain is not a mere passive chronicler of external events" but "an active participant in constructing what we see" (*Splendors* 30; "Neurology" 174). Dreams and reality are not opposed but contiguous in *Cities*, as men search for what emerged from their dreams in the textual actual world: the city of Zobeide, for instance, is born of "an identical dream" by "men of various nations" about a woman running through an unknown city (*Cities* 45). Setting out in search of that city when they awakened, "they never found it, but they found one another" and "decided to build a city like the one in the dream," each following "the course of his pursuit," rearranging the spaces and walls "at the spot where they had lost the fugitive's trail" in order to prevent her escape once more (45). Yet "none of them, asleep or awake, ever saw the woman again" (45).

Accounts of Kublai and Marco's exchanges, in particular, continually imply that the mind inflects everything we experience as reality: "Marco Polo imagined answering (or Kublai Khan imagined his answer)"; "Kublai Khan interrupted him or imagined interrupting him, or Marco Polo imagined himself interrupted"; "These words and actions were perhaps only imagined, as the two, silent and motionless, watched the smoke rise slowly from their pipes" (28, 98). Unlike the weighty density created by the highly patterned lives and fortunes in *Castle*, *Cities* lightens the texture of its worlds by emphasizing a stable, ontological ambiguity, foregrounding the sense-drive's propensity toward open-endedness. Kublai/Polo does and does not speak, conversations do and do not take place, motion and stillness are not mutually exclusive, while speech/travel is not privileged over silence/stillness.

TRANSITIONS: BETWEEN MODES OF THE SUBLIME

In keeping with Kant, philosophers including Schiller, Lyotard, and others conceive of the sublime as a conflict between "imagination and reason" (i.e., the sense- and moral-drives), suggesting that the supersensible faculty of *reason* defines the sublime.[16] My account reverses this emphasis by grounding the postmodern literary sublime in the *imagination,* revising the binary relationship between the sublime's dual modes as being on a continuum, in increasing degrees of conflict between the sense- and moral-drives as we move from the mathematical to the dynamical sublime. Unlike novels that fall within the mode of the dynamical sublime,[17] I argue that postmodern fictional texts aligned with the mathematical mode (such as *Cities*; *Policeman*; Jorge Luis Borges's "The Aleph," "The Garden of Forking Paths," "The Library of Babel," and others) only minimally engage readers' moral-drive and are far more invested in engaging our sense-drive. To clarify my argument, I draw on existing critical scholarship about Calvino's and O'Brien's novels to explain how the moral-drive's functions are subordinate to the workings of the sense-drive.

In her book *Italo Calvino's Architecture of Lightness* (2011), Letizia Modena argues that Calvino uses the concept of utopia in *Cities* to make an ethical and social intervention in Italy's crisis on urban renewal during the 1960s and '70s. Documenting Calvino's engagement with the work of Italian architects and urban planners, Modena positions *Cities* as "a deliberate foray into public and professional discussions around the city and civic life during [the] full-blown crisis" on urban renewal, as a way of "envision[ing] alternatives to existing urban forms and social conventions" (90, 62).

In architecture and urban planning and design as a whole, [. . .] utopia shared three fundamental characteristics: first, the idea that

---

16. See Philip Shaw, *Sublime* 6; Kant, "From" 393; Schiller 182; Lyotard, *Sublime* 58, 109, 125; Prager 115; Gilbert-Rolfe, *Beauty* 63; Derrida 43.

17. Examples of engagements with the dynamical sublime include Arundhati Roy's *The God of Small Things,* Cormac McCarthy's *Blood Meridian,* Salman Rushdie's *Midnight's Children,* José Saramago's *Baltasar & Blimunda,* Milan Kundera's *The Unbearable Lightness of Being,* and so on.

utopia, by going beyond ascertainable reality, makes it possible for people to observe their reality in a defamiliarized way; second, the recognition that the imagination as well as logic are fundamental to the process of exploring possibilities; and third, the awareness of utopia's vigorously dynamic character—of the dialectics of utopia and topia (i.e., the existing order). (64)

Though it is now "primarily imagined as an aesthetic project," Modena notes that "in the '60s and '70s, utopia was a question of engagement, that is, an ethical and social stance or commitment" (62).

The notion of "utopia as a critical construct and social instrument" resonates distinctly with the visionary cities in Calvino's novel, particularly in its engagements with the sublime: in the "voluptuous," imaginative potentialities for "seductions, copulations, [and] orgies" among Chloe's chaste strangers; in the ephemerality of Despina's camel-ship mirage; and in Marco's discarding of existing signifying orders so that Hypatia's own indeterminate system might emerge (Modena 64; *Cities* 51, 17, 48). Given that the "education of vision and the imagination" was "a central preoccupation of intellectuals in the '60s," just as Calvino's novel was being conceptualized and written, Modena's argument that the novel's ethical thrust lies in guiding readers "to see anew" (91) dovetails with my analysis of the text as dominantly engaging the sense-drive. I thus argue that Calvino's channeling of the imagination in this manner engages readers' moral-drive vis-à-vis their sense-drive.

To return to *Policeman,* for a novel that opens with an admission of murder, its critical scholarship has been remarkably devoid of an explicit moral thrust—a quality critics attribute to O'Brien's own textual construction. Anthony Adams observes that "if the bulk of the action takes place in a hellish afterlife, or at least an intellectual purgatory, then *The Third Policeman* presents a curiously confusing hell in which inventiveness and verbosity pose greater dangers than any corporal punishment" (106–7). In fact, Thomas Shea remarks, "I doubt that O'Brien is even mildly interested in moral themes of crime and punishment" (120). Pointing to the moment of Mathers's murder, for instance, Shea notes that what "in a realistic novel might be a gruesome scene is here a comic vehicle for verbal play. The nonsense of 'celery' and 'scullery' diverts us from any serious contemplation of the characters' sin" (120).[18] Furthermore, Hugh Kenner observes that "the great Irish writers" like O'Brien and Beckett have always been able to regard the "human dilemma as essentially an epistemological, not an ethical, comedy" (qtd. in *Policeman* xi). Even the Sisyphean eternal recurrence of the narrator's punishment remains—in typical postmodernist fashion—an ambivalent moral lesson, since the narrator does not retain the knowledge that this is hell and that he (and, later, Divney) is reaping the evil fruits of greed, whether of knowledge or of wealth.

I consider part of *Policeman*'s sublime effect to be minimally reliant on the reader's sense of the moral. Knowing that the narrator committed a heinous crime and is suffering the poetic justice of his actions in the infinitude/eternity of hell potentially alleviates residual guilt that readers might experience at enjoying the dizzying ride that is the afterlife, as we take O'Brien up on his implicit invitation to make an affective about-turn: from the disorienting bewilderment of the narrative audience's incomprehension, to the diverting pleasure the authorial audience derives from O'Brien's lively imagination. Though I do not go so far as to suggest that O'Brien is uninterested in moral themes of crime and punishment, I argue that the novel's sublime mode engages readers' moral-drive much more minimally as compared to the sense-drive.

I suggest in part that the cognitive load demanded by the mathematical sublime—the necessity of attempting to assimilate magnitude or infinitude at the sensory level—is likely to be less conducive to sustained conflicts between *reason* (moral-drive) and the *imagination* (sense-drive). As we move from the mathematical to the dynamical sublime, however, conflicts between the sense- and moral-drives are increasingly foregrounded. The next chapter examines texts approaching the other end of the sublime continuum, in which such conflicts operate at maximal levels.

---

18. "As he [Mathers] collapsed full-length in the mud he did not cry out. Instead I heard him say something softly in a conversational tone—something like 'I do not care for celery' or 'I left my glasses in the scullery'" (*Policeman* 16). Taaffe likewise agrees that "Mathers's murder is coldly and grotesquely comic" (80).

CHAPTER 4

Literary Sublime (II)

Imaginative Engagements of Our Moralistic Minds

IN THIS second of two chapters devoted to the sublime, I turn my attention to the dynamical sublime, in which tensions between the sense- and moral-drives operate at maximal conflict. Looking to developments in the cognitive sciences, evolutionary and moral psychology, I draw on Jonathan Haidt's six moral foundations to shape my conception of the moral-drive. Unlike "normative ethics," which is concerned with standards of ethical action, Haidt's model is "functionalist" or "*descriptive*"—defining "morality by what it *does*, rather than by specifying what content counts as moral" (270–71). My conception of the moral-drive is in turn underpinned by both descriptive and normative aspects: on the one hand, I consider how authors mobilize "moral intuitions" (xiv) driven by human evolution and biology to shape readers' aesthetic experiences of fiction; on the other hand, I explore fiction's potential for enlarging our moral repertoires—for instance, by exposing how human "hivishness" (xv) is complicit in perpetuating structures of injustice. Using *The God of Small Things* and *Blood Meridian* as

---

A portion of this chapter was previously published in Wang (2019), "*Blood Meridian*, the Sublime, and Aesthetic Narrativizations of Death," in Daniel Jernigan, Walter Wadiak, and W. Michelle Wang's (eds.), *Narrating Death: The Limit of Literature* (pp. 161–75), Routledge.

my case studies, I explicate how the dynamical sublime functions as an aesthetic mode that nudges readers toward a more constructive shared vision of harmonious ultrasociality.

SOCIAL-MORAL SELVES

Haidt's moral foundations theory identifies six "universal moral 'taste receptors'" that have evolved in humans to meet "long-standing threats and opportunities in social life": interconnected moral intuitions about care/harm, fairness/cheating, loyalty/betrayal, authority/subversion, liberty/oppression, and sanctity/degradation shrink or expand over time in relation to cultural pressures (123–24).[1] As a functionalist model that takes moral systems as "interlocking sets of values, virtues, norms," and "evolved psychological mechanisms" working in tandem to "regulate self-interest and make cooperative societies possible," Haidt's moral instincts describe a type of cognitive reflex toward morality which is "finely tuned to maximize survival, not accuracy" (270, 252)—and are thus susceptible to both error and malleability.

Moral intuitions about *fairness/cheating* are based on ideas about proportionality, reciprocity, and exchange; Dutton suggests that "an intuitive economics" underlies our mind's sense of "obligations, rights, revenge, and what is deserved" (Dutton 44; Haidt 124, 138, 169). The *authority/subversion* intuition—typically associated with qualities such as respect, fear, obedience, and deference—in turn "evolved in response to the adaptive challenge of forging relations that will benefit us within social hierarchies" and "are based on perceptions of legitimate asymmetries" (Haidt 124, 153–54, 143–44). Our *loyalty/betrayal* intuition grew out of "the adaptive challenge of forming and maintaining coalitions" in defense against threats to our group(s), while the *liberty/oppression* intuition developed in "response to the adaptive challenge of living in small groups with individuals who would, if given the chance, dominate, bully, and constrain others" (172–73). Typically triggered by

---

1. In recent decades, for example, "people in many Western societies have come to feel compassion in response to many more kinds of animal suffering, and they've come to feel disgust in response to fewer kinds of sexual activity. The current triggers can change in a single generation, though it would take many generations for genetic evolution to alter the design of the module and its original triggers" (Haidt 123–24).

that which is "perceived as imposing illegitimate restraints on one's liberty," Haidt notes that social justice discourses rely heavily on the liberty/oppression foundation, as a reaction against the accumulation and potential abuse of political and economic powers (174–75).

Most commonly associated with the emotion of disgust, our moral intuitions about *sanctity/degradation* "evolved initially in response to the omnivore's dilemma and then to the broader challenge of living in a world of pathogens and parasites" (148–49, 153–54).[2] Shimamura explains the anterior insula's function in relation to disgust:

> Connected to critical emotional centers, such as the amygdala and orbitofrontal cortex, [the anterior insula] is where neural impulses activated by taste buds on the tongue first enter the cerebral cortex. [. . .] Yet not only does this region respond to taste, but like mirror neurons, the insula is active when we watch someone else eat something disgusting or show the facial expression of disgust. It appears that our brains have co-opted these taste regions to respond generally to disgusting stimuli—real or imagined. In this way, the insula is a part of the emotional circuit involved in empathetic emotions. (249)

Research in moral psychology suggests "a two-way street between our bodies and our righteous minds," identifying positive correlations between physical cleanliness and moralistic attitudes (Haidt 60–61, 44–45). A study at the University of Toronto, for instance, found that "people made harsher judgments when they were breathing in foul air," implying disgust's relevance to our formations of moral judgments (44). The "ancient food-processing center" of the "gustatory cortex" has thus "taken on new duties" in humans and "now guides our taste in people. It gets more active when we see something morally fishy, particularly something disgusting, as well as garden-variety unfairness" (60–61).

Haidt notes that current triggers of the sanctity/degradation foundation "are extraordinarily variable and expandable across cultures

---

2. The omnivore's dilemma is driven by "competing motives" of "neophilia (an attraction to new things) and neophobia (a fear of new things). [. . .] The emotion of disgust evolved initially to optimize responses to the omnivore's dilemma," driven by the adaptive challenge of "avoid[ing] pathogens, parasites, and other threats that spread by physical touch or proximity" (Haidt 148–49).

and eras. A common and direct expansion is to out-group members" (148–49)—a point explicitly thematized in *The God of Small Things*, where Roy illustrates the devastating effects of India's caste system vis-à-vis Ammu and Velutha's "transgressive" relationship. When Inspector Thomas Mathew realizes that Velutha is not Ammu's rapist but her lover, the narrator sardonically notes that the Inspector takes it upon himself "to instil order into a world gone wrong" in his calculated acts "to humiliate and terrorize" Ammu and the twins (259–60). (In my subsequent analysis, I return to address this relationship between narrative voice and the novel's ethical tensions.)

Moral intuitions about *care/harm* in turn grew out of the adaptive challenge of protecting and caring for our offspring, initially triggered by "suffering, distress, or neediness expressed by one's child" (Haidt 124). Typically associated with the emotion of compassion, "it makes us despise cruelty" and celebrates virtues such as caring and kindness (153, 124). Haidt links oxytocin ("a hormone and neurotransmitter produced by the hypothalamus") to our propensity for care or for preventing harm, particularly in its relation to attachment feelings such as intimacy, trust, and loyalty toward one's mate/partner and offspring (233–34). Oxytocin levels also rise when we experience impulses of helping behavior in empathetic response to others' suffering: we "feel each other's pain and joy to a much greater degree than do other primates," since "in humans the mirror neurons have a much stronger connection to emotion-related areas of the brain," including the insula cortex, "the amygdala, and other limbic areas" (234–35).

An important caveat Haidt notes is that we empathize in a *conditional* manner, prioritizing not only our partners and members of our in-groups, but also those who act in ways that conform to rather than violate our own moral matrix (234–36). Our general tendency to empathize with like-minded others who adopt similar moral matrices is congruent with cautionary warnings about fiction's limited efficacy for moral education,[3] but one of literature's unique values lies in its ability to create resonance across moral divides. I argue that an important way fiction orchestrates such resonance is in its use of affective tensions, when it provokes conflicting moral intuitions and/or mixes aesthetic

---

3. See chapter 2 of this book.

registers, as I demonstrate in my analyses of Roy's and McCarthy's novels. Haidt notes that controversial issues often rouse "multiple" and/or "conflicting intuitions" whereby one's "judgment may flip back and forth" depending on "which victim, which argument, or which friend you are thinking about at a particular moment" (59, 68–69)—that is, whom we empathize or identify with—making fiction a fertile site on which such moral thought experiments can be endlessly and imaginatively unfolded.

Given that my concept of the moral-drive relates to the way it functions as an ordering system,[4] in which the self is considered in relation to others within social structures, Haidt's approach to morality—as a system which underpins human ultrasociality in our ability to form and sustain groups (xii–xiii)—offers a pragmatic framework for me to elucidate how authors employ moral intuitions in their aesthetic shapings of fictional worlds. Since literature is continually invested in facilitating novel ways of seeing, experiencing, knowing, and understanding the world, I argue that an important dimension of our interest in fiction lies in its ability to expand (and not simply confirm) our moral horizons. Haidt notes that to persuade someone to approach issues with a revised moral lens requires "elicit[ing] new intuitions" (48). Using *The God of Small Things* and *Blood Meridian* as my case studies, I explain how the aesthetic mode of the dynamical sublime enlarges readers' moral repertoires by facilitating moments of awe, conflicting affect, and tensions between representation and the unpresentable.

The use of fMRI technology in neuroaesthetics experiments has revealed that when participants reported sublime experiences, the superior frontal gyrus was unexpectedly found to be the "most prominently deactivated area," which signifies "a suppression of self-awareness during such processing" (Ishizu and Zeki 9). Given that the sublime has traditionally been regarded "as leading to an *awareness of one's insignificance in relation to the immensity and grandeur of Nature*" (9; emphasis added), such deactivations invite reconsiderations for how we are to understand the aesthetic mode of the sublime. I suggest that one way to explain this diminishing sense of self-awareness relates to what Haidt terms our *hivish inclinations*. Haidt and others

---

4. See the introduction of this book.

argue that as an ultrasocial species, "human nature was produced by natural selection" operating at two simultaneous levels: competitively within *and* between groups (xv). We thus "have the ability (under special conditions) to transcend self-interest and lose ourselves (temporarily and ecstatically) in something larger than ourselves," working "like bees in a hive [...] for the good of the group"—what Haidt terms "*the hive switch*" (223).

Haidt explains that "there are many ways" to trigger our hivish inclinations, noting that "awe is one of the emotions most closely linked to the hive switch, along with collective love and collective joy," which opens us "to new possibilities, values, and directions in life," making us feel "*part of a whole*" (227–28). Conversely, however, such "hivishness can blind us to other moral concerns" as we close ranks with like-minded members of our in-group; our "bee-like nature" thus "facilitates altruism, heroism, war, and genocide" (xv). I attend to both of these dimensions in my analyses: on the one hand, I demonstrate how characters' hivishness can perpetuate structural violence against non/out-group members; on the other hand, I highlight moments that facilitate experiences of the dynamical sublime, triggering readers' hive switch vis-à-vis tensions between the sense- and moral-drives. By inviting readers across moral divides, I explain how the dynamical sublime relates to what Kant terms *practical reason*, especially in the readerly responsibilities to which the text implicitly calls us, or even demands of us.

THE GOD OF SMALL THINGS

Arundhati Roy's *The God of Small Things* (1997; hereafter *Small Things*) centers on how a series of events that happens to a family living in Ayemenem in 1969 ripples across two decades, irrevocably changing the lives of the novel's twin child protagonists, Rahel and Estha(ppen). Despite the seemingly circumscribed nature of their personal tragedies—in which the twins lose in succession their cousin Sophie Mol, their friend Velutha, and eventually their mother Ammu—the novel takes on an "a-historicity" and "timelessness," given the narrative's "circular structure and the evocation of legendary subjects" from Hindu epics (Célérier-Vitasse 69). Though critical scholarship about the novel tends to be dominated by postcolonial readings, Roy explains that for her, this "is not a book specifically about 'our culture'—it's a book about human nature" (Abraham 91; Aldama, *User's* 57, 64). "Spun from the ungodly, human heart," Roy's novel illustrates the range and power of the "boundless, infinitely inventive art of human hatred" that pervades the everyday, in which personal tragedies take on a terrifying limitlessness, "lurk[ing] for ever in ordinary things" (*Small Things* 55, 230, 236).

The narration's matter-of-fact quality functions in stark tension with the "hideous grief" that the twins experience (328). The "uneasy octopus" of silence that eventually chokes Estha into muteness rocks him "to the rhythm of an ancient, foetal heartbeat," timeless and steady; Rahel's return, however, bursts the dam of silence as "savage waters swept everything up in a swirling. Comets, violins, parades, loneliness, clouds, beards, bigots, lists, flags, earthquakes, despair were all swept up in a scrambled swirling" in Estha's mind (12, 15). Rahel in turn imagines Velutha "dropping like a dark star out of the sky that he had made" at her cousin Sophie Mol's funeral: "Lying broken on the hot church floor, dark blood spilling from his skull like a secret. By then Esthappen and Rahel had learned that the world had other ways of breaking men" (6). The twins' despair and loneliness reverberate with cosmic references to comets, earthquakes, stars falling out of the sky, and an almost default mode of cruelty that generally characterizes the world in its varied ways of breaking people.

The dynamical sublime is further facilitated by Roy's skillful orchestration of conflicting affective registers. For instance, upon seeing her dead mother "wrapped in a dirty bedsheet and laid out on a stretcher,"

> Rahel thought she looked like a Roman Senator. *Et tu, Ammu!* she thought and smiled, remembering Estha.
> It was odd driving through bright, busy streets with a dead Roman senator on the floor of the van. [. . .] Outside the van windows, people, like cut-out paper puppets, went on with their paper-puppet lives. Real life was inside the van. Where real death was. Over the jarring bumps and potholes in the road, Ammu's body jiggled and slid off the stretcher. Her head hit an iron bolt on the floor. She didn't wince or wake up. [. . .]
> The steel door of the incinerator went up and the muted hum of the eternal fire became a red roaring. The heat lunged out at them like

a famished beast. Then Rahel's Ammu was fed to it. Her hair, her skin, her smile. Her voice. [. . .]

The door of the furnace clanged shut. There were no tears. (162–63)

The narrative voice switches seamlessly between irony, nostalgia, black humor, and clinical objectivity, threaded all the way through by seven-year-old Rahel's frozen and inarticulable grief. It is a sublime moment of wrenching intimacy, as Rahel once again witnesses loss first-hand: first of her nine-year-old cousin to the rushing Meenachal waters, then of her friend Velutha to the forces of "history," followed by her twin brother who is sent away to live with their estranged father, and, since "the church refused to bury Ammu" (162), the crematorial flames are indelibly etched in Rahel's memory as a roaring eternal fire that devours her mother's smile and voice.

In particular, the body becomes a "site upon which the spatial meanings of the social order are [cruelly] written" (Friedman 202). The central scene of violence where Velutha is beaten to within an inch of his life, soon dying of his grievous injuries afterward, is rendered in the novel's characteristic conflicting mix of affective registers. Described as "man's subliminal urge to destroy what he could neither subdue nor defy," Estha and Rahel become involuntary witnesses to

> human nature's pursuit of ascendancy. Structure. Order. Complete monopoly. It was human history, masquerading as God's Purpose, revealing herself to an under-age audience. [. . .] The posse of Touchable Policemen acted with economy, not frenzy. Efficiency, not anarchy. Responsibility, not hysteria. They didn't tear out his hair or burn him alive. They didn't hack off his genitals and stuff them in his mouth. They didn't rape him. Or behead him. [. . .] They were merely inoculating a community against an outbreak. (*Small Things* 308–9)

Relying heavily on language that invokes moral intuitions about *sanctity/degradation* and *authority/subversion* in the juxtapositions between those considered Touchable and Untouchable, between policemen and transgressor, Roy's ironic narrative voice exposes how moral discourses are hijacked in the service of reinforcing social caste structures used to justify the subjugation of individuals like Velutha.

Such tensions between the sense- and moral-drives are evident in early reviews of the novel. Alice Truax remarks that the "extraordinary" quality of the narration—"at once so morally strenuous and so imaginatively supple"—emerges in part from "the exuberant, almost acrobatic nature of the writing," which "refuses to allow the reader to view the proceedings from any single vantage point: time and again, [Roy] lures us toward some glib judgment only to twist away at the last minute, thereby exposing our moral laziness and shaming us with it" (*New York Times Book Review* 5). I add that the novel resists simplistic moral judgments by weaving a thick web of culpability, proliferating from individuals to entire social structures complicit in sustaining and perpetuating injustice. When the Ipe family learns of Ammu and Velutha's relationship, a hivish closing of ranks grips members of the "Touchable Kingdom," who patrol moral and social structures "like a team of trolls," fortifying "Edges, Borders, Boundaries, Brinks and Limits," so as to keep "transgressors" like Velutha, Ammu, Estha, and Rahel in line (*Small Things* 260, 309, 3, 31).

Mammachi is enraged Ammu has "defiled generations of breeding [...] and brought the family to its knees," and "nearly vomited" when she thought of her naked daughter with a man whom (with "his particular Paravan smell") "was nothing but a filthy *coolie*" (257–58). Baby Kochamma rides on Mammachi's rage to hatch a vicious plan which eventually "spun out of control like a deranged top," falsely accusing Velutha of (attempted) rape and kidnap—a ploy she sanctimoniously considers "God's Way of punishing Ammu for her sins [while] simultaneously avenging her (Baby Kochamma's) humiliation" (257–62). Velutha's "crimes" are unquestionably taken as given and he is beaten to near-death before he ever hears of (not to mention responds to) the charges, as the Inspector and "Touchable Policemen" work "to instil order into a world gone wrong" (309, 260). The reader's moral-drive is feverishly overloaded as characters' invocations of *sanctity/degradation* ("filthy," "smell," "defiled," "vomited"), *fairness/cheating* ("avenging," "punishing," "sins"), and *authority/subversion* ("instil order," "God's Way") clash violently with readers' moral intuitions about *care/harm, fairness/cheating,* and *liberty/oppression,* in our recognition of the cruel violence, unjust discrimination, and legal deprivation that Velutha suffers.

When the Inspector discovers Baby Kochamma's lies after his subordinates have almost beaten Velutha to death, she uses Sophie Mol's death to blackmail the twins into identifying Velutha as their kidnapper in order to retrospectively substantiate her false accusations.

> In the years to come they would replay this scene in their heads. As children. As teenagers. As adults. Had they been tricked into condemnation?
>
> In a way, yes. But it wasn't as simple as that. They both knew that they had been given a choice. And how quick they had been in the choosing! They hadn't given it more than a second of thought before they looked up and said (not together, but almost)—"Save Ammu." Save us. Save our mother.
> [. . .]
> The Inspector asked his question. Estha's mouth said Yes.
> Childhood tiptoed out.
> Silence slid in like a bolt.
> Someone switched off the light and Velutha disappeared. (318–20)

The twins' inarticulable sense of having violated moral foundations of *care/harm* and *loyalty/betrayal* haunts them endlessly, even though they "both knew that there were several perpetrators (besides themselves)": "It would have helped if they could have made that crossing. If only they could have worn, even temporarily, the tragic hood of victimhood" (191). But "like an imaginary orange" that "wasn't theirs to give away," this unnamable sense of shame "would have to be held. Carefully and for ever" (191).[5]

The sublime force of Velutha's death "left behind a hole in the Universe through which darkness poured like liquid tar. Through which their mother followed without even turning to wave goodbye. She left them behind, spinning in the dark, with no moorings, in a place with no foundation" (191–92). Our sense- and moral-drives are at maximal conflict as readers recognize the partial misguidedness of the twins' limitless grief and self-blame, unleashing alternate waves of pathos for

---

5. The reference to "an imaginary orange" explicitly invokes the traumatic shame and guilt Estha experiences when he is sexually abused by the "Orangedrink Lemondrink Man": Estha "held his Other Hand [which the drink-seller used for masturbation] away from his body. It wasn't supposed to touch anything. [. . .] Estha held his Other Hand carefully (upwards, as though he was holding an imagined orange)" (105).

the children and outrage at the adults and social structures that enable such injustice. *Small Things* continually resists easy moral judgments or assignations of culpability—and, in so doing, indicts the social structures that continue to subjugate individuals under the guise of morality.

Attending to the dynamical sublime not only reveals how the sense- and moral-drives operate in tension with each other, but also allows me to respond to several perhaps well-intentioned but ultimately misguided readings of the text. Aldama has highlighted several of these problems, noting that some critics use Roy's novel as a "reflective surface [. . .] to sound out a particular theoretical reading: feminist, postcolonial (Bhabhaean *inter dicta* or Saidean orientalism), deconstructivist, Marxist, New Historicist, Bakhtinean, post-Freudianist, nativist," and so on—to the point that "Praveen Swami remarked how all the criticism was telling us more about the critics than about 'the book itself'" (Aldama, *User's* 58, 55). My aesthetic lens responds in part to Aldama's exhortation to offer a different type of reading that "account[s] for its accomplishments as a literary work of art" (58). Focusing on the sublime moment of Velutha's and Ammu's mutual recognition of desire, I read back against interpretations that reduce Velutha to "an object of desire and nostalgic longing" (Nandi 181) or "the object of upper-caste men's victimizing masculinist power and an upper-caste woman's gaze" (Mittapalli 54).

Miriam Nandi notes that "Velutha is represented as a stereotypically beautiful labourer" ("strong, muscular, and sexually attractive") whom we see "through Ammu's gaze" (181). "Despite the feminist statement implied in this role reversal," Nandi argues, "the fact that it is a lower caste, underprivileged man who is sexualized and feminized here" renders the act of looking "strongly reminiscent of colonial narratives in which the native and/or the colonized space become the object of the gaze" (181). Rajeshwar Mittapalli goes further, considering Ammu's "sexualized gaze" a "misuse of erotic capital," which "infantilizes" and "objectifies Velutha"; at one point, Mittapalli characterizes Ammu as "a sex-starved woman" who "suffers from sexual deprivation" and remains deeply skeptical about the nature of the relationship given the unequal power dynamics: "Depending on how one defines love, there might be an element of love, better described as 'romantic casteism' in her relationship with Velutha" (61–63).

Such interpretations vividly contradict my own reading of *Small Things,* particularly if readers attend closely to the novel's sublime energies, especially in the scene where Ammu and Velutha mutely recognize their mutual desire.

> It was his smile that reminded Ammu of Velutha as a little boy. [. . .] Holding out little gifts he had made for her, flat on the palm of his hand so that she could take them without touching him. [. . .] she couldn't help thinking that the man he had become bore so little resemblance to the boy he had been. His smile was the only piece of baggage he had carried with him from boyhood into manhood.
>
> [. . .]
>
> The man standing in the shade of the rubber trees with coins of sunshine dancing on his body, holding her daughter in his arms, glanced up and caught Ammu's gaze. Centuries telescoped into one evanescent moment. History was wrong-footed, caught off guard. Sloughed off like a snakeskin. Its marks, its scars, its wounds from old wars and the walking backwards days all fell away. In its absence it left an aura, a palpable shimmering that was as plain to see as the water in a river or the sun in the sky. [. . .]
>
> In that brief moment, Velutha looked up and saw things that he hadn't seen before. Things that had been out of bounds by far, obscured by history's blinkers. [. . .] For instance, he saw that Rahel's mother was a woman. [. . .] He saw too that he was not necessarily the only bearer of gifts. That *she* had gifts to give him too.
>
> This knowing slid into him cleanly, like the sharp edge of a knife. Cold and hot at once. It only took a moment.
>
> Ammu saw that he saw. She looked away. He did too. History's fiends returned to claim them. To rewrap them in its old, scarred pelt and drag them back to where they really lived. Where the Love Laws lay down who should be loved. And how. And how much.
>
> Ammu walked up to the verandah, back into the Play. Shaking.
>
> Velutha looked down at Ambassador S. Insect in his arms. He put her down. Shaking too. (175–77)

While sexual attraction is undeniably crucial to the moment, I remain unconvinced by the argument that Ammu's gaze is a colonizing or infantilizing act of objectification. Such criticism seems to miss the vital point that Velutha's and Ammu's acts of seeing and recognitions of desire are reciprocal, and it is this mutuality that stuns both and leaves them "shaking." Mittapalli and Nandi rightly observe the power imbalance created by historical and social pressures of the caste system, but they fail to recognize that though Ammu and Velutha's relationship may be hampered by "history's fiends" and "obscured by history's blinkers," more important, it *unfetters* itself from these pressures for "one evanescent moment," sloughing off history's "scars" and "wounds," leaving a "palpable shimmering" "aura" in the mutual recognition of love that was as natural and "plain to see as the water in a river or the sun in the sky."

Still more troubling is Mittapalli's assertion that Ammu takes "advantage of the asymmetrical social order" to "exploit" and "victimize" Velutha (54)—a reading that actively strips Velutha of his agency in the relationship, strips him of his ability and choice to having voluntarily loved Ammu. I remain similarly disturbed by Mittapalli's assessment that "like any healthy young man of his age," Velutha "is ruled by hormones and uncontrollable sexual urge," "hardwired to respond to Ammu's sexual overtures," and "thus becomes a pawn in her psychological game" to "get even with her family" (64–65). I argue that such an interpretation flattens and dehumanizes Velutha and Ammu, reducing both characters to passive objects obeying only the dictates of primal sexual urges, perpetuating a kind of theoretical violence in a severe misreading of Roy's novel.

Nandi's interpretation is much more measured, rightly noting that the afore-quoted scene is "among the few in which Velutha serves as a focalizer," since he is typically viewed through other characters' eyes for "most of the novel" (181). However, I disagree with her corresponding assessment that "the reader hardly ever learns about Velutha's own feelings or thoughts; until his death he remains mysterious and unreachable, an object of desire and nostalgic longing" (181). Readers learn a good deal about Velutha given his rapport with and kindness toward the twins—an intimacy that escalates the twins' sense of their eventual betrayal. Sensitive to their emotional needs, he swings delighted seven-year-old Rahel (who has been feeling neglected and insecure) into the air and is the only one who notices Estha's absence amidst the family's fawning over Sophie Mol (*Small Things* 175, 178). When the children visit him "in saris, clumping gracelessly through red mud and long grass," he "greeted them with the utmost courtesy," "introduced them to his surly hen," "gave them fresh coconut water to drink," and playfully remarks that "the ladies in Ayemenem" were "getting shorter by the year. [. . .] It is only now, these years later, that Rahel with adult hindsight recognized the sweetness of that gesture. A grown man entertaining three raccoons, treating them like real ladies," instead of decimating their fictional world "with adult carelessness" (190)—revealing Velutha's loving patience and playful sense of humor.

Rather than being "mysterious and unreachable" (Nandi 181), Velutha is arguably one of the novel's most fully humanized and well-fleshed-out characters with a rich emotional life. Following the sublime moment of his and Ammu's mutual recognition, Velutha wrestles with his feelings for her when he sees the twins: "something clenched in him. [. . .] He saw them every day. He loved them without knowing it," beginning to see Ammu's eyes, mouth, and teeth in her children—thoughts he tried to drive "away angrily," only to have them return (*Small Things* 214). When their relationship is exposed, Velutha quietly stands his ground in the face of Mammachi's outburst, awash in worry for Ammu on the one hand ("*What had they done to her? Had they hurt her?*") and burying his hurt within on the other, as "the rain washed Mammachi's spit off his face" but couldn't stop the "vomit dribbling down his insides. Over his heart. His lungs. [. . .] All his organs awash in vomit. There was nothing that rain could do about that" (286).

The final chapter of Velutha and Ammu's lovemaking transforms the tenderness of remembering each other as children into "aching desire," shared laughter, and "small promise[s]" that temporarily stay the "abyss" beyond (334, 337–39). Velutha's limited focalization results from Roy's strategic narrative choice of dominantly framing the novel through the twins' minds, rather than depriving Velutha of agency as some postcolonial readings suggest. In the eagerness to inscribe dichotomies between colonizer and colonized, oppressor and oppressed, subject and object, such criticism at times offers heavily skewed readings—ironically, by neglecting Velutha's agency—in turn perpetuating a postcolonial theoretical violence on the characters in such misinterpretations.

By attending to the aesthetic mode of the dynamical sublime, readers are better able to vividly share in Roy's sense of the book not (merely) as "an angry critique of 'our society,'" but more crucially as "a way of seeing, a way of presenting the irreconcilable sides of our nature, our ability to love so deeply yet be so brutal" (Abraham 91). That Ammu and Velutha grew up together is a crucial detail of their shared history which undercuts readings that dismiss their relationship as exclusively based in *eros*: having for years internalized society's hierarchized expectations of how they should be around one another, Velutha and Ammu's ability to imagine and realize a different way of being with each other—in the clear knowledge of what it would likely cost them eventually—speaks to the potential promise and possibilities of subverting an unjust social-moral system that seeks to discipline bodies, hearts, and minds.

BLOOD MERIDIAN

Like *Small Things,* Cormac McCarthy's *Blood Meridian* (1985) is similarly shaped by the dynamical sublime's engagement with the forces of history. Richly fashioned from a wealth of historical and geographical sources, McCarthy's novel is a rewriting and partial fictionalization of events involving a gang of scalp hunters along the Texas-Mexico border around the mid-nineteenth century, populated by "historically verifiable characters, places, and events" (Sepich 1). Scholars dominantly discuss *Blood Meridian* (hereafter *Meridian*) in relation to American exceptionalism, the American dream and manifest destiny, colonial/imperial expansion, and racial domination.[6] Critics like Barcley Owens, Steven Shaviro, Rick Wallach, and Ronja Vieth have variously attended to the novel's "sublime realism," "sublime prose style," or "sublime effects," in relation to the American Gothic (Owens 54, 7; Shaviro 153; Josyph 109; Vieth 47, 51–53).

The novel's "ubiquitous violence" is most often understood "as a demythologizing of the American West": a "revisionist western" or "postmodern form of the historical romance," which "challenges and

---

6. See Jarrett 74–75; Masters 25; Michael Evans, "Second" 81; Cant 5, 157; Bowers 8–9, 46; Campbell 221; Parrish, *Civil* 93; Jonathan Imber Shaw, "Evil" 209.

critiques the once-popular view of the West as a place of romance and honor" (Peebles 231; Jarrett 69; Frye 109; Snyder 127; Snyder and Snyder 31, 34). However, even this "revisionist reading" is beset with difficulty, in that "savagery is independent of race" in *Meridian* and massacres are committed by Anglo-Americans, African Americans, Native Americans, and Mexicans alike (Cant 159; Owens 38–39; David Evans, "True West"). Some critics suggest that the novel is both a narrative about a distinctly "American violence" *and* a universal narrative about humankind's enduring propensity for violence (Jarrett 88; Bowers 26; Michael Evans, "Second" 81–82; Bloom, *How* 255; Parrish, "History" 68)—an assessment borne out by the novel's invocation of limitlessness.

Meridian specifically engenders a sense of limitlessness in McCarthy's treatment of space and time. Events in the novel are set against "celestial motions and divine plottings"—a gesture that invokes the cosmic in ways that resonate with the sublime's etymological root "from the Latin *sublimis*" meaning elevated or lofty (Masters 34; Morley 14). The novel opens with the image of the 1833 Leonids meteor shower, as the unnamed protagonist's father recalls the year of his son's birth: "God how the stars did fall. I looked for blackness, holes in the heavens" (*Meridian* 3). Recurrent gestures to the cosmic are evident in descriptions of the Glanton gang as "a patrol condemned to ride out some ancient curse" (157) and of Sproule letting out a "howl of such outrage as to stitch a caesura in the pulsebeat of the world" (69). The cosmos becomes McCarthy's canvas for situating humankind and our (mis)deeds, as human insignificance is made apparent against the sublime vastness of the landscape. Seeing the characters as "pilgrims exhausted upon the face of the planet Anareta, clutched to a namelessness wheeling in the night" (47–48),[7] or as "migrants under a drifting star" with "the star spent reaches of the galaxies hung in a vast aura above" their heads (160) reminds readers time and again of the inconsequentiality of the human species and our deeds, even in our most unremitting acts of violence against one another.

Distinctly calling the novel's subtitle *The Evening Redness in the West* to mind, the scalp hunters' bloody deeds are implied in the very landscape, as the earth is "drained up into the sky at the edge of cre-

---

7. "Anareta was believed in the Renaissance to be 'the planet which destroys life'" (Daugherty 163).

ation" to run like blood across the firmament (47). The world "is a great stained altarstone," with a thirst that cannot be slaked even by the "blood of a thousand Christs" (108)—the single man who in Christian understanding was sent for the redemption of all humankind. The chilling proportions of a bloodthirsty world—one in which readers are inescapably implicated given the text's historical underpinnings—are vividly invoked as the entire world is channeled into the single image of an altarstone, a grotesque inversion of celebratory sacrifice with no possible hope of redemption.

Cosmic indifference is further evoked in what Dana Phillips terms the novel's "lack of human implication," whereby nature and humankind "are equally violent and indifferent to each other" (Phillips 33; Andreasen 23). Following the brutal slaughter of the peaceful Tiguas, readers are confronted with the awful reality that "in the days to come the frail black rebuses of blood in those sands would crack and break and drift away so that in the circuit of few suns all trace of the destruction of these people would be erased [. . .] and there would be nothing, nor ghost nor scribe, to tell any pilgrim in his passing how it was that people had lived in this place and in this place died" (*Meridian* 182). Such inconsequentiality in the face of the perpetual destruction heightens the conflict between readers' sense- and moral-drives in our response to McCarthy's work—a point to which I will return. *Meridian* itself, I suggest, works as a fictional historical testimony against such cosmic indifference and forgetting.

Critics observe that events "take place with a circular or cyclical repetitiveness" in *Meridian,* whereby historical figures such as Glanton and Angel Trias "are merely props for McCarthy's portrayal of history as the eternal return of violence" (Andreasen 19; Parrish, *Civil* 85). The ubiquitous recurrence of violence gives the novel epic proportions that fail to be contained either by geographic space or by the passage of time, as implied by the choice of epigraph from *The Yuma Daily Sun* emphasizing the perpetuity of violence across continents and the span of 300,000 years. Judge Holden's terrible mantra of war—the "ultimate trade awaiting" humankind, "its ultimate practitioner" (*Meridian* 259)—resounds throughout the novel in the unrelenting, historically based violence with which readers are repeatedly confronted.

Shaviro notes that *Meridian* manifests "a sublime visionary power" in its epic scope and its obsession with open space, exploring "vast uncharted distances with a fanatically patient minuteness" (146). Though McCarthy's novel traces the scalp hunters' historical journey "through real places like Ures, Chihuahua, and the Hueco tanks near El Paso," Stacey Peebles observes that "the landscapes that surround them are cosmic and otherworldly" (235). Bernard Schopen remarks that the open topography perpetuates a sense of "inexorable onwardness," stylistically reflected in the repetition of phrases such as "He went on," "They rode on," or the exhortation "to go on" (Schopen 188–89; *Meridian* 47–48). Such gestures toward limitlessness are reinforced in the epilogue's final sentence ("Then they all move on again" [*Meridian* 351]), facilitating a sense of cosmic open-endedness unto perpetuity.[8]

Extradiegetic prolepses scattered throughout the novel—typically insinuations or bald-faced statements about how gang members will meet their end[9]—alongside summaries/blurbs at the beginning of each chapter impart an ominous sense of prophetic doom. Passages such as "now come days of begging, days of theft" (16) or "for each fire is all fires, the first fire and the last ever to be" (255) give the narration an ever-present quality, as though channeling an underlying cosmic consciousness. This cosmic quality is reinforced by sudden switches in verb tense that recur throughout the novel, particularly in the awful refrain that repeatedly emphasizes the judge "never sleeps" and that "he'll never die" (348–49). McCarthy's use of the present tense in the chilling celebratory refrain and the epilogue keeps this violent chapter of US-Mexican history alive and in the present, as something that readers need to continue to grapple with, rather than that which is known, dead, and buried in the past.

The cyclical sense of infinitude is facilitated by the recurrence of meteors that the unnamed protagonist observes in his final vision of the open skies before encountering the judge in the jakes: "Stars were

---

8. Mark Busby remarks on the epilogue's Sisyphean resonances: "The significant elements that McCarthy's epilogue shares with Camus' discussion of Sisyphus are repetition of seeming endless acts (rolling the rock up the hill, digging holes in the ground), rock imagery, mechanical actions, and narratives that confirm the irrevocable reality of death relieved by consciousness and will" (91).

9. For instance, on the inside of the Vandiemenlander's "lower arm was there tattooed a number which Toadvine would see [. . .] when he would cut down the man's torso where it hung skewered by its heels from a treelimb in the wastes of Pimeria Alta in the fall of that year" (*Meridian* 92; cf. 237). For other examples, see pp. 85, 96–97, 111–13.

falling across the sky myriad and random, speeding along brief vectors from their origins in night to their destinies in dust and nothingness" (347). The protagonist's birth and end then are finally tied to the cosmic and the fallen stars' destinies in dust and nothingness. This sense of perpetuity is reinforced in the narration's switch from past to present tense as the scene moves from the unwritten episode in the jakes back to the hall, where the judge's dance resonates with the rhythmic chant of a limitless diabolism. However, it is not the person of the judge that never sleeps or dies[10] but all that he stands for: the insatiable human appetite for perpetual power over others—evolutionarily rooted in our moral intuitions about *liberty/oppression*—and its corresponding cycle of violence in a world doomed to eternal recurrence.

Though McCarthy's allusions to the cosmic, recurrence, and limitlessness in *Meridian* reinforce existing understandings of the sublime, postmodern fiction and contemporary fiction also tend to complicate the aesthetic category. While verbosity and garrulousness in *The Third Policeman* emphasize language's inadequacy for bringing experience to account, *Meridian* subverts this traditional notion of "lack" (in perceptual or imaginative terms) that attends the Kantian sublime by reinvesting readers' faith in the representability and power of words to vividly call experience to the mind's eye.[11] "In an age in which we have been made increasingly aware of the limits of language, of its inability to 'signify the real,'" *Meridian* makes McCarthy's "profound love of language" and "his confidence in its ability to do what he wants it to" startlingly clear in the novel's highly stylized renditions of violence (Cant 3; Snyder and Snyder 32).

The scene most frequently referenced as a powerful instance of aestheticized violence is when the kid rides out with Captain White for the first (and last) time, against Comanche archers who are

> half naked or clad in costumes attic or biblical or wardrobed out of a fevered dream with the skins of animals and silk finery and pieces

---

10. Some critics read the judge as a Satanic, otherworldly figure in light of the diabolical qualities associated with his character, including the insinuation that he will never die. I argue that it is ultimately necessary to read the judge as inescapably *human* (abhorrent as the idea may be) to avoid the easy displacement of evil as something otherworldly. McCarthy makes it explicit in *Meridian* that evil is very much of this world and of the human race.

11. See Crowther 11; Philip Shaw, *Sublime* 10, 138–39; Morley 16.

of uniform still tracked with the blood of prior owners, coats of slain dragoons, frogged and braided cavalry jackets, one in a stovepipe hat and one with an umbrella and one in white stockings and a bloodstained weddingveil [. . .] and one in a pigeontailed coat worn backwards and otherwise naked and one in the armor of a Spanish conquistador, the breastplate and pauldrons deeply dented with old blows of mace or sabre done in another country by men whose very bones were dust [. . .] and all the horsemen's faces gaudy and grotesque with daubings like a company of mounted clowns, death hilarious, [. . .] screeching and yammering and clothed in smoke like those vaporous beings in regions beyond right knowing where the eye wanders and the lip jerks and drools.

Oh my god, said the sergeant. (*Meridian* 54–55)

McCarthy's lengthy sentence captures the scene's anarchy with minute, painstaking detail, in the chaotic, incongruous mishmash of outfits and accessories that vividly invoke times, places, and peoples past, from the slain bride's wedding veil to the "men whose very bones were dust."

Robert Jarrett points out that from an aesthetic point of view, several of *Meridian*'s most violent scenes "probably comprise the best writing in the novel" (75, 88). The sublime beauty of McCarthy's prose emerges from highly stylized yet heterogeneous configurations of violence that fuel the sense-drive, which thrives on change and variation. The violence is at times characterized by visual chaos and sensory overload—with "bits of broken mirrorglass that cast a thousand unpieced suns against the eyes" in the "fevered dream" of the Comanche attack (*Meridian* 54–55)—but ephemeral and surrealistic at other points in the narrative. The dreamlike confrontation with the Apaches in chapter 9, for instance, blends man and landscape, as the "thin frieze of mounted archers," "immense and chimeric," "trembled and veered in the rising heat" like "burnt phantoms" out of a "vanished sea," kicking up "spume that was not real," "shimmer[ing] and slurr[ing] together" as they were "lost in the sun" and the lake (115). As the kid fires at them, they begin to "crumble in the serried planes of heat and to break up silently," vanishing and "dissolving in the [. . .] hallucinatory void" (115, 119).

At other times still, the highly contrived, almost theatrical, images of death function like stylized, visual choreography. During the confrontation with the Chiricahuas, for instance, Glanton spins around to see the gang "frozen in deadlock with the savages, they and their arms wired into a construction taut and fragile as those puzzles wherein the placement of each piece is predicated upon every other and they in turn so that none can move for bringing down the structure entire" (239). When the gang arbitrarily runs a group of mercury-bearing muleteers off into an abyss, the animals drop "silently as martyrs, turning sedately in the empty air and explod[e] on the rocks below in startling bursts of blood and silver as the flasks broke open," and "small trembling satellites" of mercury race in the stone arroyos, as though "some ultimate alchemic work" was being decocted in "the secret dark of the earth's heart" (203). Such savage fireworks that pervade *Meridian* attest to McCarthy's mastery of aesthetic technique—and facilitate a corresponding unease many readers experience in the gratuitous spectatorship of violence in which we are thus implicated when reading the novel.

Most readers likely experience a sensory overdrive after 350 pages of unrelenting violence, as we are continually confronted by partially eaten human bodies and other corporeal desecrations that are wrenching in their intimacy. Our mind's eye is forced to participate in co-constructing images of "eyes cooked in their sockets" (63) and sickening, gut-wrenching acts of scalping that recur throughout the novel.[12] The sense- and moral-drives operate at maximal conflict as readers experience "visceral revulsion" (Eddins 32; Attridge 330) in the sensory overstimulation that violates our moral intuitions about *sanctity/ degradation, liberty/oppression,* and *care/harm.*

Following the confrontation with the Comanches, Sproule and the kid come to a bush hanging "with dead babies. [. . .] These small victims, seven, eight of them, had holes punched in their underjaws and were hung so by their throats from the broken stobs of a mesquite to

---

12. "Passing their blades about the skulls of the living and the dead alike and snatching aloft the bloody wigs and hacking and chopping at the naked bodies, ripping off limbs, heads, gutting the strange white torsos and holding up great handfuls of viscera, genitals, some of the savages so slathered up with gore they might have rolled in it like dogs and some who fell upon the dying and sodomized them with loud cries to their fellows. [. . .] Dust stanched the wet and naked heads of the scalped who with the fringe of hair below their wounds and tonsured to the bone now lay like maimed and naked monks in the bloodslaked dust and everywhere the dying groaned and gibbered and horses lay screaming" (56–57).

stare eyeless at the naked sky. Bald and pale and bloated, larval to some unreckonable being" (*Meridian* 60). George Guillemin notes that this "terrible vignette of the bush hung with dead infants, then, translates into a pure memento mori motif [. . .], reminding us not only that even infants may be subject to murder, let alone death, but also that the world is essentially indifferent to this fact and to such incidents" (243–44, 258). The exactitude of McCarthy's representation likely causes readers to reel with sickening disgust, the recount and specialized diction[13] stumbling us momentarily as we are forced to dwell with the number of dead babies and the precision with which they are calculatedly hung from the tree. Scrupulous in its description of not only the cruel method—where each hole and string goes—the narration takes the reader's mind's eye over the infants' bodies, moving our gaze from throat to eye socket to scalp, forcing us to confront the very corporeality of these babies in an excruciating fashion.

Nor are such descriptions sporadic or infrequent. In yet another massacre,

> one of the Delawares emerged from the smoke with a naked infant dangling in each hand and squatted at a ring of midden stones and swung them by the heels each in turn and bashed their heads against the stones so that the brains burst forth through the fontanel in a bloody spew and humans on fire came shrieking forth like berserkers and the riders hacked them down with their enormous knives and a young woman ran up and embraced the bloodied forefeet of Glanton's warhorse. (*Meridian* 162)

The methodical deliberateness of the description (squatting, swinging, bashing, bursting forth, hacking) and the unexpectedly, almost tender gesture of embrace at the end—which emerges from the use of a completely "different aesthetic register" (Attridge 336) that elicits conflicting moral intuitions about *care/harm*—become overwhelming. The dynamical sublime is facilitated by such tensions between the sense- and moral-drives, as readers are frequently torn between

---

13. *Stob* is dialect for a broken branch while a *mesquite* is a shrub or tree native to Southwest US and Mexico.

staying with the scene/text and feeling compelled to avert our vision from the mental carnage. McCarthy shows that words are more than adequate—perhaps too much so for many readers, who reel from the visions of exacting cruelty; Owens contends that *Meridian* is "pure anoesis, sensation without understanding, devoid of ethical or mythic comfort" (7).[14] McCarthy thus reinvests in the representability of words but emphasizes language's capacity for sensuousness rather than understanding, dominantly engaging the sense- rather than the form-drive.

Schiller's version of the dynamical sublime (otherwise known as the "pathetically sublime") consists of two laws: "to represent suffering nature" *and* "to represent the resistance of morality opposed to suffering" (Schiller 77; Guyer 106). Schiller proposes that suffering is depicted in sublime works of art *in order to* represent "moral freedom," in its "resistance to painful affections" or "the violence of feelings" (75–77). I suggest that in sublime works of postmodern and contemporary fiction, Schiller's second law is deferred/transferred to the reader, such that negotiating the conflicting affective response that attends the sublime becomes a means by which readers are (implicitly) invited to more active engagements with the text. Such affective conflicts are staged in idiosyncratic ways, in line with each novel's specific thematic concerns and overall textual design: *Meridian*, for example, is characterized by continual oscillations between nihilism and sense-making, between beauty and violence, between aesthetic appreciation and ethical dissent, and between the sense- and moral-drives (i.e., *imagination* and *reason*).

Critics point overwhelmingly to *Meridian*'s capacity for vividly engendering conflicting affective states—evident in references to its "blood music" or "difficult beauty"—given "the novel's outlandish aesthetic and moral territories" (Josyph 51; Donoghue, *Practice* 277; Phillips 18). Frye positions the novel as being broadly "informed by the Burkean sublime" (109, 117) while Eddins reads it through a Schopenhauerian sublime, alternating "between awe at the sumptuous prose and the haunting vignettes and visceral revulsion at the heinous atrocities unremittingly depicted in them" (32). Donoghue's experience of

---

14. Other critics observe that "*Blood Meridian* comes at the reader like a slap in the face" and its "unremitting slaughter [. . .] was simply too much" for many readers (Caryn James, "Everybody" 31; Arnold xii).

reading and teaching the novel entails an acute awareness of the difficulties of speaking about *Meridian*'s "language, form, style, and tone without appearing decadent [and] ethically irresponsible" (*Practice* 258)—a struggle I personally experience in writing about and teaching the novel.

Meridian is a troubling book because it has the appearance of being "ethically bereft" in the conspicuous absence of ethical comment or judgment that pervades the text (Josyph 70).[15] The novel's lack of ethical commentary is stylistically reinforced by the distance at which the narration holds us—where we are given very limited access to characters' minds or inner lives, and all is treated with the same "thoroughly dispassionate" equanimity (Phillips 35–37)—a narratorial distance fortified by McCarthy's use of the cosmic to foster readers' sense of infinitude. Moral issues are inevitably foregrounded and exacerbated by the text's own strange dearth of ethical comment, compelling readers to question the degree to which our acts of readerly spectatorship become complicit with the monstrous deeds enacted.[16] That the novel is driven by historically based sources only serves to make such refusal to engage in moral conversations even more disturbing; critics like David Holmberg and Steven Shaviro thus note that "*Blood Meridian* seems to have nothing to do with actively righting the wrongs of history," since readers "are called to no responsibility" (Holmberg 141; Shaviro 148).

My proposal of a postmodern literary dynamical sublime—which posits the reader's active role in resisting *Meridian*'s explicit represen-

---

15. Frye comments on the novel's "amoral relativism" (7), while Donoghue observes that the barbarous events "seem to be protected from any ethical comment" (*Practice* 264). Richard Selzer perhaps passes the most damning judgment: "Most of the violence is egregious, rising out of some manic cruelty and flung in the face of the reader with all the bravado and defiance of a smart-aleck teenager [. . .]. And I continue to be nonplussed by his egregious love of depravity and violence for its own sake. What a waste! All that great gift laid at the feet of cruelty" (qtd. in Josyph 59–60).

16. Jarrett observes that *Meridian*'s violence is "'historical' in the fullest sense of the term; it is used so as to represent the dynamic ethnic, racial, and social tensions of this period of Western history." It is "not an ex nihilo creation of the imagination but based on historical men and deeds. This is not to say that we take no pleasure in this violence, for its linguistic 'rendering' is neither unadorned nor unesthetic. This very esthetic pleasure may compel the reader to a guilty consciousness of his or her own esthetic consumption of narrated violence" (90).

tations of suffering—pushes back against such judgments. Instead, I argue that the novel itself is an act of fictionalized historical testimony in which readers are called to the responsibility of *exercising* our moral freedom, in both senses of the word: the active use/application of our *practical reason* (i.e., our concern with morality and ethical judgments as we grapple with the atrocities represented) and the fictional text as a means of training and stretching such capacities for ethical response. Like Frye and Donoghue, I consider McCarthy's refusal to pass explicit moral comment an ethical stance in and of itself—and one that requires no mean aesthetic feat.[17] The usual catharsis associated with poetic justice, for instance, fails to resonate here.

One of the Delawares, earlier shown to be responsible for brutal infant mutilation, meets his own grisly end along with numerous other scalp hunters: "They were skewered through the cords of their heels with sharpened shuttles of green wood and they hung gray and naked above the dead ashes of the coals where they'd been roasted until their heads had charred and the brains bubbled in the skulls and steam sang from their noseholes" (*Meridian* 237). The bubbling brains and singing steam are clearly meant to resonate with his own earlier act of bashing the infants' "heads against the stones so that the brains burst forth through the fontanel in a bloody spew" (162), yet readers likely find it nauseatingly difficult to rejoice in the potential act of implicit poetic justice; only a further sickening sensation registers as we struggle with the excessive violence that marks the deed, unsettled by the sense that there is something terribly wrong with it all.

Such gut-wrenching scenes of apparent poetic justice—combined with the narration's withholding of explicit ethical judgments in its refusal to attribute causality—force readers to confront the meaning (or lack thereof) of these violent deaths over and over again, of both aggressors and innocents alike. *Meridian*'s moral reticence thus stages implicit conflicts between ethics and aesthetics and between historical representation and artful narration. I suggest that such dialectical energies function in two distinct ways: first, in the refusal to allow the value

---

17. For Donoghue, the work's "remarkable creative power [. . .] seems to be at one with McCarthy's refusal to bring in a moral verdict on the characters and actions of the book," where *Meridian* "raises an ethical issue mainly by not speaking of it" (*Practice* 259, 264). Frye in turn observes that "moral and ethical questions lie at the heart of [this] novel that seems on the surface deaf to them" (108).

and meaning of violence to be assimilated with the *understanding*, which some historians and critics rightly identify as a type of violence in and of itself;[18] and, second, in confronting the possible fundamental nonrationality of the world, especially in an age of increasing secularity and agnosticism in certain cultures and regions.

In seeking "to guard critical thought against transforming painful [. . .] histories into a field of enjoyment," historians like Dominick LaCapra view "the aesthetic of the sublime, as theorized by Jean-François Lyotard and Slavoj Žižek," as a troubling "effort to transform the violent and traumatic histories of the twentieth century into sacred objects that can comfort us through their aesthetic value" (Slade, "Violence" 90). Notwithstanding its aesthetic merits, however, *Meridian* works against such a model since the aestheticized violence serves to disconcert rather than comfort readers. Slade notes that "sublime figurations avoid complicity with repetitions of terror and death by refusing to pass from feeling to knowledge" (*Lyotard* 90). McCarthy's act of withholding ostensible ethical judgment in *Meridian* thus "short-circuit[s] easy assimilation" (Hooker 51) and works against readers' consumption of its historically based violence as a tidy object of knowledge, understood and settled once and for all. Guillemin remarks that "McCarthy's fiction belongs to what Roland Barthes designated 'writerly' (as opposed to 'readerly') literature, the meaning of his writings being dependent on what we make of them and their epidemic destructiveness" (262).

I suggest that this active co-construction of meaning, which twentieth- and twenty-first-century literature invites readers to participate in, constitutes the dominant shift in updating our understanding of aesthetic paradigms in the present moment. In chapters 1 and 2, I show that texts falling within the aesthetic mode of play partly shift the onus of co-constructing formal coherence and meaning onto readers (i.e., in relation to tensions between the form- and sense-drives). In chapters 3 and 4, I propose that texts exemplifying an aesthetics of the sublime likewise invite readers to participate in meaning-making via our rene-

---

18. Nancy Scheper-Hughes observes that "ideas of 'acceptable death' and of 'meaningful,' rather than useless, suffering extinguish rage and grief for those whose lives are taken [. . .]. Whenever we allow ourselves to attribute some meaning, whether political or spiritual, to the useless suffering of others we behave a bit like public executioners" (19).

gotiations of their affective and ethical implications (i.e., in relation to tensions between the sense- and moral-drives).

A second function of the sublime in *Meridian* is its implication of the world's nonrationality. Guyer notes that "if we take the Dionysian as Nietzsche's version of the sublime, then Nietzsche has radically reconceived the experience of the sublime as an intimation of the fundamental nonrationality of existence, rather than its rationality" (115). Anthropologist Nancy Scheper-Hughes observes that "the one thing humans seem unable to accept is the idea that the world may be deficient in meaning" (23). This nonrationality certainly seems to be the position implied both by the novel and by McCarthy's remarks in an interview that there is "no such thing as life without bloodshed" and "the notion that the species can be improved in some way, that everyone could live in harmony, is a really dangerous idea" (qtd. in Woodward, "Venomous"). Many readers struggle with *Meridian*, partly because we want the terrible violence to mean something at the end—such as condemnation of racism, for instance—but McCarthy offers the chilling alternative that there may be no such compensatory significance, or at least that vindication or meaning is not his to offer. *Meridian* ultimately implies that the only available ethical move is one that is up to the reader to make, not the author; in so doing, McCarthy ensures that the literary art object itself does not pass from feeling into knowledge. The move from feeling to knowledge, from nihilism to meaning-making, is ours to make—and the corresponding accountability that comes with this knowledge, the responsibility for co-building a better world, the readers' as well.

CONCLUSION: EXERCISING MORAL AUTONOMY

In a collection of essays that deals topically with the sublime through categories such as the unpresentable, transcendence, technology, terror, the uncanny, and so on, Simon Morley argues that the sublime is ultimately "an experience looking for a context. In the pre-modern period, this context was mostly provided by religion," and in recent times by "spectacle and the mass media," concluding that the "sublime is an experience that can serve many interests; it is now for us to decide what it holds for the future" (21). Morley's remarks point to an important underlying dimension of my project in this book: though certain aesthetic categories and/or terminology fall in and out of critical/scholarly favor, the experience that underpins these categories remains pertinent and integral to our encounter with the (literary) art object—even if the models used to describe and explain such experiences may at times be in need of updating or further finessing.[19] Accordingly, aesthetic evaluations of literature serve not only to account for authors' artistic strategies, as informed by the novel's broader situational and historical contexts, but also to illuminate our frequently shared or common affective experiences of reading.

Though theorists tend to advocate that "no determinable concept" or "single figure or trope" will stand "as a definitive example of the sublime" (Lyotard, *Sublime* 59; Philip Shaw, *Sublime* 47), that has not stopped others, including me, from attempting to find ways to articulate the distinctive experience of the sublime, as evident from the reemergence of critical interest in the concept over the course of the twentieth century. My own endeavor involves using four diverse texts to demonstrate the range and rich complexities that characterize the spectrum of the sublime, while positing several key attributes I consider to be definitive of a (postmodern) literary sublime: namely, limitlessness and the infinite, unresolved tensions between representation and the unpresentable, and the process of negotiating conflicting affective states idiosyncratically staged in a given work depending on its thematic and aesthetic concerns.

In his analysis of Yeats's poetry, Ramazani suggests that death is an "occasion of the sublime": in a variety of guises and names, "death precipitates the emotional turning called the sublime" and is the "recurrent obsession" for theorists "from Longinus to Heidegger and Bloom" (173–74, 164). Ramazani observes that death is Longinus's "organizing trope" and interprets the sublime as "a *staged* confrontation," an

---

19. Beyond critical/scholarly favor, Morley points to two crucial reasons for resistance to the sublime: first, "the heady rhetoric of the sublime was often employed by totalitarian regimes in order to seduce the masses" in the twentieth century; second, kitsch trades "on the ersatz experience of the sublime [. . .] designed to stimulate an increasingly jaded consumer" in contemporary society. "The discourse of the sublime is therefore tainted by association with both malevolent politics and inauthentic mass culture. Not surprisingly, contemporary artists are often wary of attributing to their practices lofty or grandiose intentions that may seem polluted by such associations" (19).

"ecstatic encounter with death" (164). Since the sublime is predominantly concerned with the unpresentable (including what remains ultimately unknowable), it seems inextricably linked to death. The play with the posthumous in *Lanark, Policeman,* and other postmodernist texts makes the relationship between death and the sublime a potential avenue of further study, especially in light of McHale's remark that "postmodernist fiction is *about* death in a way that other writing, of other periods, is not. Indeed, insofar as postmodernist fiction foregrounds ontological themes and ontological structure, we might say that it is *always* about death" (*Postmodernist* 231). Examining associated literary tropes and/or their relationships to the unknowable may offer productive avenues for future explorations of the sublime.

Though the sublime has traditionally been underpinned by relations to the moral-drive, Schiller rightly notes that the "praiseworthy object of pursuing everywhere moral good as the supreme aim" has already "brought forth in art so much mediocrity": "if it is the aim that is moral, art loses all that by which it is powerful,—I mean its freedom, and that which gives it so much influence over us—the charm of pleasure" (181). By positing the (postmodern) literary sublime as principally driven by the sense-drive/*imagination* in increasing degrees of conflict with the moral-drive/*reason* as we move from the mathematical to the dynamical sublime, my revised proposal foregrounds the active exercise of readers' moral freedom—in its resistance to representations of suffering—more effectively accounting for our sublime experiences of the literary art object. Art's autonomy thus takes on a new dimension in the aesthetic practices of twentieth- and twenty-first-century novelists, whose orchestrations of the sublime invite readers to participate in these always unfinished acts of meaning-making.

CHAPTER 5

Muted Beauty

Complex Harmonies

IN CONTEMPORARY WORKS such as Milan Kundera's *The Unbearable Lightness of Being* (1979), Gabriel García Márquez's *Love in the Time of Cholera* (1985/88), J. M. Coetzee's *Disgrace* (1999), Ian McEwan's *Atonement* (2001) and *On Chesil Beach* (2007), John Banville's *The Sea* (2005), and Julian Barnes's *The Sense of an Ending* (2011), among others, we witness a (re)turn to fragmentary or incongruous beauty. A key issue in these texts is how literature might reconcile the brokenness of human experience with beauty, especially given the radical skepticism that characterizes the postmodern period and the loss of faith in grand narratives—including those associated with the quality or experience of beauty. By drawing attention to the workings of the form-drive and its concern with pattern isolation, shape, grouping, repetition, rhythm, symmetry, and textual architecture more generally, I propose that much of contemporary fiction is strikingly beautiful in its muting of contexts, in what texts leave unarticulated and the gaps readers are thus called upon to fill.

Galen A. Johnson observes that "it is a serious loss for philosophical thought, our lives with others, and our openness to the world and nature that throughout the twentieth century beauty has been a nearly completely neglected idea. Nevertheless, this very philosophical trope must itself be worked and reconfigured in an altered cultural climate" (xviii). As noted in the introduction of this book, my theoretical frame reworks Kant's and Schiller's definitions to account for both formal and moral modes of ordering associated with experiencing beauty. This revision is further underpinned by neuroscientists' belief in "the existence of brain mechanisms shared between moral and aesthetic appreciation" (Cela-Conde et al. 10458)—a notion that partly explains the enduring relationship over millennia between ethics and aesthetics.

Scholars working in the field of neuroaesthetics—which examines common neural configurations of aesthetic experience and behavior—have found that the part of our "emotional brain known as the medial orbito-frontal cortex (mOFC) [. . .] is consistently active when subjects, irrespective of race or culture, report having an experience of the beautiful, regardless of whether the source is visual, musical, or mathematical" (Zeki, "Clive Bell's" 1–2). The "strength of activity in the mOFC" is further "proportional to the declared intensity" of experiencing beauty (3). As "part of the brain's reward system," the OFC is more generally "known to be critical for social cognition processes, moral decisions, and emotion control" (Zeki, *Splendors* 17; Brink et al. 2). In their use of functional near-infrared spectroscopy[1] to understand the OFC's role in young children's processing of stories eliciting empathy, Tila Tabea Brink et al. found that the OFC is involved in "moral appraisals" and the exercise of "affective empathy," while the mOFC is "especially engaged in socio-affective processing" (9, 13)—results that lend credence to the notion of shared brain mechanisms used in moral and aesthetic appreciation (Cela-Conde et al. 10458).

I propose that twentieth- and twenty-first-century fiction manifests the aesthetic category of beauty in at least two distinct ways. My first case study, Jeanette Winterson's *Written on the Body* (1992), deals with a more traditional conception of beauty as the harmony of the form- and sense-drives, while the second, Kazuo Ishiguro's *Never Let Me Go* (2005), complicates classical understandings of beauty by foregrounding both harmony *and* tension between the form- and moral-drives. I

---

1. Functional near-infrared spectroscopy is a noninvasive, optical imaging method of "assessing changes in cortical oxygenation by applying near-infrared light" to measure "concentrations of oxygenated and deoxygenated hemoglobin" (Brink et al. 3).

suggest that beauty is ultimately grounded in the form-drive, variously engaged with the other two drives. My model of rooting beauty in the form-drive and the sublime in the sense-drive also reinforces the distinction that theorists like Burke and Kant have made between the two aesthetic categories—a contrast that has gained neurobiological corroboration in fMRI experiments.[2] By examining a cluster of features gleaned from multiple aesthetic traditions, I outline an aesthetics of literary beauty in postwar fiction, suggesting that readers likely experience local moments of beauty even as they apprehend beauty in the work's global form.

THEORIZING BEAUTY

The third-century Neoplatonist philosopher Plotinus remarked that the experience of beauty is attended by an amalgamation of "astonishment, and a sweet shock, and longing, and erotic thrill, and a feeling of being overwhelmed with pleasure" (59). Of these, pleasure is the affect that has received the most sustained scholarly inquiry in contemporary aesthetics.[3] Danto, in fact, suggests that the resurgence of interest in beauty in the final decade of the twentieth century was in part so exciting because "beauty was proxy for something that had almost disappeared from most of one's encounters with art, namely enjoyment and pleasure" ("Aesthetics" 61). A key development in our understanding of the relationship between beauty and pleasure comes from what we now understand about reward neurons, which are crucial to evolution as "the genetic memory of successful positive or negative experiences

---

2. Ishizu and Zeki found "a distinctly different pattern of brain activity" when participants were exposed to visual stimuli evoking representations of the beautiful and the sublime, which suggests that the two aesthetic modes "engage separate and distinct brain systems" (1).

3. Dutton identifies *direct pleasure* as one of numerous characteristics found cross-culturally in the arts from an evolutionary perspective (51). Using "positron emission tomography to study neural mechanisms underlying intensely pleasant emotional responses to music," Anne J. Blood and Robert J. Zatorre link our pleasure in music with "biologically relevant, survival-related stimuli via their common recruitment of brain circuitry involved in pleasure and reward," noting that regional cerebral blood flow increases in the "left ventral striatum and dorsomedial midbrain" (11818–23).

from the phylogenetic history," thus enabling an organism to maximize its experiences for reward or punishment (Changeux 56–57). The desire to repeat or return to such experiences in order to maximize cognitive rewards likely bears out what many of us encounter in our experiences of artistic beauty—a feature Étienne Gilson associates with beauty's *radiance* (Gilson 35; Galen A. Johnson, *Retrieval* 170).[4]

I focus in particular on beauty's dialectical nature, which has received relatively scant attention[5] but persists across a variety of cultures and aesthetic traditions. Eco notes that when the "Grand Theory" of beauty (consisting in proportion of the parts) reached its zenith during the Renaissance, there were simultaneously "centrifugal forces whose thrust was toward a disquieting, nebulous, and surprising Beauty"—a dialectical tension reflecting the fragile and transient equilibrium of its historical moment (*History* 214, 216). This emphasis on beauty's dialecticism was taken up in the eighteenth century by British writer and painter William Hogarth, who identifies *variety* and *uniformity*, *intricacy* and *simplicity*, as principles which "co-operate in the production of beauty, mutually correcting and restraining each other" (Davis, "Introduction"; Hogarth 12).

The concern with beauty's dialectical energies was likewise evident in the German aesthetic tradition: Kant and Schiller conceived of beauty as harmony between liberatory energies of the imagination/sense-drive and ordering qualities of the form- and/or moral-drives. Eco notes that the German "Romantics—particularly Novalis and Friedrich Hölderlin—were not looking for a static and harmonious Beauty, but a dynamic one, in the process of becoming" (*History* 315). Nietzsche famously pointed to the unresolved antithesis inherited from the Greek concept of beauty, between the *Apollonian* (understood in terms of "serene harmony," "order and measure") and the *Dionysian* (a chaotic, "joyous and dangerous" beauty that breaches all rules) (Nietzsche 222; Eco, *History* 53–55, 58).

---

4. Beauty's inexhaustibility relates to the desire to repeat such experiences: "You can never get to the bottom of something beautiful, because it always finds space inside itself for a new and surprising recapitulation of its idea that adds fresh feeling to the familiar pattern" (Turner 2; see also Scarry 50).

5. More recently, Paul Armstrong engages with this dynamic between harmony and dissonance, though his focus is not specifically on beauty but more broadly on literary experience.

Beauty's dialecticism (re)gained emphasis from the twentieth century forward,[6] especially in light of interest in Nietzschean philosophy and Marxist critical thought. Dewey "repeatedly insists" from a pragmatist stance that "the permanence of experienced unity is not only impossible, it is aesthetically undesirable; for art requires the challenge of tension and disruptive novelty and the rhythmic struggle of achievement and breakdown of order" (Shusterman 32). Susanne Langer situates this tension in affective terms, observing that "the power of artistic forms to be emotionally ambivalent springs from the fact that emotional opposites—joy and grief, desire and fear, and so forth—are often very similar in their dynamic structure, and reminiscent of each other" (242). Though artistic form is now considered in some quarters of literary studies as having largely fallen out of critical/scholarly favor—particularly given the rise and fall of movements such as New Criticism and New Formalism toward the end of the twentieth century—I argue for form's continued relevance to aesthetics and beauty, explicating its relation to fundamental cognitive processes such as object recognition.

Beauty's dynamism depends not only on expectation/predictability enabled by *pattern* and *object recognition* but also on their disruptions—facilitated by concealment, violation, or surprise. Developmental psychologists learn a great deal about our brains' existing predispositions by "invent[ing] ways to look into infant minds": the trick is "to see what surprises babies" (Haidt 63). "Infants as young as two months old will look longer at an event that surprises them," since "'surprise, pleasant or unpleasant, is more informative than predictability.' Neurons in the substantia nigra and the ventral tegmental area of the brain secrete dopamine in reaction to the surprising but not to the expected" (Haidt 63; Boyd 184). Boyd further observes that "children seem to understand the value of the rewards of surprise and how to produce them in their first attempts at story," long before they are able to articulate their intentions for doing so (184). The process of object

---

6. Santayana, for instance, notes that beauty and the art of words "comes from the wealth of suggestion, or the refinement of sentiment" (*Sense* 110). This tension between the centrifugal (variety or wealth of suggestion) and the centripetal (refinement or narrowing of sentiment) implies Santayana's concern with beauty's dialectical energies. Calvino in turn attends to the tension between weight and lightness (*Six Memos* 15), while Frederick Turner calls beauty "the paradoxical coexistence of chaos with order" (4). Galen A. Johnson observes that "repetition and difference, theme and variations, structure the beautiful" (169).

recognition underpins surprise since children "become interested in testing and overturning expectations" after they "gain confidence in identifying and distinguishing objects and situations" (183).

Many qualities traditionally identified with form (including rhythm, symmetry, and coherence) drive the process of object recognition.[7] "In the first few months of life," for example, infants "pay special attention to the rhythm of their native language, heard in utero during the last months of pregnancy" (Dehaene 197). Neuroscientist Stanislas Dehaene observes, "From birth on, we all seem to possess an uncanny sense of mirror symmetry" whereby "our visual system, before formal schooling, already conforms to a strong symmetry constraint"—such that we have to unlearn this innate view-invariance or "mirror generalization in order to process 'b' and 'd' as distinct letters" (278, 266, 263). "Very young infants are also sensitive to aesthetic features in forms" such as coherence and "patterns of symmetry" (Sheridan and Gardner 281). Object recognition depends partly on determining figure-ground segregation—primarily cued by symmetry and "the grouping of perceptual features," such as color, edges, and motion—whereby the "end point of form perception is the ability to recognize familiar objects" (Shimamura 55, 63). Discerning form is thus integral to the process of object recognition, which I argue in turn underpins beauty's dynamism. Such dialectical tensions are evolutionarily linked to attention, interest, reward, and information processing.

My framework for articulating an aesthetics of literary beauty posits that readers likely experience either *local* moments of beauty and/or apprehend a *global* "architecture of the beautiful" (Galen A. Johnson, *Retrieval* 145)[8] in the work's formal shape/structure. Boyd notes that "as we mature, the right hemispheres of our brains seek explanation at a deeper level and coherence on both a local and a larger scale" (151). Neuroscientists point to the temporoparietal junction (TPJ) as a key region "implicated in exerting attentional control over switches

---

7. Dehaene argues that our very "ability to recognize words in reading uses the species' evolutionarily older circuitry that is specialised for object recognition" (Wolf 13–14; see Dehaene 195, 263, 285).

8. "We speak of an architecture of the beautiful," Johnson notes, "in order to indicate a certain understanding of the relation of parts and wholes in the meaning of the beautiful" (*Retrieval* 145).

from local to global processing"; Hideaki Kawabata and Semir Zeki's fMRI experiments reveal that the left TPJ is also activated by paintings that we find beautiful, suggesting the importance of this region for aesthetic appreciation (Ishai 348). Beauty may be manifest in stylistic expression, individual episodes, artful characterization, and innumerable other local aspects of narrative: *Written on the Body*, for instance, is notable for its artful use of poetic devices (including alliteration, assonance, repetition, and rhyme), which not only emphasizes the lyricality and aural pleasure of Winterson's prose but further facilitates "processing fluency" by reinforcing "the impression of familiarity" (Reber 228; Bohrn et al. 6).

Inspired by Donoghue's discussion in *On Eloquence*, I examine various local modes of literary beauty relating to beauty's dialecticism and its quality of surprise. The first type of eloquence "comes in flashes, sometimes in a phrase or two," sometimes breaking "forth in a single word"; such local instances of beauty are "sudden gestures, flares of spirit, words breaking free from every expectation, audacities of diction and syntax" (*Eloquence* 19–20). An "eloquence of situation" in turn "issue[s] from something memorably done," whereby "the words don't matter" and "could easily have been replaced by different ones: what matters is the gesture, the little unpredictable thing done" (62–64). The third is an eloquence of the unsaid or of something "almost being said," alluding to larger muted contexts which are only hinted at or remain unarticulated (70).

Despite being very different types of eloquence—one pivoted on locution, one heedless of it, and the third implying absent utterance—all three depend on dynamic energies between expected syntax/diction/development of events and their pleasurable violations that attend our experience of beauty. Hogan notes that "reward system activation is linked with expectancy and violations of expectancy," such that "aesthetic pleasure is more likely to derive from partial unexpectedness that, within some window, allows for retrospective pattern recognition" (*Beauty* 30, 26; see also Starr 119–20). This "necessary element of pure surprise" is paradoxically "followed by a realization of the appropriateness, the necessity," the fitness, and "even the inevitability of the surprising element" (Turner 4). Artists, writers, and philosophers return repeatedly to the quality of surprise when writing about beauty, and

Dutton further identifies art's "capacity to surprise its audience" as one of numerous characteristics found cross-culturally in the arts (51, 54).[9]

Apart from *local* moments, I propose that readers also discern literary beauty in relation to *global* form/shape/architecture.[10] Early considerations of global form may be traced to the ancient Greeks, who emphasized "the correspondence between Form and Beauty" in terms of "conceptual formalisms such as order, symmetry and proportion"—qualities deemed "objective standards of beauty" that "persisted throughout the Renaissance and beyond" (Eco, *History* 61; Benezra, Viso, and Danto 87).[11] Philosophers including the Third Earl of Shaftesbury (1711), Kant (1790), Santayana (1896), and Clive Bell (1913), among others, have continued to explicate ancient Greek and Hellenistic understandings of beauty in various ways, emphasizing formal elements of design, composition, unity, and the relation of elements to each other.[12]

Shusterman, however, rightly notes that such notions of organic unity have been "radically challenged by recent developments in postmodern art and aesthetics" as an overly "rigid ideal which stifles creativity and formal experiment, and can induce in us an overly facile and complacent sense of harmony in the world" (63)—a unity/harmony radically contradicted by our heightened awareness of rupture and violence in the twentieth and twenty-first centuries, a cognizance markedly enabled by the advent of the Internet and proliferation of media

---

9. I am grateful to Neil Murphy, who first drew my attention to the significance of surprise in relation to beauty. For further remarks on beauty's relation to surprise, see Plotinus 59; Schjeldahl 53. Other cross-cultural aesthetic features Dutton identifies include direct pleasure, skill and virtuosity, style, novelty and creativity, criticism, representation, special focus, expressive individuality, emotional saturation, intellectual challenge, art traditions and institutions, and imaginative experience (51–58).

10. For discussions on global form/shape/architecture, see also Schelling 174–75; Clive Bell, "Art" 262–63; Shusterman 92; Aldama and Hogan 116–18.

11. Eco notes in *A History of Beauty* that Pythagoras's philosophical thought marked the birth of this "aesthetico-mathematical view" from the sixth to fifth century BC, which in turn influenced Plato's conception of beauty as "harmony and proportion between the parts" from the fifth to fourth century BC (61). These ideals of unity, order, and beauty "by participation in Form" were taken up by Plotinus in the third century AD (58).

12. See Third Earl of Shaftesbury 80; Kant, *Aesthetics*, "Critique" 139; Santayana, *Sense* 50, 93; Clive Bell, *Art* 13.

technologies. It is precisely in light of these challenges that the issue of how we are to understand the form-drive and its role in making aesthetic sense of (literary) art becomes even more pertinent. Our ability to sort and make sense of data—impulses of the form-drive—is an evermore crucial cognitive skill in the present age, not only for processing aesthetic experiences but also for attending to the informational glut of everyday life and experience. Adorno notes, "less and less does the beautiful actualize itself in a particular purified shape; more and more does it manifest itself in the *dynamic totality* of the work of art" ("Concept" 80; emphases added)—in what Shusterman terms "complex forms of coherence" (76).[13]

I suggest in chapter 2 of this book that readers discern such complex coherence in the text's global form/structure when we engage in the (game) task of determining the shapes of postmodern textual worlds vis-à-vis the use of possible worlds theory. In this chapter, I propose that global forms also relate to fitness or proportion (parts in relation to the whole), and interrelated principles of *grouping, orderliness,* and *symmetry*—which neuroscientist V. S. Ramachandran identifies as "universal laws of aesthetics" (199).[14] By combining Kantian and Deweyan approaches to aesthetics, I argue that determining global forms through such "interpretive holism" (Shusterman 77) serves as a pragmatic reading strategy for framing contemporary understandings of form's relevance to beauty.

---

13. Shusterman observes, "If our human need to perceive and experience satisfying unities in the disordered flux of experience is what motivates our interest in art, this need should not be rejected. What we should reject is the repressive limitation of art to the expression of only such unity, the prohibition of jarring fragmentation and incoherencies which can have their own stimulating aesthetic (and cognitive) effect, and which can result in more complex forms of coherence" (76).

14. Ramachandran notes that "'artistic' principles [such] as grouping by color, contrast, and symmetry are in evidence" even in nature (194). Discovered by Gestalt psychologists and subsequently identified as an evolutionary adaptation, such "successful grouping feels good" since you experience "an internal 'Aha!' sensation as if you have just solved a problem [. . .]. It's this 'Aha!' signal that the artist or designer exploits" when using the law of grouping (201–6). Orderliness in turn has to do with "our love of visual repetition or rhythm" (233). Other universal laws of aesthetics Ramachandran identifies include principles of peak shift, contrast, isolation, perceptual problem solving, abhorrence of coincidences, and metaphor (200).

WRITTEN ON THE BODY

In Jeanette Winterson's *Written on the Body* (hereafter *Written*), an autodiegetic narrator of indeterminate gender recounts her/his relationship with a married woman named Louise, interpolating their story with past affairs, which creates the effect of an intercalated narration continually oscillating back and forth in time as the narrator first recalls "a certain September," then "a hot August Sunday," followed by "the wettest June on record" (9, 10, 20). Such chaotic, Dionysiac tendencies of the sense-drive in Winterson's presentation of time are countered by the repetitive telling[15] that establishes a poetic order foregrounding the form-drive, as the narrator turns his/her memories of Louise's remarks into refrains that resound throughout the novel. The repetitions of "I love you and my love for you makes any other life a lie" (18–19, 98); "I will never let you go" (69, 76, 96, 163); and "It's the clichés that cause the trouble" (10, 155, 189) repeatedly cycle the narrative back to specific moments in their relationship, turning time and memory into rich palimpsests, as the narrator tries "to find the place to go back to where things went wrong. Where I went wrong" (17).

Though *Written* was the British novelist's "first international success" to reach "millions of readers in translation," scholars observe that it was, ironically, also the text that turned the tide of reviews and criticism "against Winterson and her work" (Kostkowska 57; Finney 23).[16] Numerous critics have judged the novel deficient on several counts, suggesting that it "lacks subtle character shading and emotional authenticity," particularly given the "self-indulgent" autodiegetic narrator (Miner 21; Vaux 20). Following an initial need to "defend the text" against hostile public reception, Lynne Pearce eventually found narrative descriptions of "Louise's disease as seductively attractive" to be "personally alienating," making it difficult "to engage emotionally" for both personal and academic reasons: "Having had the personal experience of watching cancer's depredations created the first difficulty and the text's similarity to Pre-Raphaelite glamorisation of female suffering

---

15. *Repetitive telling* is "telling several times what happened once" (Herman, Jahn, and Ryan 189).

16. See Annan; Ellam 105; Stowers 89. Brian Finney, Jennifer Smith, Merja Makinen, and Sonya Andermahr offer comprehensive summaries of the positions taken by various critical camps about *Written*.

[...] compounded the difficulty" (Makinen 119; Pearce 29–40). Andrea Harris argues that the "narrator violates Louise from a metaphorical standpoint" in the anatomical annotations, and her/his literal abandonment of Louise makes "this violent rewriting" of her body "all the more violent" (138–39).

Though Harris's and Pearce's reactions are not the dominant critical position on Winterson's novel, their responses—which have largely gone unaddressed—raise important challenges and correspondingly present a worthwhile theoretical opportunity to test the efficacy of an aesthetic interpretation against such criticisms of ethical deficiency. By attending to the beauty of *Written*'s anatomical annotations—characterized by diverse energies of the sense-drive operating in harmony with ordering impulses of the form-drive—I contend that the narrator's imaginative transfigurations of Louise in this manner function as a literary recourse against death's certainty.

The novel's anatomical annotations literalize the convention of the *blason*, where each subsection employs different motifs in its exploration of the body's CELLS, TISSUES, and CAVITIES, exhibiting beauty's mutually cooperative principles of uniformity and variety. The narrator likens leukemia cells in Louise's body to "rebelling security forces" that stage "a coup," a "blind tide" that bypasses the sleeping keeper, carrying its murderous cargo through her portal veins and artery canals (*Written* 115–16). The subsection TISSUES in turn takes on a different aesthetic register, turning from the metaphor of besiegement to emphasis on the sensuousness of Louise's body, as the lining of her mouth becomes the narrator's "landing strip" (117) in the intimacy of a remembered kiss. The narrator's sinuous memories—"My eyes are brown, they have *f*luttered across your *b*ody like *b*utter*f*lies. I have *f*lown the distance of your *b*ody from side to side of your ivory coast. I know the *f*orests where I can rest and *f*eed" (117; emphases added)—are suffused with lyrical voluptuousness, accentuated by the alliterative brown butterflies, the end rhyme in "eyes" and "butterflies," and repetitions of the fricative *f*-consonants. The beloved's life-giving body is thus transfigured into familiar forests that nourish the narrator's longing for the absent Louise.

The subsection CAVITIES features the narrator as coroner, "embalm[er]," and "archaeologist of tombs," who explores the "mausoleum" of Louise's body and its susceptibility to decay when her illness drastically accelerates its deterioration (119–20). This metaphor of Louise's debilitating body is taken up again at the end of the next section, "*The Skin*," as the narrator ponders: "You were milk-white and fresh to drink. Will your skin discolour, its brightness blurring? Will your neck and spleen distend? Will the rigorous contours of your stomach swell under an infertile load? It may be so and the private drawing I keep of you will be a poor reproduction then. It may be so but if you are broken then so am I" (124–25). These musings invoke the earlier subsection T1ssues, as the "ivory coast" of Louise's "milk-white," life-giving body becomes distended and "infertile." The novel thus presents a "unity in diversity" (Dutton 12) through the forging of such complex coherences between sections and subsections, which remain tethered to each other despite the imaginative diversity of tropes taken up in the narrator's mapping of Louise's anatomy.

Ruminations on the scapula and clavicle (subsections of "*The Skeleton*") begin with a similar reverie on bone shapes, which then play out in very different ways. Reimagining the triangular-shaped scapula/shoulder blade as "shuttered [. . .] blades of wings," the narrator transfigures Louise into the glorious "winged horse Pegasus who would not be saddled" and "a fallen angel" whose "great gold wings cut across the sun" (*Written* 131)—in fitting homage to Louise's strongly independent character. Though the narrator calls Louise his/her "Pre-Raphaelite beauty" (159), Louise is far from the glamorized, suffering victim that some critics make her out to be. More than capable of holding her own in confrontations with Elgin and the narrator, it is Louise who proactively pursues the narrator and reveals that she chose to marry Elgin because she knew "I could control him, that I would be the one in charge" (34; see also 49, 84–85, 87, 90). The narrator's imaginative transfiguration of Louise in this manner thus actively *resists* rather than fulfills the passive victimhood of a suffering Pre-Raphaelite female.

The subsection on the clavicle/collarbone fleshes out etymological dimensions of the root word *clavis* or "key," unfolding both its musical and its functional definitions. The narrator associates the clavicle with musical keys, given its graceful shape (a "balletic" bone with "the double curve lithe and flowing with movement") and the memory of lovingly fastening her/his fingers over the recesses behind Louise's collarbone, like keys on a clavichord (129). These musings then blend into a markedly different meaning of *clavis*/key as an implement or tool:

> Thus she was, here and here. The physical memory *b*lunders through the *d*oors the mind has tried to seal. A skeleton key to *B*luebeard's cham*b*er. The *b*loody key that unlocks pain. Wisdom says f*o*rget, the *b*ody howls. The *b*olts of your collar *b*one und*o* me. Thus she was, here and here. (130; emphases added)

The echoing refrain of the first and final lines frame the harmonious repetitions of plosive *b*-consonants and assonant *o*-vowels. The assonance, in particular, emphasizes the narrator's implicit howl of pain at losing Louise ("the body howls")—a thread subsequently taken up in the subsection HEARING AND THE EAR, where the narrator "call[s] Louise from the doorstep because I know she can't hear me. I keen in the fields to the moon. Animals in the zoo do the same, hoping that another of their kind will call back. The zoo at night is the saddest place [. . .]. I wish I could hear your voice again" (135). Such local threads of eloquent beauty lend the narrator's meandering musings a rich coherence within the novel's global form.

The passage's references to "Bluebeard's chamber," "bolts," "bloody key," "body," and sealed "doors" further invoke the folktale of Bluebeard and Angela Carter's rewriting of it in *The Bloody Chamber*—a text which, like *Written*, lingers on the voluptuous pleasures of the female body. Bluebeard's literal mausoleum of women's bodies forms a sinister parallel to the narrator's annotated memories of Louise's body, evoking the earlier subsection CAVITIES, since both function as an embalmer of sorts. However, while the former depicts perverse love(?) that ends in heinous acts of murders, the latter emerges from an eulogistic act of love in the remembered physicality of an absent Louise. Like the clavicle which functions as a "link between the upper extremity and the axial skeleton" (129), the implicit reference to Carter's transfigured Bluebeard folktale bridges the two divergent meanings of *clavis*/key (as a device to un/lock or a musical instrument): Carter's protagonist, to whom the murderous Marquis hands the keys to his bloody chamber, is herself a pianist who later falls in love with a blind piano tuner, brought together by the tune *The Well-Tempered Clavier* (Carter 30). These complex threads of coherence foreground the implicit orderliness of Winterson's text despite the narrator's apparent freely meandering associations, emphasizing the harmony of the form- and sense-drives.

Though it is certainly possible to read the narrator's annotations as a problematic appropriation of Louise's body—critics point out that Louise "does not even have to be present for the narrator to engage in this fantasy of proprietary knowledge" (Detloff 154)—her absence is precisely the point of these reveries: they are the narrator's mechanism for coping with the beloved's loss. *Written*'s anatomical annotations expand the typical relationship drawn between love and the body, projecting it not merely in terms of sexual pleasure but as an exploration of the ways in which disease rewrites the body (initial bruises of passionate lovemaking, for instance, now mark Louise's increasing debilitation instead),[17] which recasts the relationship between self and lover. An implicit process of object recognition emerges from readers' processing of the anatomical ruminations, where Louise's body is identified as a dialectical site on which struggles between what is life-giving and what is death-marked play out. Stroking Louise "with necrophiliac obsession" in the section "*The Skin*," the narrator adores even parts of her that are already dead (i.e., the epidermis): "The dead you is constantly being rubbed away by the dead me. Your cells fall and flake away, fodder to dust mites and bed bugs. Your droppings support colonies of life that graze on skin and hair no longer wanted" (*Written* 123)—remarks that take on new valences in light of Louise's diagnosis.

While I acknowledge and sympathize with the difficult emotional experience Pearce and other readers have encountered in reading the novel, it is important to note that the sensuous annotations of Louise's body have more to do with the narrator's imaginative transfiguration of his/her *memories* of Louise than with aestheticizing her disease. In writing her/his longing on the memory of rich "palimpsest" (51) that is Louise's body, the narrator as anatomist, archaeologist, coroner, and embalmer attempts to stage her/his own narrative defenses against the certainty of Louise's death, whether by disease or eventual old age. In fact, the narrator does not shy away from squarely facing cancer's debilitating effects, but actively trains himself/herself "as a cancer specialist" by reading medical textbooks and visiting terminal ward patients where he/she "listened to their stories, found ones who'd got well and sat by ones who died" (149, 175). Against the irrefutable reality of suffering and limited existing knowledge about cancer's causes,

---

17. See *Written* 89, 111, 124.

prevention, or cure—as Louise asserts of Elgin's work, reinforced by the narrator's conversation with a junior doctor at the terminal ward (67, 149–50)—imagination is perhaps the only defense we can mount against despair. The narrator's imaginative transfigurations of the beloved become her/his way of hanging on to Louise, of temporarily holding disease and death at bay.

Christy Burns notes that "Winterson revitalizes postmodern" culture's exhaustion of imagination and language "*through* an emphasis on pleasure" (279), as the narrator's play with the imaginative possibilities of words prompts readers to excavate their layers of meanings. The narrator muses as he/she recalls a past affair with Bathsheba the dentist: "Against your white coat, their heads on your breast, no-one fears the needle and syringe. I came to you for a crown and you offered me a kingdom. Unfortunately I could only take possession between five and seven, weekdays, and the odd weekend when he was away playing football" (*Written* 47). The innocuous alignment of patients' heads at the dentist's chest level is metaphorically transfigured into the sensual act of laying their heads on Bathsheba's breast—a literal act in the narrator's case, given their affair. Winterson's choice of the name Uriah for Bathsheba's husband invokes the biblical narrative of King David seizing Uriah the Hittite's wife for himself, whom he later makes his queen. The wordplay on *crown* not only refers to the dental procedure but also is paired with *kingdom* to invoke the biblical narrative, as well as fairy tales, princes/ses, and happily-ever-afters—promptly subverted by the declaration of effective visiting hours.

These local moments of eloquence are partly driven by the sense-drive's propensity for indirection, generativity, and open-endedness, allowing readers to luxuriate in Winterson's prose as she eases her way among the multiple valences of each word. The phrase *take possession,* referring to a player's temporary control of the ball in sports, not only channels Uriah's pastime of playing football—time that effectively allows Bathsheba and the narrator to conduct their affair—but further highlights the temporary nature of the narrator's demands on Bathsheba's time, even as it exposes all three characters as players, for whom love is a sport. (The sporting metaphor is extended in contrast with the narrator's later description of her/his relationship with Louise: "I don't want to be your sport nor you to be mine" [88].) By foregrounding readers' task of attending to language's imaginative possibilities, the novel emphasizes workings of the sense-drive in rejuvenating the "postmodern exhaustion" of language (Andermahr 167)—a project that gains further momentum in Winterson's choice of narratorial persona.

Critics have been split in their judgments of how well Winterson handles construction of the narrator's persona: Anna Vaux suggests that "there is something unpleasant at the centre of the book," a "self-indulgent [. . .] sensibility" and "deep self-satisfaction behind all the mourning," especially in the autodiegetic narrator's dismissal of other characters' feelings "as one-dimensional or comic" while "dwell[ing] so much on its own high passions" (20). Even those who defend Winterson's artistic choice remark on the risks of employing such a persona: Andrea Stuart observes that adopting the autodiegetic narrator's exclusive perspective, "with all its attendant dangers of seeming preachy and narcissistic, could have gone horribly wrong. With characteristic cheek, she just about gets away with it; and the solipsism of Winterson's storyteller fits in almost entirely with her depiction of the self-referential world of love" (38). Even more problematic is the implied equation of this narratorial persona with Winterson's authorial persona—partly influenced not only by Winterson's candid admission that the novel was based on her affair with Pat Kavanagh[18] but also by the reception of her first book, *Oranges Are Not the Only Fruit*, which "was widely received as autobiographical" and "has installed the expectation [. . .] that subsequent texts by Winterson can be read within the context of an autobiographical project" (Gilmore 227; Annan, "Devil").

Rather than reading the narrator as an extension of Winterson's autobiographical self, I suggest that it is more pertinent to consider the narrator's persona in light of the overall aesthetic project at stake in *Written*—that is, by considering its "fitness" in relation to the novel's global form.[19] James Hillman's use of the term *kosmos* offers a useful way to consider the notion of global form: adopting a contemporary ecological approach to beauty, Hillman notes that the Greek word "is an aesthetic term, best translated into English as fitting order—appropriate, right arrangement [. . .]. Cosmos does not present itself

---

18. Kavanagh was married to novelist Julian Barnes at the time; she died of brain cancer almost two decades after the publication of *Written* (Harris 174, 144; Field 38).

19. Santayana notes, "like a word in a poem, more effective by its fitness than by its intrinsic beauty," our apperception of form and aesthetic value also depends on fitness (*Sense* 74).

as an all-embracing whole, but as the appearance of fittingness of each thing as and where it is; how well, how decorously, how appropriately it displays. And its beauty is that very display" (268–69). Fitness in *Written* thus relates to understanding how the solipsistic, "self-indulgent" narrator is appropriate to Winterson's larger aesthetic project of reinvigorating the "postmodern exhaustion" of language using "hybridized discourses," in order to redeem or recuperate what Catherine Belsey has termed conflicted "postmodern love" (Andermahr 167, 83; Burns 279; Belsey 685).

Though "'postmodernism . . . has tended to imply a refusal of the possibility of romantic love because of its presumed status as an illusionary discourse of authenticity,'" Antje Lindenmeyer and others rightly point out that the novel scrupulously "avoids rejecting love as mere illusion" (59), even as the book's ambition and scope are revealed in Winterson's choice of narrator. As a Don Juan/a compulsively addicted to relationships with married women, the narrator attempts to articulate love from a position of constant treachery, in an age where language's banality and/or inauthenticity relentlessly betrays us: "'I love you' is always a quotation" (*Written* 11). Drunk on the excessive, Dionysiac frenzy of affairs and emotional turbulence that accompanies them, the narrator encompasses liberatory energies of the sense-drive: "This is the voluptuous exile freely chosen. [. . .] we're drugged out on danger, where to meet, when to speak, what happens when we see each other publicly" (72). Given this persona, readers are meant to hold the narrator's words (with its at-times hollow "stream of superlatives" [52] and smug sanctimoniousness)[20] at a distance and rightly be suspicious of it, as Louise herself initially does. Yet, by the same token, the narrator's unexpected gems of beauty and truth that manage to break through the clichés and our suspicions of her/his self-indulgent grand sentiments are what make these moments so powerful in the novel's pleasurable eloquence.

Such dialectical tensions between authenticity and insincerity attest to the challenges of writing love in our present age—of Winterson's

---

20. For instance: "I mumbled something about yes as usual but things had changed. THINGS HAD CHANGED, what an arsehole comment, I had changed things. Things don't change, they're not like the seasons moving on a diurnal round. People change things. There are victims of change but not victims of things. Why do I collude in this mis-use of language?" (*Written* 56–57; see also 29–30, 46, 86, 159).

endeavors to recuperate the subject from exhausted clichés and the postmodern suspicion of grand narratives—even as *Written* brazenly explores possibilities of love that ride incessantly on demolishing the sanctums of heterosexual marriage. Adultery becomes the normative position in Winterson's novel, as readers confront a confluence of perspectives from the cheater, the cheated upon, and the one who enables the cheating:

> I've never been the slippers; never been the one to sit at home and desperately believe in another late office meeting [. . .] and felt the cold weight of those lost hours ticking in my stomach.
>
> Plenty of times I've been the dancing shoes and how those women have wanted to play. Friday night, a weekend conference. Yes, in my flat. Off with the business suit, legs apart, pulling me down on them [. . .]. And while we're doing that somebody is looking out of the window watching the weather change. Watching the clock, watching the phone, she said she'd ring after the last session. She does ring. She lifts herself off me and dials the number [. . .] wet with sex and sweat. "Hello darling, yes fine, it's raining outside." (71–72)

The complex affective layers that readers encounter in such passages resist easy judgments: on the one hand, the muted nuance and sympathetic eloquence with which the narrator portrays the forlorn waiting partner—veering constantly between desperation, anxiety, and passivity as the "cold weight of those lost hours" tick away—suggests a certain tender-hearted sensibility; on the other hand, the narrator's decision to continue enabling the cheating partner despite such emotional clarity heightens our sense of his/her callousness.

Readers encounter such flashes of eloquence everywhere in the novel: Brian Finney notes that the narrator's rendition of a "two-page scene from an imaginary melodramatic playscript"—wherein a married woman's "series of clichéd excuses" are "neatly undercut" by the "Beckettian silence" of her lover's lone figure crying silently in the bathroom—creates a sophisticated affective "mixture of the genuine and the secondhand" (Finney 26; cf. *Written* 14–15). This amalgamation of illusoriness and authenticity, of melodrama and silent restraint, of cliché and unexpected gesture, irresistibly draws readers to dwell with or return repeatedly to these sites of complex beauty, as we lovingly unravel the novel's intricately woven textures. The project of exploring postmodern love in *Written* depends on such dialectical energies and nuanced character portrayals, as Winterson sympathetically articulates the emotional struggles of fidelity and commitment, richly rendering love's complexities from the challenging and unexpected position of adultery.

The narrator contrasts Louise's careful articulations of love (solemn as before a "private altar") with her/his own careless use of *I love you* as quotation, "dropping them like coins into a wishing well, hoping they would make me come true. [. . .] I had given them as forget-me-nots to girls who should have known better. I had used them as bullets and barter" (*Written* 9, 11–12). The prosaic, timeworn phrase *I love you* acquires a lively, unexpected eloquence in being rendered as a futile act akin to coins discarded in wells that could not possibly fulfill wishes, in being handed out like forget-me-nots (both in the words' literal meaning and as a floral species) to one lover after another, and in being used as currency to wound and trade. Such local flashes of eloquent beauty create a nuanced portrayal of the narrator, exposing not only his/her flawed character but paradoxically revealing an almost childlike naïveté in the knowingly futile act of dropping *I love you* as "coins into a wishing well," hoping against hope that "they would make me come true."

Reading the narrator in relation to the book's global form thus shifts critical attention from woolly speculations about Winterson's authorial persona back to the literary work, as we consider the narratorial persona's fittingness to the novel's ambition of articulating postmodern love from a default position of infidelity (both of character and language). The journey from cliché, self-satisfaction, and love as quotation, to what Louise eventually teaches the narrator about love, commitment, and respecting the beloved's choice, is crucial to her/his emotional maturation over the course of the novel. By attending to its aesthetic dimensions—showing how *Written* fittingly harmonizes sensuous excesses of language and the imagination within the dynamic totality of its global form—I contend that Winterson defies the radical skepticism inherited from postmodernism to offer readers a beautiful work of art that enlarges the possibilities of articulating love in the present age.

NEVER LET ME GO

Unlike *Written*'s voluptuous linguistic pleasures, Kazuo Ishiguro's *Never Let Me Go* (hereafter *Never*) is a "quietly devastating, beautifully written novel" that embodies a remarkable type of beauty given that it is "so mundanely told, so excruciatingly ordinary in transit" (Dalfonzo 54; James Wood, "Human" 36). Compared to the narrative complexities encountered in novels earlier examined in this book, *Never* appears deceptively straightforward, but coming to terms with its ethical implications is fraught with difficulty. Premised on a fictitious society that sanctions the genocide of cloned young adults, the novel robustly engages the reader's moral-drive in the text's underlying bioethical travesties. Ishiguro's masterful pace of withholding/disclosing information further exacerbates the authorial audience's sense of the novel's ethical stakes, particularly in its eloquence of muted allusions to something "almost being said" (Donoghue, *Eloquence* 70).

Since the moral-drive tends to be foregrounded when readers detect injustice, speaking of beauty in such cases becomes ethically tricky terrain to navigate. I suggest that representations of injustice as mediated by beauty tend to be characterized by complex harmonies between the form- and moral-drives, where "the unity of aesthetic experience is not a closed and permanent haven in which we can rest at length in satisfied contemplation. It is rather a moving, fragile, and vanishing event," as Shusterman notes, where the artist cultivates "moments of resistance and tension" in "the rhythmic struggle of achievement and breakdown of order" (32). Since "the moment of passage from disturbance to harmony is that of intensest life" (32), *Never*'s powerful dialectical energies emerge in these transitions from resistance and disorder to complex harmonies.

"Form, as it is present in the fine arts," Dewey explains, is "the art of making clear" how moments and places become "charged with accumulations of long-gathering energy" in the "course of a developing life-experience" (303). The beauty of Ishiguro's novel depends crucially on such "developing organization of meanings and energies" (Shusterman 27), particularly in its accretions of complex ethical momentum. By explicating the ethical nuances that underlie Kathy H. and Madame Marie-Claude's interactions in Part One of *Never*, I explain how complex harmonies between the form- and moral-drives propel the eloquence of situation/gesture and affective energies eventually generated in Part Three.

Early in the novel, the autodiegetic narrator Kathy recalls how a lighthearted dare among her friends to swarm past the "snooty" Madame together took an unexpected turn:

> I'll never forget the strange change that came over us [...]. And I can still see it now, the shudder she seemed to be suppressing, the real dread that one of us would accidentally brush against her. [...] Ruth had been right: Madame *was* afraid of us. But she was afraid of us in the same way someone might be afraid of spiders. We hadn't been ready for that. [...] So you're waiting, even if you don't quite know it, waiting for the moment when you realise that you really are different to them; that there are people out there, like Madame, who don't hate you or wish you any harm, but who nevertheless shudder at the very thought of you—of how you were brought into this world and why—and who dread the idea of your hand brushing against theirs. [...] It's like walking past a mirror you've walked past every day of your life, and suddenly it shows you something else, something troubling and strange. (*Never* 31, 35–36)

Kathy's vivid memory of that troubling day ("I can still see it now") collapses her two emotional selves situated more than two decades apart, the eight-year-old experiencing-I with the thirty-one-year-old narrating-I, in the moment's muted emotional intensity.[21] Because the children's identities as clones—which Miss Lucy explains about seven years (four chapters) later—has not yet been disclosed, readers likely identify with eight-year-old Kathy and her friends' bewilderment at being treated as not even someone but some*thing* to be dreaded. That the gesture of brushing against someone's arm is so innocuous reinforces our sense of the children's vulnerability while highlighting the inadvertent cruelty of Madame and other "normals" (non-clones): despite their lack of malice or ill-will, they wield a powerful influence over Kathy and her friends' fragile sense of selves, as evident in Kathy's consistent mental image of herself thereafter as a spider or "something"

---

21. "In retrospective first-person narration," the narrating-I "is the older self who recounts the experiences undergone by the earlier 'experiencing-I'" (Herman, Jahn, and Ryan 339).

physically repulsive "that gave [Madame] the creeps" in all their subsequent interactions (35, 72).[22]

Madame's physical reactions—her "shudder [. . .] of real dread," "tuck[ing] her shoulders in tightly," "almost shrinking back," "stiffen[ing]," and "trembling" (35, 251, 270, 248, 272)—offer the clearest insight into most normals' relations to the cloned children. That this rejection is not maliciously intended complicates readers' moral judgments of Madame and, by extension, of the society she represents. These ethical complexities are exacerbated by the fact that such acts of uncaring (treating clones as nonhuman "shadowy objects" from "test tubes" [263]) are paradoxically founded on the normals' ethics of care for themselves and their loved ones,[23] triggering readers' conflicting moral intuitions about *care/harm*. The tentative confessions of vulnerability that Kathy occasionally volunteers with great restraint create a poignant tension in the delicate concert of clones' and normals' relations to and mutual fears of each other, such as Kathy's abashed admission that "somewhere underneath, a part of us stayed like that: fearful of the world around us, and—no matter how much we despised ourselves for it—unable quite to let each other go" (120).

Such ethically charged relations climax with Miss Emily's heartbreaking admission in Part Three: "We're *all* afraid of you. I myself had to fight back my dread of you *all* almost *every day* I was at Hailsham. There were times I'd look down at you all from my study window and I'd feel such revulsion . . ." (269; emphases added). Her unexpected self-disclosure is particularly challenging for the authorial audience, who up to this point have judged Miss Emily and Madame's Hailsham enterprise as essentially well-meaning (striving toward "more humane and better" relations between normals and clones in a largely uncaring world [259]) though nonetheless complicit in enabling the systematic butchering of clones. Their comparative kindness partially hones the children's passive acceptance of their fates, in part by sheltering them from the truth, timing disclosures (as Tommy later realizes) "very

---

22. "As her[Madame's] gaze fell on us, a chill passed through me, much like the one I'd felt years ago"; "without doubt, she saw and decided in a second *what we were*, because you could see her stiffen—as if a pair of large spiders was set to crawl towards her. Then something changed in her expression. It didn't become warmer exactly. But that revulsion got put away somewhere, and she studied us carefully, squinting in the setting sun" (*Never* 248).

23. See Whitehead 77; Levy 13.

carefully and deliberately [. . .], so that we were always just too young to understand properly the latest piece of information" (82). Notwithstanding their shortcomings, Miss Emily and Madame invite readers' complex ethical judgments in the conflicting moral intuitions orchestrated between *care/harm, liberty/oppression,* and *authority/subversion,* because they belong to a handful of figures in the novel who actively devoted their lives to improving the clones' living conditions, intervening in the existing system of uncaring—even at personal costs to themselves, as implied by their selling of furniture and the "mountain of debt" they are eventually saddled with (265).

Miss Emily's stark disclosure (which comes as a surprise or blow, since she has never previously demonstrated her fears) forces readers to reevaluate the relationships among knowledge, affect, and ethical choice—that is, the value of knowledge/honesty when it is emotionally so crushingly cruel and the value of the *"sheltering"* protection Hailsham did offer the children against the world's indifference (268). Ishiguro deftly choreographs these complex ethical tensions between ignorance and knowledge, kindness and cruelty, care and harm, as Tommy and Kathy's muteness in the face of Miss Emily's honest self-disclosure speaks volumes. Such dialectical tensions are further epitomized in ideological differences between how members of the staff felt Hailsham should have been run: though similarly invested in care for the children's welfare, Miss Emily favors a kind-ignorance/cruel-knowledge dynamic whereas Miss Lucy believes in cruel-ignorance/kind-knowledge (267–68, 273).

In Part One, when Madame unexpectedly chances upon Kathy at Hailsham dancing to the song "Never Let Me Go," Kathy notes "the odd thing" was that Madame was "sobbing and sobbing, staring at me [. . .] with that same look in her eyes she always had when she looked at us, like she was seeing something that gave her the creeps. Except this time there was something else, something extra in that look I couldn't fathom" (71–72). Two decades later, in Part Three, both recall the encounter as Madame shares her interpretation of that moment in light of the truth Kathy and Tommy have just learned about Hailsham's purpose and eventual closure:

> "I saw a new world coming rapidly. More scientific, efficient, yes. More cures for the old sicknesses. Very good. But a harsh, cruel world. And

I saw a little girl, her eyes tightly closed, holding to her breast the old kind world, one that she knew in her heart could not remain, and she was holding it and pleading, never to let her go. That is what I saw. It wasn't really you, what you were doing, I know that. But I saw you and it broke my heart. And I've never forgotten. [. . .] Poor creatures. I wish I could help you. But now you're by yourselves."

She reached out her hand, all the while staring into my face, and placed it on my cheek. I could feel a trembling go all through her body, but she kept her hand where it was, and I could see again tears appearing in her eyes.

"You poor creatures," she repeated, almost in a whisper. (271–72)

Madame's response here echoes her earlier reaction when Tommy earnestly explains that they have come to apply for a "donation" deferral (i.e., a deferment of death) because he and Kathy are certain of their love for each other: "'You say you're *sure*? Sure that you're in love? How can you know it?' [. . .] I saw, with a kind of shock, little tears in her eyes as she looked from one to the other of us. [. . .] 'Poor creatures. What did we do to you? With all our schemes and plans?'" (252–53).

The configuration of events—repeated references to Madame's tears and her repetition of the phrase "poor creatures," jarring in its nonhuman implications—points to Madame's bittersweet recognition that at the very moment when Hailsham's political and social failure seemed sealed (movers coming to sell their furniture that very day being a pointed reminder), Kathy and Tommy emerge as living proof of how their labors at Hailsham have succeeded on another level. Madame and Miss Emily's efforts to convince the world of the children's humanity, that their lives mean more than the sum of four "donations," is affirmed through Kathy and Tommy's love for each other—at a cruelly ironic moment when the world has decided it no longer has any need or desire for it.

Madame also seems to intuit now that their enterprise was perhaps more cruel than kind: even as they gave the children hope that the "old kind world" still existed (vis-à-vis Hailsham's sheltering them from the world's uncaring indifference, a hope leading to Tommy and Kathy's present application for a "deferral"), that vision was ultimately always a sham. Madame's tearful remark, "What did we do to you? With all our schemes and plans?" (253), implicitly acknowledges the paradox of the Hailsham enterprise, since there was never going to be any alteration of the children's course toward premature death. In other words, Hailsham's ethics of care created a fallacious sense of liberty that helped cement normals' illegitimate authority over the cloned children's oppression. The false hope of a potentially different course for their lives, of a better way for things to be, of more equitable relations between normals and clones—a prospect that the narrative audience gradually invests in over the course of the novel—is poignantly borne out by Tommy's question about whether the deferral rumor was ever true, to which "Miss Emily said gently: 'No, Tommy. There's nothing like that. Your life must now run the course that's been set for it'" (266).

Despite the muted futility characterizing Kathy's and her friends' circumstances, *Never* ultimately offers the implicit promise of a somewhat kinder world, not at the global sociopolitical level of the storyworld but carefully circumscribed in the locally evolving relations between two women. Madame's unexpectedly gentle act of reaching out to place her hand on Kathy's cheek is charged with what Shusterman terms the "internal integration and fulfillment" of the text's "meanings and energies" (27). Riding on that single tentative touch is the cumulative weight of unjust relations between clones and normals that has been gathering force throughout the novel, reaching its climax in Miss Emily's disclosures. It represents Madame's changed understanding and perspective ("I saw you and it broke my heart") as she takes a tentative step past her personal fears, of even inadvertently brushing up against eight-year-old Kathy and her friends in Part One, to offer her own unexpectedly ordinary solicitude in Part Three. That Madame remains fearful—"I could feel a trembling go all through her body, but she kept her hand where it was"—heightens the moment's poignancy.

As I explain in the introduction, an essential component of the form-drive within my aesthetic framework relates to the cognitive process of target encoding, where emotions serve as "relevance detectors" as "our mind selects elements of experience and structures them into relations with one another" (Kanske 2; Hogan, *Beauty* 55). The authorial audience's implicit readerly undertaking of selecting and structuring Kathy and Madame's evolving relationship in this manner (which depends in turn on Ishiguro's masterly shaping of these elements) culminates in our sense of Madame's surprising yet fitting eloquence of gesture—an act that carries the entire weight of what lies at the core of this heartbreaking novel. The beauty of Madame's gesture comes as close as the novel gets to an affirmation of the possibility of changed relations between normals and clones, in a way that sustains *Never*'s complex ethical tensions rather than simplistically erasing or resolving them. Such changed relations are borne out by Kathy's and Tommy's retrospective sense of intimacy with Madame: "The strange thing was—and Tommy agreed when we discussed it afterwards—although at Hailsham she'd been like this hostile stranger from the outside [. . .], Madame now appeared to me like an intimate, someone much closer to us" (*Never* 252). The novel's beauty thus emerges from such complex harmonies of the form- and moral-drives, in its eloquence of situation/gesture that sustains the book's layered ethical tensions.

Just as *Written* is characterized by a sense of harmonious fitness between the form- and sense-drives—personified by a Don Juan/a narrator drunk on the Dionysiac excesses of love and on language's sensuous possibilities—I contend that *Never*'s complex harmonies of the form- and moral-drives are similarly marked by the authorial audience's sense of fitness between narrative form and the text's "ethicism" (Gaut 589).[24] As with Winterson's novel, Kathy's narratorial persona in *Never* has triggered contentious and divergent critical attitudes, highlighting tensions in readerly reception, whereby some critics detect a misfit between the author's chosen narrative forms and (implicit/explicit) ethical positions and attitudes expressed by the text. In the analysis that follows, I explain how such interpretations are not at odds with but fuel the kind of complex harmonies that Ishiguro's novel is invested in.

Almost all critics point to the "disjuncture between Kathy's unaffected manner and the horror of her fate," where her "very even,

---

24. Berys Gaut explains: "Ethicism is the thesis that the ethical assessment of attitudes manifested by works of art [and not necessarily attitudes of characters in the work] is a legitimate aspect of the aesthetic evaluation of those works" (589). "For instance, a work of art may be judged to be aesthetically good *insofar as* it is beautiful, is formally unified and strongly expressive, but aesthetically bad *insofar as* it trivializes the issues with which it deals and manifests ethically reprehensible attitudes [. . .]. What is relevant for ethicism are the attitudes *really* possessed by a work, not those it merely claims to possess [. . .]. Just as we can distinguish between the attitudes people really have and those they merely claim to have by looking at their behavior, so we can distinguish between real and claimed attitudes of works by looking at the detailed manner in which events are presented" (589–90).

unemotional, matter-of-fact style" and "uninflected tone" are "at odds with the disconcerting content of the narrative," representing a "calculated risk" on Ishiguro's part: for the "more one learns about this underclass of organ donors, the more disturbing the casual blandness of Kathy H.'s voice becomes, leading to an ever increasing divide between her disaffected tone and one's own growing horror and outrage" (Garlick 150; Desai 51; James Wood, "Human" 37; Puchner 36). This risk has paid off with readers who recognize "Ishiguro's matching of Kathy's voice to her experience" as "a feat of imaginative sympathy and technique," where the "consistently battened-down tone is key to the powerful emotional impact of *Never Let Me Go*" (Beedham 138; Kerr, "*Never*"; Sim 81)—that is, by readers who discern the fitting dialectical energies that underlie the novel's jarring juxtaposition of voice and ethically charged subject matter.

Others, however, have judged the "simply bland and inept" Kathy to be an authorial failing, her "pale narration" and "somewhat anxiously ingratiating" manner pointing to a "lack of plausibility in the style," which Philip Hensher attributes to Ishiguro's "limited linguistic inventiveness" (Jennings 44; James Wood, "Human" 37; Hensher 32–33). Such criticisms of Kathy's narratorial voice are exacerbated by what critics judge as having been left problematically unarticulated in the novel, at the level of both the characters' and Ishiguro's authorial discourses; in other words, they take issue with the "ethics of the told" and "ethics of the telling" (Phelan, *Experiencing* 11).[25] By explicating the functions of character and authorial reticence in conversation with such critical readings, I draw on Donoghue's notion of eloquence to illustrate the beauty of *Never*'s muted allusions in the dialectical oscillations of harmony and tension thus generated between the form- and moral-drives.

For all that Kathy does say in her 288-page narration, for the most part, *Never* is characterized by a sense of great reticence, reinforced by Kathy and her friends' largely innocent collusions in collective (childhood) fantasies—which become ethically problematic within the

---

25. "Ethics of the told" refers to ethical positions that involve "character-character relations," while "ethics of the telling" cumulatively relates to ethical positions that have to do with "the narrator's relation to the characters, the task of narrating, and to the audience; and the implied author's relation to these things" (Phelan, *Experiencing* 11).

unarticulated global context of their circumstances as systematically oppressed organ suppliers trapped in an unjust social system. From Ruth's formation of Miss Geraldine's "secret guard"[26] to hypotheses about "Madame's gallery," "dream futures," "possibles" (human clone models), "donations" (mandatory organ extractions), and "completions" (dying), Kathy and those around her remain continually fearful of confronting truths about their circumstances and, by extension, the system that oppresses them: "we all sensed that to probe any further [. . .] would get us into territory we weren't ready for yet"; or "we'd all sense we were near territory we didn't want to enter, and the arguments would fizzle out" (*Never* 37, 139).

Most poignantly, when the blatantly unfair system of relations they are caught up in is exposed toward the end of the novel, Kathy and Tommy remain quite unable to overcome these childhood fears:

> "You know why it is, Kath, why everyone worries so much about the fourth? It's because they're not sure they'll really complete. If you knew for certain you'd complete, it would be easier. But they never tell us for sure." [. . .] How maybe, after the fourth donation, even if you've technically completed, you're still conscious in some sort of way; how then you find there are more donations, plenty of them, on the other side of that line; how there are no more recovery centres, no carers, no friends; how there's nothing to do except watch your remaining donations until they switch you off. It's horror movie stuff, and most of the time people don't want to think about it. [. . .] As it was, after I dismissed it as rubbish, we both shrank back from the whole territory. (279)

The terrifying prospect of having to give endlessly, of being unable to die even after the fourth "donation," is one which Tommy is ultimately unable to fully articulate; it is left to the narrator Kathy to expli-

---

26. The children form a "secret guard" at Hailsham to foil a supposed "plot to kidnap Miss Geraldine," their favorite guardian: "And yet, all the time, I think we must have had an idea of how precarious the foundations of our fantasy were, because we always avoided any confrontation"; "Moira was suggesting she and I cross some line together, and I wasn't prepared for that yet. I think I sensed how beyond that line, there was something harder and darker and I didn't want that. Not for me, not for any of us" (*Never* 52, 55).

cate (for the reader) their shared anguish and unspoken fears of dying alone. Such understatement of their emotional lives—comparing their circumstances to the banal affect of "horror movie stuff," where the colloquial choice of the word *stuff* emphasizes the everyday nature of their appalling realities—has led numerous critics to judge the characters as being complicit in a system that oppresses them through similar understatements, euphemisms, and nondisclosures ("But they never tell us for sure") to the point of literal death. Valerie Sayers notes that Kathy's and her friends' "quiet responses may roil readers more than open rebellion" (28).

Hensher, for instance, lashes out at what he perceives to be *Never*'s implausibility of situation with a barrage of questions that the novel fails to account for, suggesting that the plot's muted context is not much more convincing than its style: "It is an awful thing to say, but I believed so little in any of the people, their situation, or the way they spoke that I didn't really care about what happened to them" (32–33). Shameem Black remarks that "the *complacency* of the cloned students has provoked intense outrage among Ishiguro's readers, who cannot understand why Kathy and virtually all other characters in the novel express so little explicit anger at their condition and take so few steps to contest their fate" (791; emphasis added. See also McDonald 81; Sawyer 239; Tsao 224). On the one hand, the novel fosters readers' conflicting moral intuitions about *care/harm* given Kathy's role as both victim and enabler, as we judge the pride she takes in her work as a "carer" (which comes through vividly in her discourse)[27] to be an internalization of and complicitous with the system of oppression. On the other hand, it is precisely this choice of narratorial voice that heightens our moral revulsion and outrage at a system that makes the victims into enablers of their own and others' victimization.

In her use of evolutionary psychology to approach the study of narratives, Spolsky asserts that "it is not the truth or falsehood of stories" nor the "production of any one moral or another," "but their *indirection* that is crucial to their usefulness" (180–81, 194). Such indirection characterizes "the complexity, the indeterminacy, [and] the *sheer* difficulty" (Gaut 594) of readers' moral judgments in *Never,* where Ishiguro's masterly configuration of these ethical challenges into the text's

---

27. For instance, see *Never* 282.

formal design through its narratorial voice attests to the novel's aesthetic merit. By sustaining these dialectical oscillations of conflict and harmony between the form- and moral-drives, Ishiguro achieves a complex form of beauty in *Never* that many late twentieth- and twenty-first-century novels seem partial to.

Given the book's bioethical premise, critics offer mixed reactions to its noticeable absence "of wider sociopolitical debates about cloning and organ harvesting" (Eatough 136).[28] Mike Godwin argues that "the cloning aspect of Ishiguro's novel is almost tangential," such that "even a casual reader [. . .] can see how little the author (who has become known in his other work for painstaking craftsmanship) cares for whether this whole cloning-for-spare-parts scenario is politically or scientifically credible. [. . .] Nevertheless, the story is emotionally credible" (56). Anita Desai, on the other hand, is troubled by such contextual muteness, noting that horrifying as the novel may be, it "makes no mention of a far greater and more real horror, which is the trafficking in organs of donors in the desperately poor countries of Africa, Asia, and Latin America, compelled by their poverty to provide organs for which the first world with its obscene wealth can pay" (51). Simon Cooper suggests that "the book's *weakness* lies in the fact that it is able to say nothing about the society that would sanction this kind of living organ factory" (20; emphasis added). Characters' affective muteness and Ishiguro's muting of contexts thus take on complex valences in *Never*, working both for *and* against the novel in terms of readerly engagements.

Contrary to such readings, I argue that character and authorial reticence function as part of the novel's indictment; it is in the stripping away or muting of these contexts that I detect *Never*'s affinities with "mute radiance" or an eloquence of "something almost being said" (Galen A. Johnson, *Retrieval* 231; Donoghue, *Eloquence* 70). Drawing on Louise Glück's notion of the power and potency of the "ellipsis," "suggestion," and "deliberate silence," Donoghue's eloquence of the unsaid is "analogous to the unseen; for example, to the power of ruins, to works of art either damaged or incomplete," which haunt us

---

28. For criticisms in a similar vein, see Messud 31; Black 797, 803; Gabriele Griffin, "Science" 652; Whitehead 62–63. Ishiguro candidly remarks, "ultimately I'm not that interested in saying things about specific societies; and, if I were, I think I'd prefer to do it through nonfiction" (Shaffer and Wong 75).

in their inevitable allusions to larger unseen or unarticulated contexts (*Eloquence* 70). For Maurice Merleau-Ponty, "'mute radiance' (*le rayonnement muet*) [. . .] means that silence and vacuity are not defects, but the occasion for solitude and contemplation, a sense of fullness rather than emptiness" (Galen A. Johnson, *Retrieval* 231). *Never*'s muted beauty creates occasions for ethical contemplation in the dialectical readerly tensions generated between simultaneously interpreting Kathy's and her friends' behaviors as both passive acceptance *and* active resistance.

Judgments of the novel's aesthetic deficiencies tend to be linked to unanswered questions, such as why do the clones take "so few steps to contest their fate" (Black 791), "why don't any of them ever run away" (Hensher 32–33), and more generally to the absence of information about forms of resistance available to them. In other words, these critics partly link the book's aesthetic failures to its refusal to fully flesh out contextual circumstances that would allow readers to definitively judge the degree to which victims resist or are complicit with the system— a critical line of questioning which further implies that only political resistance (which is certainly important) is dominantly valid or justifiable. I contend that *Never* aligns with plural forms of resistance, adopting not only political but local and nongrandiose lines of defense.

Kathy's and her friends' acts of resistance tend to take place at an individual level, for the self and their loved ones, achingly rendered in the fragility of their modest dreams: "Maybe once Hailsham was behind us, it was possible, just for that half year or so," to "ponder our lives without the usual boundaries. [. . .] Mind you, none of us pushed it *too* far. I don't remember anyone saying they were going to be a movie star or anything like that. The talk was more likely to be about becoming a postman or working on a farm" (*Never* 143). Ruth scrambles to atone for past mistakes by finding Madame's address (though it "wasn't easy" and took "a long time," including running "a few risks" [233]), seeking to give Kathy and Tommy a chance to live and love a little longer despite her own impending death. When they return from the final meeting with Madame and Miss Emily (made possible by Ruth's efforts), Tommy persists with his art despite its apparent futility in granting him a death deferral, while Kathy's story serves as her form of narrative defense against the cruel reality of her circumstances over which she has little control, except to never let those she loves go, holding them both in her memory and narrative: "The memories I value most, I don't see them ever fading. I lost Ruth, then I lost Tommy, but I won't lose my memories of them. [. . .] that'll be something no one can take away" (286–87).

Henry Carrigan Jr. observes, "Above all, [Ishiguro's] characters strive to forge an enduring self-identity that can withstand the blows of an uncaring world" (98). Ruth's, Tommy's, and Kathy's modest forms of resistance serve not the greater good of all clones or other grand narratives of justice, equality, or rights, but only their own local narratives of love and friendship—endeavors that the novel validates in its nuanced portrayals of their quiet resilience. Ironically, the main form of political resistance staged by Madame and Miss Emily (imperfect and inadequate as it was) is ultimately subverted, ending in Hailsham's closure and the two well-intentioned women's disillusionment. In the end, Ishiguro's beautifully shaped novel suggests that perhaps we can each only stage forms of resistance within the best reach of our abilities, by treating one another with greater love and kindness, and holding on to the people and things that matter with an ever greater persistence; all lines of resistance are equally valid, so long as they are grounded in a loving and constructive vision of how we are to live and act, with and toward others.[29]

CONCLUSION: SHAPING READERLY CAPACITIES FOR NUANCE

Many late twentieth- and twenty-first-century novelists have found the issue of beauty to be crucially tangled with the moral and have

---

29. Ishiguro's comments about the nature of his aesthetic project are worth noting: "I was much more interested in the extent to which we accepted our fates [. . .] rather than focus on the rebellious spirit we gain and try to move out of our lives. I think this is predominantly what takes place in the world, that people take the life they feel they've been handed. They try their best to make it good. [. . .] Nothing is a perfect metaphor for the human condition. This is just one metaphor for one aspect of how people are. The strategy here is that we're looking at a very strange world, at a very strange group of people, and gradually, I wanted people to feel they're not looking at such a strange world, that this is everybody's story" (Shaffer and Wong 215). Ishiguro ultimately sees *Never* as "an allegory about the human lifespan and our inability to escape it" (Nick James, "Art" 39).

correspondingly shaped literary projects that reflect this entanglement; however, even texts that are *not* explicitly concerned with ethical issues have found an eager critical audience that remains engaged with attending to the moral-drive. Despite the apparent ethical challenges several critics have raised, I emphasize the form/sense (rather than form/moral) facets of *Written*'s engagements with beauty, since Winterson uses aesthetic strategies that are invested in formal and sensuous dimensions of her prose rather than the moral or ethical.

Relative to the other two drives, the moral-drive is comparatively more susceptible to change, as mediated by continually evolving social and cultural contextual understandings. When Winterson's novel was first published in 1992, the implicit challenge to engage readers at the thematic level—to enlarge our understandings of the moral and of "permissible" loves (whether it be adulterous love or the ungendered narrator's potentially homosexual, bisexual, or transgender perspective on love)—takes on slightly different implications for a reader who picks it up now, a quarter-century later, given the altered social landscape.[30] The text's formal and sensual engagements, on the other hand, have remained relatively resistant to such contextual changes. Winterson herself has remarked that she is far less interested in these thematic engagements and this authorial vision translates into her choice of aesthetic strategies.[31]

What then does this mean in terms of the form/moral engagement of beauty that I use to characterize Ishiguro's aesthetic project? While *Written*'s engagement of the moral-drive is heavily anchored in thematic dimensions, *Never*'s ethical engagement is implicit in its entire aesthetic design, including Ishiguro's shaping of narrative forms and voice—which invite conflicting moral intuitions about *care/harm, liberty/oppression,* and *authority/subversion.* Though *Never* is likewise susceptible to contextual changes that the moral-drive is always subject to (such as our evolving perceptions of bioethical boundaries), its ethical engagements are more persistent because they are not domi-

---

30. For instance, LGBTQ+ individuals have gained slow but greater visibility and acceptance in some cultures, while adultery is generally somewhat less prevalently frowned upon socially in a number of cultures than it would have been two decades ago.

31. "In a written interview she [Winterson] claimed bluntly that 'the story is nothing, the language is everything'" (Petro 112).

nantly issues-driven and hence "time-sensitive." *Never*'s engagements of the form- and moral-drives remain as poignantly moving more than a decade after its publication; in fact, Anne Whitehead points out that by the time Ishiguro was writing the novel, the "reality" of its context was already becoming somewhat "obsolete," allowing him "to shift perspective from the actuality of scientific practice to the moral and ethical questions that it raises" (61). When we connect such authorial choices with Ishiguro's decision to set this fictional world in the recent past—that is, England in the late 1990s, predating the book's publication in 2005—his deliberate muting of such contexts dislodge the novel from continually changing social, political, and scientific landscapes in order to shape an enduring novel of timeless beauty.

Never further illustrates that there is no simple or straightforward continuity between ethics and aesthetics, but that a sensitivity to beauty enlarges our capacity for ethical response, especially in the final exquisite exchanges among Madame, Miss Emily, Kathy, and Tommy. While the Hailsham enterprise was essentially a move in the direction of doing what was good/right/ethical, Miss Emily's startlingly honest revelations at the end are likewise moments of crushing cruelty. To miss the novel's beauty is to miss the opportunity to be profoundly moved by the strength of these ethical moments. Kathleen Marie Higgins notes that "beauty allows moral insight to develop further," because it "develops our capacity for nuance" in a way that "moral outrage typically does not. [. . .] Without a sense of degrees, moral indignation is stupid and dangerous. Beauty may indeed have limits as a moral arm, but it is indispensable to reflective and responsible moral outrage" (34–35). I suggest that beauty ultimately enlarges our capacity for ethical response, but can neither will it nor dictate it. Beauty works to tutor the faculties (including those responsible for the moral-drive) in the long run.

In response to Lyotard's notion that an aesthetic of the sublime rather than beauty characterizes mid- to late twentieth-century works of art, I propose in turn that in the post-postmodern era of the contemporary we may be making a cyclical re-turn to beauty. At stake is not simply an inherited beauty, but rather a return that resurrects the value of Platonic beauty alongside Kantian beauty. Platonic beauty, as reconceived by Nehamas, is committed to beauty as love/*erōs*, emphasizing an invested, interested, and passionate attitude toward beauty, while Kantian beauty is more strongly affiliated with an analytical, disinterested,[32] and contemplative attitude; notwithstanding their differences, both share a commitment to liberty and free play of the faculties (Nehamas 6–7; Kant, "Critique" 134). Thus, beauty cannot be a matter of propaganda, even when its purpose is a worthy one (such as fostering a more ethical outlook on the world); instead, it works at the height of its powers when the form-drive swings into freewheeling harmony with the sense- or moral-drives. Beauty's calling is ultimately to a poetic truth.

---

32. Adorno remarks that "the route to aesthetic autonomy proceeds by way of disinterestedness [. . .]. Yet art does not come to rest in disinterestedness" (*Aesthetic* 12–13).

CODA

Between Borders

> And then they learned that dominant obsessions can prevail against death.
>
> The history of the family was a machine with unavoidable repetitions, a turning wheel that would have gone on spilling into eternity were it not for the progressive and irremediable wearing of the axle.
> —GABRIEL GARCÍA MÁRQUEZ, *ONE HUNDRED YEARS OF SOLITUDE*

IN TRACING and updating the modes of play, sublime, and beauty, I hope to have shown how the history of aesthetics is itself a machine with unavoidable repetitions; as with the cyclical unfolding of the Buendía family history in *One Hundred Years of Solitude*, dominant obsessions (e.g., with beauty) tend to recur across literary eras. The spinning wheels of the sense-, form-, and moral-drives, held together by axles of aesthetic modes/theories, do progressively wear out—given shifting sociopolitical and cultural contexts over time—though not irremediably so, requiring only timely revisions for the aesthetic apparatus to remain functional and pertinent to the field of literary inquiry. Though the three modes explored in this book do not exhaust the diverse aesthetics organizing postwar literature in English, they can be viewed as junctures that offer us an alternative trajectory for thinking about forms of literary practice during this period. Orchestrations of the sublime, beauty, and play in the work of twentieth- and twenty-first-century novelists invite readers to participate in their always unfinished acts of meaning-making—an active co-construction,

I contend, which constitutes the dominant shift in updating our understanding of aesthetic paradigms in the present moment.

In chapters 1 and 2, I identified tensions between the form- and sense-drives, suggesting that through our participation in the game-like structures and textual mayhem of postmodern fictional worlds, texts like *The Castle of Crossed Destinies* and *Lanark* partially shift the onus of creating narrative form onto readers. Chapters 3 and 4 posit that the postmodern literary sublime is propelled by the sense-drive in increasing degrees of conflict with the moral-drive as we move from the mathematical to the dynamical sublime, foregrounding the active exercise of readers' moral freedom (e.g., in our resistance to representations of suffering in *Blood Meridian*). Chapter 5 responds in part to Adorno's proposition that the beautiful increasingly manifests itself "in the dynamic totality of the work of art" ("Concept" 80), such that grasping these energies in the text's complex coherences becomes the reader's key task in our discernments of beauty. Novels like *Written on the Body* and *Never Let Me Go* stage encounters with literary beauty in a dynamic plurality of ways—in the form-drive's complex harmonies with the sense- or moral-drive—faithful to beauty's very spirit of polysemy.

Categories also shade off into one another, with porous rather than rigid borders. The proliferation of highly antimimetic worlds in radically playful texts such as *At Swim-Two-Birds,* for instance, tends to verge on the mathematical sublime's postulation of infinite worlds, while others like *Invisible Cities* straddle multiple aesthetic modes, in a textual universe that hovers between the beautiful and sublime—at once both "the sum of all wonders" and "an endless, formless ruin" (*Cities* 5). A "zodiac of the mind's phantasms," Calvino's cities flicker in and out of sight at the chapter level, even as eloquent blazes of beauty at the sentence level sear readers with eternalized images of Despina the camel-ship city, Ersilia's city of strings progressively rendering its inhabitants eternal nomads, and Armilla's "forest of pipes" where nymphs and naiads luxuriate "under showers suspended in the void" in a city without walls, ceilings, or doors (22, 17, 76, 49).

In this final chapter, I turn my attention to interstices between aesthetic modes, explaining how all three drives function in dynamic interplay. Shimamura describes our experience of art as "a whole brain phenomenon," but with "no *art center* in the brain"; instead, highly interconnected neurons "dynamically interact to drive experiences. There is, however, a division of labor as different brain regions serve different functions" (258)—and it is this labor division that I work to capture using my heuristic tools of the sense-, form-, and moral-drives. Dutton makes a similar point when he explains that what he terms "the art instinct" is "not a single genetically driven impulse [. . .] but a complicated ensemble of impulses" or "sub-instincts" (6). Distinctions among modes of play, sublime, and beauty—in relation to the tension/harmony between dominant drives and implicit readerly tasks thus engendered—are valuable to the extent that they shed light on readers' aesthetic experiences and enhance our appreciation of previously under-considered dimensions of literary works. There are, however, works like Gabriel García Márquez's *One Hundred Years of Solitude* (1967/70) which seem to elide such distinctions: not only because they challenge or defy easy categorization (most postmodern fictional texts I discuss in this book similarly resist pinning down), but because they fit comfortably within *all* of these modes.

I argue that the cognitive load demanded by such texts—in their stacking of aesthetic modes and in the range and complexity of the subject matter they deal with—creates a seesawing effect in which various drives (and modes) take turns to dominate. I posit that literary works of such complex artistry simulate the workings of the human brain's "well-developed network,"[1] mimicking its "global workspace that allows for the confrontation, synthesis, and distribution of information arising from other brain processors. This system is further endowed with a fringe of spontaneous fluctuation that allows for the testing of new ideas," particularly in the prefrontal regions, which Dehaene is "tempt[ed] to associate [. . .] with the spontaneous flow of consciousness and imagination" (321)—or what I term the *sense-drive* in my aesthetic model.

Maryanne Wolf explains reading as "a neuronally and intellectually circuitous act," wherein information processing and comprehension are facilitated by "associative dimension[s]" that are "part of

---

1. Dehaene observes that "a great number of researchers have arrived, via different routes, at the conclusion that our species has a gift for putting thoughts together": the human brain's "special knack for mental recombination" distinguishes us from other species, whereby the full development of our prefrontal cortex allows us to integrate varying sources of information with a high degree of flexibility (322–24).

the generative quality at the heart of reading," and that "the proportion of our brain devoted to these association areas is a major difference between the human brain" and those of other primates (16, 29).[2] Readers (implicitly) engage in such associative processes via ordering systems of the form- and moral-drives. The *form-drive*, for example, facilitates readerly comprehension in our attempts to impose temporal coherence in *A Visit from the Goon Squad* or ontological coherence in *At Swim-Two-Birds*. The *moral-drive* is in turn engaged when we consider how asymmetrical character relations—for instance, between clones and "normals" in *Never Let Me Go* or those created by the caste system and gender inequalities in *The God of Small Things*—lay bare the inherent injustice of such institutionalized systems, exposing how moral discourses are hijacked in order to reinforce the subjugation of specific groups.

My three-drive model partly responds to Changeux's notion of "the search for a harmonious synthesis between brain processors as the very essence of art" (Dehaene 323) and to cognitive psychologists Hans Kreitler and Shulamith Kreitler's belief that the experience of art is characterized by dialectical energies of tension and relief.[3] Like Starr, I am convinced that "rewards exist in [such] dynamic interplay," where aesthetic experience "makes possible the unexpected valuation of objects, ideas, and perceptions and enables new configurations of what is known, new frameworks for interpretation," since "the *hedonic value* assigned to those perceptions and ideas at a neural level enables powerful connections that had not existed before" (129, 20). In this final chapter, I examine the seesawing tensions and harmonies between drives in *One Hundred Years of Solitude*—and, in so doing, explain how García Márquez's complex ethics of telling broadens readers' capacities for ethical nuance through complex figurations of motifs such as

---

2. Spolsky explicates a similar process in literary inquiry when she observes that a "large amount of the work of literary theory can be understood as investigating the possibility that experiences of narrative" offer "practice in repatterning, recategorizing, reinferencing and reanalogizing"—associative processes that "teach us that very generativity that we need to counterbalance the rigidities that life so often requires of us" (196).

3. Kreitler and Kreitler suggest that "all art forms, including visual, musical, dramatic, and literary artworks, create tension which we try to resolve" (Shimamura 203; cf. Kreitler and Kreitler 16–21, 251–56).

incest, solitude, and nostalgia, even as its eloquent beauty refracts the social and political realities that underpin the novel's construction.

ONE HUNDRED YEARS OF SOLITUDE

Steven Boldy positions García Márquez's magnum opus as a novel that "generously invites reading, offers great textual pleasure, but merely *tolerates* interpretation" (258; emphasis added). Such hermeneutic instabilities relate partly to the way *One Hundred Years of Solitude* (hereafter *Solitude*) "slips constantly and deftly" between "mythical narration" and "the story of real Colombian history"—one that is "not so different from that of other Latin American republics: the struggle between Liberals and Conservatives and the Civil War of 1899–1902, the treaty of Neerlandia, the banana boom of the first decades of the century, the transfer of power from the criollos to multinational companies, the strike and massacre of workers in 1928, and the economic ruin of the area by the Caribbean coast" (Boldy 259). This leveling of the real and fantastic simultaneously engages modes of play and beauty (in the respective tension and harmony between the sense- and form-drives), even as its engagements of the sense- and moral-drives propel the novel's political satire and its sublime energies.

Tensions between Drives: Playfulness, Sublimity, and Authorial Compassion

Akin to *The Third Policeman*'s revelry with stretching laws of physics to their breaking points, *Solitude*'s textual universe is characterized by persistent departures from "physical compatibility" with the AW: a world in which an Armenian hawking invisibility syrups turns into an evaporating puddle and where bones in a sack follow exasperated workmen around the Buendía house with a "dull rattle" and the "clucking of a brooding hen" (Ryan, *Possible* 32; *Solitude* 17, 56, 43). *Solitude*'s dimensions of play are encapsulated in the founding José Arcadio Buendía's invitation to "his offspring to read with their imaginations": "in a room plastered with unrealistic maps and fabulous drawings, he teaches them to read by telling them of 'the wonders of the world' ('las maravillas del mundo')" (Swanson 57). Philip Swanson suggests that "this prompting to read in a 'marvellous' or magical way is a possible invitation to the reader to approach the work they are about to read as a playful fictional adventure" (57). Michael Wood observes a "philosophical playfulness" and "so much deadpan mischief" in García Márquez's writing—a "nonsense" or nonrationality that Wood argues "is precious and should not be recklessly converted into meaning on all occasions" (46, 39). While Wood's call to suspend (or defer) interpretation is sound advice, Solitude's engagement of our form- and sense-drives remains an unresolved tension as readers attempt to navigate the novel's labyrinthine webs of character relations—a readerly challenge that begins almost immediately on the opening page with the Buendía family tree.[4]

The incessant repetition of character names in varying configurations—an Amaranta, an Úrsula, and an Amaranta Úrsula; three Remedioses; four José Arcadios (plus another Arcadio); and twenty-two Aurelianos—echo up and down the family line, perpetuating a Dionysiac frenzy which is exacerbated by parallel events readers discern between namesakes. It is difficult to shake an ominous sense of foreboding when we suspect that Meme (whose name is a diminutive of her aunt's, Remedios the Beauty) is clandestinely meeting her lover in the bathroom, given that the voyeur who watches her aunt bathe falls to his death while taking aside broken roof tiles "in order to drop down into the bathroom" (*Solitude* 218, 297, 239). When Meme's lover Mauricio Babilonia is shot down from the roof "as he was lifting up the tiles to get into the bathroom where Meme was waiting for him," readers are struck by an inevitable sense of fatalism impelled by the form-drive's patterning of names with destinies—a fatalism that seems to bear out Úrsula's suspicion that the family's "long history of [. . .] insistent repetition of names" led to "some conclusions that seemed to be certain" (297, 186).

---

4. It is worth noting that García Márquez had initially "made a family tree, but [later] tore it up" (Poniatowska 215). Editors decided to include a family tree in the English translation, which *Solitude*'s translator Gregory Rabassa initially "thought [was] a good idea, something to help readers keep all the characters straight and to let them see the complex inter-relationships" ("Gabriel" 245–46). Rabassa later "had second thoughts," since "confusion (and fusion) was meant to be a part of the novel" (246).

The prophetic end of the Buendía line in the (unwitting) incestuous union of Amaranta Úrsula and her nephew Aureliano reverberates with echoes from Amaranta's "autumnal passion" with both her nephew Aureliano José and her great-grandnephew José Arcadio (147, 282–83). *Solitude* maintains dialectical tensions between the sense- and form-drives in García Márquez's endlessly generative figurations of motifs such as incest, solitude, and nostalgia, even as such sensuous impulsions are countered by an inherent dialectical energy—where Wood points to incest's function as "the sexual form of solitude, a failure to imagine the way out of the family, to make contact with the world" (Michael Wood, *Gabriel* 85), in a gyroscopic inward turning toward the past. García Márquez's operationalization of incest in *Solitude* thus is not narrowly hinged only to the moral-drive but is further implicated in the form- and sense-drives: in the symmetrical paralleling of desire across generations between aunts and nephews, and the resultant inexorable march toward the family's doomed inward rather than outward generativity, completing the circle of an Aureliano being the first and last Buendía to be born and to die in Macondo.

Death in *Solitude* is characterized by sensuous impulsions tending toward the sublime:[5] from the devastating circus that leaves "onlookers peering into the precipice of uncertainty" marking Colonel Aureliano Buendía's passing, to Remedios the Beauty's "fatal emanation" that penetrates the body of her doomed voyeur and "kept on torturing men beyond death, right down to the dust of their bones" (*Solitude* 273, 239). In particular, José Arcadio Buendía's demise—his failure to return to "the room of reality" during his recurring "dream of the infinite rooms" (143–44)—instantiates the relationship I posit between death and the sublime in chapters 3 and 4, where I argue for the aes-

---

5. *Solitude* gestures unceasingly toward the sublime not only in relation to death but also with reference to outward journeys into the "enchanted region"—a place where "the world became eternally sad" and men found themselves "overwhelmed by their most ancient memories [. . .] going back to before original sin" (11–12)—as well as characters' interior journeys of delirium and sexual awakening. For instance, Colonel Aureliano Buendía attempts to find relief from his unbridled love for little Remedios Moscote with Pilar Ternera, in whose lovemaking he "found Remedios changed into a swamp without horizons," while his elder brother José Arcadio likewise finds himself at Pilar's door, "wondering in fright how he had ever got to that abyss of abandonment" (69, 27).

thetic mode's significance in representing the unknowable and how a revised emphasis on the sublime's imaginative dimensions (such as awe) works to foreground readers' profound awareness of the limits of human knowledge.

Unresolved tensions between the sense- and moral-drives further facilitate the mode of the dynamical sublime, where readers remain disturbed by unaddressed ethical transgressions inherent in *Solitude*'s sensuous excesses. Long-discarded rolls of Pietro Crespi's music "kept spinning and playing" endlessly in Amaranta's memory, as she first attempted to sink her nostalgias "into the swampy passion" with her nephew Aureliano José and later—in "the most desperate act of her old age"—"when she would bathe the small José Arcadio [. . .] and caress him not as a grandmother would have done with a grandchild, but as a woman would have done with a man, [. . .] as she had wanted to do with Pietro Crespi at the age of twelve, fourteen" (282–83). Given Haidt's postulation that the *care/harm* moral foundation evolved in response to the adaptive challenge of protecting and caring for (our) children, especially those who are suffering, *Solitude* provokes conflicting readerly moral intuitions particularly in the case of José Arcadio, for whom "the caresses of Amaranta in the bath and the pleasure of being powdered between the legs with a silk puff would release him from the terror" inadvertently perpetrated by his great-great-grandmother Úrsula (Haidt 124, 183; *Solitude* 375).[6]

---

6. While readers learn in chapters 10 and 13 that the hundred-year-old Úrsula takes responsibility for raising little José Arcadio amidst her worsening eyesight, its consequences are only revealed years later in chapter 18 when we realize that in order not to "lose him in the shadows" of her blindness, the "terror-filled nights" of José Arcadio's childhood were reduced to a bedroom corner in which he would remain motionless, "perspiring with fear" until bedtime, "safe from the dead people who wandered through the house after sundown. [. . .] It was useless torture because even at that time he already had a terror of everything around him and he was prepared to be frightened at anything he met in life: women on the street, who would ruin his blood; the women in the house, who bore children with the tail of a pig; fighting cocks, who brought on the death of men and remorse for the rest of one's life; firearms, which with a mere touch would bring down twenty years of war; uncertain ventures, which led only to disillusionment and madness [. . .]. When he awakened, pressed in the voice of his nightmares, [. . .] the caresses of Amaranta in the bath and the pleasure of being powdered between the legs with a silk puff would release him from the terror" (*Solitude* 194, 253, 375).

García Márquez complicates the inherent *care/harm* conflict of such sexually fraught and (potentially) abusive relationships by focalizing these episodes extensively through the minds of both Buendía men as adults, where their idealized memories of Amaranta are so potent that Aureliano José "tried to drown that image in the bloody bog of war," while José Arcadio—later murdered by drowning—is found "floating on the perfumed mirror of the pool, enormous and bloated and still thinking about Amaranta" (*Solitude* 374, 381). Such tensions between the moral- and form-drives recur throughout the novel—for instance, when (Colonel) Aureliano encounters "the matron of the rocking chair" (53) who prostitutes her granddaughter—in the dissonance orchestrated between the "ethics of the told" and "ethics of the telling" (Phelan, "Narrative Ethics"). The "adolescent mulatto girl with a forlorn look" explains to Aureliano that she had caused her grandmother's house to burn down two years earlier when she fell asleep without putting out the candle:

> Since then her grandmother carried her from town to town, putting her to bed for twenty cents in order to make up for the value of the burned house. According to the girl's calculations, she still had ten years of seventy men per night, because she also had to pay the expenses of the trip and food for both of them as well as the pay of the Indians who carried the rocking chair. (*Solitude* 53–54)

Filled "with a mixture of desire and pity" for the girl, Aureliano "felt an irresistible need to love her and protect her" (54). When he decides "to marry her in order to free her from the despotism of her grandmother and to enjoy all the nights of satisfaction that she would give the seventy men," he learns that the girl had left Macondo (54).

The ethics of the told—which pertain to events and "ethical dimensions of characters' actions, especially the conflicts they face and the choices they make about those conflicts" (Phelan, "Narrative Ethics")—violate readerly moral intuitions about *care/harm, liberty/oppression,* and *fairness/cheating,* in the matron's perverse decision to prostitute her granddaughter under the false auspices of fair dealing. Our disgust is compounded by the nefarious reasoning that in addition to making up "for the value of the house," the adolescent girl is responsible for the expenses of her sexual slavery. The fleetingness of the encounter—Macondo as a one-night stop in twelve abominable years of sexual servitude the girl is being subjected to—frames Aureliano's intended intervention within a complex ethics of the told: while his potentially altruistic act (driven at least in part by the *care/harm* intuition of wanting to "love her and protect her") offers a significant amelioration of the girl's abhorrent circumstances, it simultaneously exchanges the grandmother's despotism for a husband's prerogative to sex (the enjoyment of "all the nights of satisfaction that she would give the seventy men"), in which the girl remains left without or with little agency, trading one form of authority over her body for another.

Difficult as the ethics of the told may be, the dissonance created by conflicts between the form- and moral-drives in the ethics of the telling—which relate to "ethical dimensions of the narrative's techniques," and the values thus implied/conveyed about the narrator and/or implied author's relations "to their materials (events and characters) and their audiences" (Phelan, "Narrative Ethics")—is still more disconcerting. Akin to Kathy's measured account of clone genocide in *Never Let Me Go* or the methodical explication of slaughtered infants in *Blood Meridian*, the girl's quiet resignation is palpable in the free indirect discourse, as her suffering and the atrocious math underlying her debt are narrated as matters of fact: "The girl thanked him in silence. Her back was raw. Her skin was stuck to her ribs and her breathing was forced because of an immeasurable exhaustion" (*Solitude* 54). Wood notes that like much of Franz Kafka's writing, *Solitude*'s narration is notable for its "calm, [. . .] extraordinary refusal to be ruffled," where "the desperate and the monstrous" are treated "as if it were the everyday, as if language could proceed untouched by what it reports, and the very modesty of the voice enhances the nightmare" (Michael Wood, *Gabriel* 62).

Solitude's characteristic employment of free indirect discourse foregrounds such tensions between the form- and moral-drives: for instance, in both Amaranta and Fernanda's murderous meanderings. "For long months" Amaranta "trembled with fright," waiting for that fateful hour "when all the resources of her imagination" to impede Rebeca and Pietro's wedding had failed, she would summon "the courage to poison" Rebeca; Fernanda, in turn, "had to tolerate" her illegitimate grandson "against her will for the rest of her life because at the moment of truth she lacked the courage to go through with her inner determination to drown him in the bathroom cistern" (*Solitude* 89,

298). Such double-voicedness in the narration—the "courage" required to follow through on plans for murder—fashions a complex ethics of telling, whereby the rich ironies that underpin characters' judgments of their actions and life-events (i.e., ethics of the told) are accentuated through the use of free indirect discourse. García Márquez's narrative strategies complicate our readerly judgments about both women, especially Fernanda, whose last vestige of withered protective instincts for her grandson—a humane act for which she despises herself—ironically leads readers to judge her a little less harshly.

The depth of Amaranta's desperate jealousy that frightens even herself offers readers intimate access to her inner life, provoking our unexpected sympathy for her, even as we remain acutely conflicted about her intended violation of the *care/harm* moral foundation in her plan to poison Rebeca, her adopted sister. Such dissonances between the form- and moral-drives shape our understanding of Úrsula's eventual realization with "the lucidity of her old age" that her daughter was "the most tender woman who had ever existed, and she understood with pitying clarity" then that so many of Amaranta's vindictive and bitter acts had in fact "been a mortal struggle between a measureless love and an invincible cowardice, and that the irrational fear that Amaranta had always had of her own tormented heart had triumphed in the end" (253–55). The paradoxical tenderness at the core of Amaranta's "hardness of heart [that had] frightened" even her own mother (*Solitude* 254) bears out Wood's observation that "there are almost no villains" in García Márquez's work, "no situations not ravelled in complexity [. . .]. Above all his vision concentrates on the way people live with themselves and with others, and the way they picture their world" (Michael Wood, *Gabriel* 9–10)—an assessment remarkably resonant with my own conception of the moral-drive.

"When asked what critics had most blatantly missed about his novel, García Márquez answered[,] 'its main quality: the author's immense compassion for all his poor creatures'" (Boldy 267). I contend that an aesthetic reading of *Solitude* opens us up to these nuances of authorial compassion, sensitizing us to characters' sufferings in spite of their flaws, in ways that lead readers to step outside their moral comfort zones. Though Haidt notes that we tend to exercise conditional empathy with those who act in ways that conform to (rather than violate) our own moral matrix, literature is also able to use such conflicting moral intuitions to create resonances across lines of moral divide.[7] Unresolved conflicts between the form- and moral-drives thus invite readers to engage in a form of difficult empathy, as we struggle to expand our moral intuitions in ways that we were initially unwilling to do or uncomfortable doing.

Harmonies between Drives: Satire and Beauty

"Though Colombia is the most obvious model" for *Solitude,* critics note that "lurking in the background of the story [is] the overall pattern of Latin American history" (Echevarría 369; see also Erickson 158, 172; Clive Griffin, "Humour" 81; Deveny Jr. and Marcos 83). Just as dynamic tensions among the three drives propel *Solitude*'s sophisticated figurations of incest, all three drives are implicated in the novel's treatment of politics and history—in the complex harmonies orchestrated between generative excess and ethicism (sense-/moral-drives), between moral intuitions and narrative forms (moral-/form-drives), and between expectations and their pleasurable ruptures (form-/sense-drives). Boldy notes that José Arcadio Segundo and Aureliano Babilonia are "the two figures most linked to censured political and historical knowledge: the massacre of the banana workers by the authorities in connivance with the United Fruit Company"—which was based on events that "took place at Ciénaga railway station in 1928," whereby the "real names of soldiers and words of the official decree" are reproduced in *Solitude* (Boldy 260).[8]

After the decree "authoriz[ing] the army" to open fire on the striking workers is read, José Arcadio Segundo gave a shout,

> which did not bring on fright but a kind of hallucination. The captain gave the order to fire and fourteen machine guns answered at once. But it all seemed like a farce. [. . .] their panting rattle could be heard and their incandescent spitting could be seen, but not the slightest reaction was perceived, not a cry, not even a sigh among the compact crowd that seemed petrified by an instantaneous invulnerability. Sud-

---

7. See chapter 4 of this book; Haidt 236, 68–69.
8. Eduardo Posada-Carbó examines these historical bases at length in his article, "Fiction as History: The *bananeras* and Gabriel García Márquez's *One Hundred Years of Solitude.*"

denly, on one side of the station, a *cry of death* tore open the *enchantment*: "Aaaagh, Mother." A *seismic* voice, a volcanic breath, the *roar of a cataclysm* broke out in the center of the crowd [. . .], and the panic became a dragon's tail [. . .], swirling about in a gigantic whirlwind. (*Solitude* 310–11; emphases added)

Rendered in sensuous terms that tend continually toward excess, the Dionysiac frenzy characterizing the moment befits the egregious violations of moral foundations on all counts. Gathering oppressed workers under false auspices of conflict mediation, the seismic proportions of the cataclysmic massacre that ensues jars readerly moral intuitions about *care/harm, fairness/cheating, authority/subversion, loyalty/betrayal,* and *liberty/oppression*. Such fitness between the sense- and moral-drives foregrounds the absurdity of the all-too-common political travesty of turning armed enforcers on those whom they were meant to protect.

Taken with more than three thousand others, José Arcadio Segundo narrowly escapes death—surrounded by "man corpses, women corpses, child corpses who would be thrown into the sea like rejected bananas"—only to discover that "he could find no trace of the massacre" upon his return and that no one, not even his twin brother, believed his version of the events (312–19). Boldy notes this as an instance of "magical realism brilliantly used as political satire" (260); to cast this in terms of my aesthetic model, the sensuous excesses of José Arcadio Segundo's solitary, nightmarish experience finds chilling accord with (and is paradoxically reinforced by) the town's collective amnesia and later vociferous denial of the massacre, in a complex harmony of the sense- and moral-drives. For the purposes of this book, I allude to the much-contested concept of *magical realism* (derived from Alejo Carpentier's *lo real maravilloso*)[9] with specific reference to ways *Solitude*'s "magical" or "marvellous" dimensions relate to my conception of the sense-drive—even as I remain cognizant of lively debates

---

9. An aspect of Carpentier's *lo real maravilloso* that resonates with my conception of the sense-drive is its "amplification of the measures and categories of reality, [which are] perceived with particular intensity" (translated in Aldama, *Postethnic* 9). For José Arcadio Segundo, the aftermath of the massacre's reality was "the train with two hundred cars loaded with dead people which left Macondo *every day* at dusk on its way to the sea" (*Solitude* 342; emphases added).

contesting the term's implications among postcolonial theorists and scholars of Latin American literature.[10]

The magical/marvellous is used as a wry criticism of the novel's—and, by extension, Colombia's and other Latin American countries'—political realities both in the lead up to and in the aftermath of the massacre, where the banana company's lawyers dismissed workers' "demands with decisions that seemed like acts of magic" (*Solitude* 306). Elaborate ruses to forestall workers from officially notifying the company of their demands include the "disappear[ance]" of Mr. Brown, the banana company representative who subsequently allows himself to be "jailed as an imposter" in order to prove "he had nothing to do with the company," forging first a birth certificate and later a

> death certificate, attested to by consuls and foreign ministers, which bore witness that on June ninth last he had been run over by a fire engine in Chicago. Tired of that hermeneutical delirium, the workers [. . .] brought their complaints up to the higher courts. It was there that the sleight-of-hand lawyers proved that the demands lacked all validity for the simple reason that the banana company did not have, never had had, and never would have any workers in its service because they were all hired on a temporary and occasional basis. [. . .] by a decision of the court it was established and set down in solemn decrees that the workers did not exist. (306–7)

Parodying the officious tone and language adopted in government documents and legal papers, García Márquez exposes the collusion between corporate interests and political authorities in the absurd unreality of their circumstances, whereby workers' rights "disappeared" like "acts of magic," and ominous decrees resound as prophetic performative acts in which the workers' very existence is later forcibly erased during the massacre.

---

10. See, for instance, Rabassa's "Beyond Magic Realism"; Brian Conniff's "The Dark Side of Magical Realism"; Edwin Williamson's "Magical Realism and the Theme of Incest in *One Hundred Years of Solitude*"; Dean J. Irvine's "Fables of the Plague Years"; Daniel Erickson's *Ghosts, Metaphor, and History in Toni Morrison's* Beloved *and Gabriel García Márquez's* One Hundred Years of Solitude; Christopher Warnes's *Magical Realism and the Postcolonial Novel*; Stephen M. Hart's "Magical Realism in the Americas"; and Hart and Wen-chin Ouyang's *A Companion to Magical Realism*, among others.

Such parody is also evident in Colonel Gerineldo Márquez's written tug-of-war for his pension, where "the voices of officialdom are expertly mimicked" (Michael Wood, *Gabriel* 67):

> With them he waged the sad war of daily humiliation, of entreaties and petitions, of come-back-tomorrow, of any-time-now, of we're-studying-your-case-with-the-most-proper-attention; the war hopelessly lost against the many yours-most-trulys who should have signed and would never sign the lifetime pensions. The other war, the bloody one of twenty years, did not cause them as much damage as the corrosive war of eternal postponements. Even Colonel Gerineldo Márquez, who escaped three attempts on his life, survived five wounds, and emerged unscathed from innumerable battles, succumbed to that atrocious siege of waiting and sank into the miserable defeat of old age, thinking of Amaranta among the diamond-shaped patches of light in a borrowed house. (*Solitude* 249)

The analogy of "the corrosive war of eternal postponements" to the bloody civil war of twenty years echoes Colonel Aureliano Buendía's earlier sense "of the vicious circle of that eternal war that always found him in the same place," where "nothing ever happened" (171). The narrative's centripetal spiraling and the rhetorical tussle Colonel Gerineldo Márquez is subjected to thus foreground the "emptiness of war" (165), highlighting the sense of disillusionment that extends to the historical realities that underpin *Solitude*.

The "atrocious siege of waiting" Colonel Gerineldo Márquez succumbs to is an overt allusion not only to the novelist's own "grandfather Colonel Márquez and his eternal wait for his veteran's pension" (García Márquez, *Living* 513–14),[11] but is also an intertextual reference to García Márquez's own novella, *No One Writes to the Colonel*, which was published five years before *Solitude*. Just as the novella is "a brilliantly terse indictment of social injustice in Latin America" (Prieto 33), where—like the author's grandfather—the titular/unnamed colonel waits in vain for a pension that never arrives, Colonel Gerineldo Márquez is worn down by the insidious weapon of bureaucratic red

---

11. García Márquez writes about his grandfather Colonel Nicolás Ricardo Márquez Mejía in his autobiography, *Living to Tell the Tale* (12).

tape and the infinite deferment of empty promises that would never be fulfilled. All he is eventually left with is his nostalgia of a lifetime's unrequited love for Amaranta—a war likewise hopelessly lost against Amaranta's fear "of her own tormented heart" (*Solitude* 255).

Christopher Warnes posits, "unlike the ambivalence that attaches to the novel's treatment of solitude, nostalgia is virtually always presented in negative terms," functioning as "illusion" and a "trap" that eventually "leads to cynicism and decline" (80–81).[12] I argue that the nostalgic beauty of Colonel Gerineldo Márquez's ruminations does not function as an escapist means of deflecting attention from his unjust circumstances, but instead serves as a mode for refracting social and political realities in ways that develop readerly capacity for ethical nuance and moral insight.[13] In other words, I suggest that our indignation at the colonels' shared plight—in the violation of moral intuitions about *fairness/cheating* and *liberty/oppression*—is partly shaped by the nostalgic beauty that follows. As with the novel's complex figurations of incest and solitude, nostalgia functions here through dialectical energies pointing not only to Colonel Gerineldo Márquez's forlorn acceptance of his hopeless defeat in the war of words against political injustice (a verbal parrying that evokes the "hermeneutical delirium" conjured by the banana company's "sleight-of-hand lawyers"), but also to the stoic beauty with which he counters such futility.

Wood observes that in its "particular mingling of despair and possibility," Latin American Boom fiction is steered by a "nobly refused but always hovering despair," such that García Márquez's magnum opus is

---

12. Warnes argues that "García Márquez recognises very clearly that the problem with nostalgia is that it 'wipe[s] away bad memories, and magnifie[s] the good ones' (*Living* 19)"—pointing specifically to incidents such as the wise Catalonian being caught between "two nostalgias facing each other like two mirrors"—and suggests "that it is nostalgia itself that later succeeds in killing the Colonel where a lifetime of wars had failed" (Warnes 80–81; cf. *Solitude* 408).

13. René Prieto notes that much of García Márquez's innovation lies in his transformation of (political) reality: "He has always repudiated the misjudgement inherent in the bending of artistic inspiration to serve political ends. [. . .] 'It is perhaps more rewarding to write honestly about what one is capable of telling for having lived it', he declares, 'than to write, with the same degree of earnestness, about that which our political position suggests must be told, even if it means inventing it'. Forcing the pen to fit the message, in other words, leads unremittingly to failure. With equal conviction, he indicates that the best means of eliciting reader response is through suggestion and challenge[,] not through pontification" (41–42).

"not so much a portrait of solitude as a portrait of the style and grace with which solitude has been and is borne" (Michael Wood, *Gabriel* 6, 103)—an assessment I extend to the novel's treatment of nostalgia. The one thing Colonel Gerineldo Márquez cannot be robbed of in his impoverishment is the rich present-ness of his unyielding devotion for Amaranta, which streams through in "diamond-shaped patches of light," even as "the sad war of daily humiliation" and "miserable defeat of old age" are relegated to the past tense; our preoccupations, as suggested in my chapter epigraph, can prevail against death and decline in the face of such apparent futility. Formal strategies of parody, intertextuality, and parallel mirrors of futility (whether in love, war, or politics) frame readers' sense of the moment's ethical stakes, where the moral- and form-drives emerge in complex harmony, marked by a sense of fitness between *Solitude*'s ethicism and its narrative forms.

Solitude's translator Gregory Rabassa notes that "García Márquez's words so often have the ring of prose poetry" as they are "strung together in rhythmic cohesion"—a quality Rabassa works to replicate in his transposition of the novel in English ("Gabriel" 245). Love is manifested in the very measure of sound, where the *e*- and *o*-vowels and the *m*- and *r*-consonants in the musical refrain of little Remedios Moscote's name accentuate the spell of entrancement that enfolds Colonel Aureliano Buendía:

> everything, even m̲usic, rem̲inded hi̲m̲ of R̲em̲edios. The house became full of love. Aurelian*o* expressed it in poetry that had n*o* beginning *o*r end. [. . .] in all of it Remedios would appear transfigured. R̲em̲edi*o*s in the sop̲o̲rific ai̲r *o*f two in the afterno*o*n, R̲em̲edios in the soft b̲r̲eath *o*f the r̲oses, R̲em̲edios in the water-clock secrets *o*f the m̲oths, R̲em̲edios in the steam̲ing m̲orning bread, Remedios everywhere and Remedios forever. (*Solitude* 67–68; emphases added)

Much of *Solitude*'s beauty emerges from such eternalized fragments of eloquence that endure in the mad excesses of characters' hearts, mirrored between pairs of characters including Amaranta and Rebeca, Pietro Crespi and Remedios the Beauty's foreign suitor, and Meme and Mauricio.

Unbeknownst to each other, Mauricio and Meme's fates unfold along parallel tracks that end in solitary old age, united in their joint muteness following their separation. Believing "Mauricio Babilonia had died," Meme "did not let herself be defeated by resignation" but "kept on thinking about him" (301). Just as Colonel Gerineldo Márquez kept "thinking of Amaranta among the diamond-shaped patches of light in a borrowed house," Meme thought about Mauricio under the yellow stream of light from the convent's stained-glass windows:

> his smell of grease, and his halo of butterflies, and she would keep on thinking about him for all the days of her life until the remote autumn morning when she died of old age, with her name changed and her head shaved and without ever having spoken a word, in a gloomy hospital in Cracow. (301–2)

The "bullet lodged in his spinal column" in turn "reduced [Mauricio] to his bed for the rest of his life," where he "died of old age in solitude, without a moan, without a protest, without a single moment of betrayal, tormented by memories and by the yellow butterflies, who did not give him a moment's peace" (297). United in what Wood terms that "nobly refused but always hovering despair," the form- and sense-drives emerge in dynamic harmony as the mirrored tenacity of the characters' spirits becomes a muted measure of love—one that exceeds Mauricio's paralysis and Meme's confinement, surpassing even Melquíades' prophetic manuscript in which the relationship is set down in terms of "a mechanic [that] satisfied his lust on a woman who was giving herself out of rebellion" (422).

Such formal mirrors are similarly erected between Rebeca and Amaranta. Having "forced the lock" on both their trunks when they suffer in turn from a feverish delirium, Úrsula finds "sixteen perfumed letters" from Pietro Crespi "tied together with pink ribbons" at the bottom of Rebeca's trunk, and "letters tied together with a pink ribbon, swollen with fresh lilies and still wet with tears, addressed and never sent to Pietro Crespi," at the bottom of Amaranta's trunk (68, 70). Though the fervor of characters' feelings does not always lead to lasting devotion or enduring happiness, these eternalized moments of eloquence are marked by a sense of autonomy or self-sufficiency—manifest in what Donoghue terms the sudden "flares of spirit," the unpredictable gestures, and the muted contexts alluded to.[14]

---

14. See chapter 5 of this book.

Rebeca's "ancestral appetite" is reawakened by her feelings for Pietro, where her hunger for earth and love converge in her furtive act of geophagia ("eating earth" [65]), marking an unexpected sense of fittingness between the unpredictable gesture and the feverish excesses of her love. The beloved is materialized in each mouthful, "as if the ground that he walked on with his fine patent leather boots in another part of the world were transmitting to her the weight and the temperature of his blood in a mineral savor that left a harsh aftertaste in her mouth and a sediment of peace in her heart" (65–66). The coherence of imagery reinforces the dynamic harmony of the form- and sense-drives, as the materiality and ferocity of Rebeca's feelings for Pietro are later mirrored in her feverish delirium for José Arcadio.

Just as Pietro's delayed love letter drives Rebeca "mad with desperation" as she eats earth "with a suicidal drive," "chewing tender earthworms and chipping her teeth on snail shells" till she "vomited until dawn" (68), when she learns that her foster brother José Arcadio reciprocates her sexual attention, "Rebeca lost control of herself" again and "went back to eating earth and the whitewash of the walls" till she "vomited up a green liquid with dead leeches in it" (95). Rather than diluting the intensity of her passions, the echoing forms of Rebeca's affections for both men paradoxically magnify the voracity of her heart, testifying against the notion of love's singularity. Just as *Written on the Body* challenges heterosexual norms by exploring postmodern love from a default position of infidelity, love in *Solitude* is marked by an open-ended generativity whereby lust, incest, and tempestuous changes of heart are not love's antinomies, but a default mode of the novel's storyworld and of the human condition.

Rebeca's change of heart leads Pietro to turn his attentions to Amaranta, whose "enveloping tenderness" wove "an invisible web" about the Italian musician before she too eventually rejects him (97, 110, 112).

> "Don't be simple, Crespi." She smiled. "I wouldn't marry you even if I were dead."
>
> Pietro Crespi lost control of himself. He wept shamelessly, almost breaking his fingers with desperation, but he could not break her down. [. . .] One night he sang. Macondo woke up in a kind of angelic stupor that was caused by a zither that deserved more than this world and a voice that led one to believe that no other person on earth could feel such love. Pietro Crespi then saw the lights go on in every

window in town except that of Amaranta. On November second, All Souls' Day, his brother opened the store and found all the lamps lighted, all the music boxes opened, and all the clocks striking an interminable hour, and in the midst of that mad concert he found Pietro Crespi at the desk in the rear with his wrists cut by a razor and his hands thrust in a basin of benzoin. (112–13)

The brevity of the line "One night he sang" enhances the musicality of the long sentences that follow, in which the ardor of Pietro's love takes on an operatic quality in its extravagant theatricality with reference to an "angelic stupor," to music "that deserved more than this world," and the conviction that "no other person on earth could feel such love." The "eloquence of situation," to borrow from Donoghue, emerges from one set of images leading rhetorically to another (*Eloquence* 64, 55): just as Pietro's eyes follow the lights that go on in every window, eventually terminating in Amaranta's darkened bedroom, readers make their way past the lighted lamps and "mad concert" of opened music boxes and resounding clocks to find Pietro's extinguished life at the end of the line. The sequence functions as a wordless aria in the operatic nature of Pietro's love, whereby readers gain access to his despair through deed rather than word, drawn into his anguish in the dynamic harmony of the form- and sense-drives.

The episode's force emerges entirely as "the result of act and gesture" (Donoghue, *Eloquence* 57), whereby Amaranta reacts to Pietro's suicide by calmly burning her hand on the coals of the kitchen stove, carrying the scarred "sores of her heart" and the "black bandage of terrible expiation" on her burned hand until her own death in old age (*Solitude* 113–14, 224). Amaranta's unpredictable gesture instantiates the complexities of love in *Solitude,* where love and rancor are not antitheses, and regret and cowardice unexpectedly magnify rather than diminish the quality of Amaranta's love. Úrsula retrospectively realizes decades later that the "unjust tortures" to which Amaranta had submitted Pietro had not merely "been dictated by a desire for vengeance," but also by a "mortal struggle between a measureless love and an invincible cowardice" (254–55). The cowardice, Wood notes, is just as significant as the love: "only great love makes the cowardice moving, and not merely abject. Amaranta's vocation is to miss love, and painfully to cherish the knowledge of all she is missing, to maintain intact her raw, intentional regret"—a regret "purified, magnified, and eternalized" by time and solitude (Michael Wood, *Gabriel* 81; *Solitude* 225).

Pietro's despondency is mirrored in Remedios the Beauty's foreign suitor, who is described as "so elegant and dignified" that "Pietro Crespi would have been a mere fop beside him" (*Solitude* 201). When the foreign gentleman offers Remedios a solitary rose after Mass, "she took it with a natural gesture, as if she had been prepared for that homage, and then she uncovered her face and gave her thanks with a smile. That was all she did. Not only for the gentleman, but for all the men who had the unfortunate privilege of seeing her, that was an eternal instant" (201). Like Pietro who sings outside Amaranta's window,

> from then on the gentleman had a band of musicians play beside the window of Remedios the Beauty, sometimes until dawn. [. . .] The saddest part of his drama was that Remedios the Beauty did not notice him, not even when he appeared in church dressed like a prince. She accepted the yellow rose without the least bit of malice, amused, rather, by the extravagance of the act, and she lifted her shawl to see his face better, not to show hers. (201–2)

The formal parallels established between both men paradoxically foreground the radical differences underlying the (apparent) indifference of both Buendía women, where the extravagance of Pietro's love irrevocably brands Amaranta's hand and heart while the unnamed gentleman's elaborate attentions merely amuse Remedios.

Solitude is suffused by such moments of poetic power, in which the force of each episode invites readers to make what we will of its beauty: as with all who are struck by Remedios the Beauty in that "eternal instant" she uncovers her face, readers too are constantly struck by such spontaneous moments of aesthetic beauty in our acts of reading, which irrevocably hold and compel our attention in the flow of life. Wood contends that one way to understand García Márquez's insistence that everything in *Solitude* is "based on reality" is that the novel is "genuinely in touch with some *fact of feeling*, however hyperbolically or metaphorically expressed" (Michael Wood, *Gabriel* 57; emphases added). These eternalized fragments of eloquence afford "the truth of a fitting image, the appropriateness of the imagination's rising to the grand occasion" (57), in a fitting harmony between the sense- and form-drives, between the excesses of love and narrative.

FINAL FRAGMENTS

In a neuroscientific study of "aesthetic judgments on written texts" using parametric fMRI technology, Isabel C. Bohrn et al. found that "spontaneous aesthetic evaluation takes place during reading," *even when participants are not tasked to do so,* as indicated by positive correlations in the ventral striatum and the medial prefrontal cortex, "likely reflecting the rewarding nature of sentences that are aesthetically pleasing" (1). In proposing my three-drive framework for explicating aesthetic impulses at work in postmodern and contemporary fiction, I point to the inherently rewarding nature of our experiences with literary works of art, which invite readers to a changed sense of the world through our participation in their purposefully unfinished acts of meaning-making. Such aesthetic experiences, Starr explains, "restructure the hierarchies of value that motivate and map daily life" by producing "paradigm shifts in how we see, hear, or think" (20).

Robert Morgan notes that "the omnipresent glut of information" in the contemporary age "has distorted our means of sensory intake," whereby the "reception of data—scientific, economic, cultural, and political—has become so overabundant as to suggest infinity" (75), which has at least two implications for our aesthetic engagements with literature. On the one hand, to paraphrase Matei Călinescu, it has become far too easy for rich literary aesthetic experiences to become lost in the glut of kitschy literature, advertisements, and other cultural artifacts that mimic and/or create abbreviated or diluted versions of the pleasures we encounter with aesthetically sophisticated literary texts like *One Hundred Years of Solitude* that demand more rigorous and complex readerly engagements.[15] On the other hand, as Morgan notes,

---

15. Călinescu notes that "in the postmodern age, kitsch represents the triumph of the principle of immediacy—immediacy of access, immediacy of effect, instant beauty"; "what constitutes the essence of kitsch is probably [. . .] its promise of an easy 'catharsis'" (8, 228). "Kitsch may be conveniently defined as a specifically aesthetic form of lying. As such, it obviously has a lot to do with the modern illusion that beauty may be bought and sold" (229).

it has become more difficult to give validity to "sensory experience" or "the rightness of the senses as a perceptual filter in determining quality in works of art," which are invariably blunted or dulled by daily informational gluts and sensory overload (75). In light of such challenges, the resurgence of interest in aesthetics and beauty over the past three decades—both in the arts and in the critical paradigms used to examine them—makes the present an opportune moment to reexamine our notions of how aesthetics has survived the postmodern age.

This book works to fill a gap that Hogan and others have identified in cognitive studies of the arts, "which tend to focus on music and visual art" ("Literary" 319). By explaining the neural correlates of the form-, sense-, and moral-drives, I begin to address the "relative neglect of literature in neurologically-based discussions of beauty," including the "almost complete absence of the sublime" in cognitive literary studies (319). Since our appreciation of the arts "recruits neural systems of reward and emotion" that overlap with those used to appraise "objects of evolutionary importance, such as the desirability of food items or the attractiveness of mates," researchers in neuroscience posit that "it is likely that artworks have co-opted" these brain areas, which "may represent an emergent property of the complexity of human cognition" (Blood and Zatorre 11823; Brown et al. 250). These growing areas of research suggest the efficacy of a neuroaesthetics of literature and the productivity of an aesthetic approach to literary studies, which I argue remains integral to contemporary experiences of fiction.

Danto observes that beauty "connects with something inherent in human nature, which would explain why aesthetic deprivation [. . .] should have taken on the importance it did in the artistic agendas of the avant-garde" (33). Danto points out that while "beauty is an option for art," "it is a necessary condition for life as we would want to live it. That is why beauty, unlike the other aesthetic qualities [. . .], is a value" (160). Precisely because beauty is implicated in life as we would want to live it, I contend it was simply a matter of time before beauty would return following the artistic agenda of aesthetic deprivation in the early twentieth century. In fact, I argue that readers' engagements with the aesthetic have never faded completely despite the waxing and waning of interest in critical aesthetic paradigms; what we need is a new conceptualization of readers' changed relationship to aesthetics in light of postmodernism—a gap I hope to have filled with this book.

The theoretical model I propose is a dynamic one since the form-, sense-, and moral-drives are continually in need of updating, with reference to the context of their particular historical moment. As explained in chapters 3 and 5, the moral-drive is particularly susceptible to change in our constantly evolving sense of ethical relations with our fellow human beings. Though aspects of the form-drive are relatively less susceptible to historical variability, the effects of formal stylistic practices that dominate particular literary periods or artistic movements are nonetheless subject to historical influence: the defamiliarizing effects of *At Swim-Two-Birds*'s metaleptic transgressions, for instance, tend to lose some of their initial disorientating power for readers accustomed to postmodern literary techniques. Writers are thus constantly challenged to manifest dynamic energies of all three drives in innovative ways that continue to surprise and engage readers.

Since aesthetics as a field of study works to explain "our basic intuitions about [literary] art and beauty" (Dutton 39), particularly the pleasures we derive from them, attending to aesthetic engagements highlights an important aspect of readerly experience that historical and sociopolitical approaches tend to overlook. The pleasures of literary fiction draw us to invest our time, attention, interest, and emotions in a wide range of thematic concerns: from the insatiable human appetite for violence in *Blood Meridian* to the sociopolitical realities that underpin *One Hundred Years of Solitude*. My three-drive model thus complements other ways of reading post–world war fiction by highlighting how authors use aesthetically sophisticated projects to engage and challenge readers' capacities for meaning-making.

Though my book works to explicate and thus defend aesthetic dimensions of fiction as integral to the reading experience, I recognize that the experience of art—especially the literary arts—is certainly not limited only to the aesthetic; but there are important reasons for focusing on aesthetics, as I hope to have shown in this book. Since critical scholarship and literary analyses are implicit attempts to claim legitimacy for, prioritize, or foreground particular interpretative payoffs, I am making the case that responding to a literary work of art's aesthetic dimensions is a particularly rich and crucial form of readerly engagement. After all, as Shusterman observes, "mere pleasure is far from a trivial thing," since as human beings we spend a significant part of our lives in pursuit of "sensual and emotional satisfaction" (29), be it through family, friendship, religion, travel, art, or love. Attending to the aesthetic enlarges and enriches our capacities for vivid experience, both in literature and in life.

WORKS CITED

Abraham, Taisha. "An Interview with Arundhati Roy." *ARIEL: A Review of International English Literature*, vol. 29, no. 1, 1998, pp. 89–92.

Adams, Anthony. "Butter-Spades, Footnotes, and Omnium: *The Third Policeman* as 'Pataphysical Fiction.'" *Review of Contemporary Fiction*, vol. 31, no. 3, 2011, pp. 106–19.

Adams, Hazard, editor. *Critical Theory since Plato*. Harcourt Brace Jovanovich, 1971.

Adorno, Theodor W. *Aesthetic Theory*. 1970. Edited by Gretel Adorno and Rolf Tiedemann. Translated by Robert Hullot-Kentor, U of Minnesota P, 1997.

———. "Aesthetic Theory." 1961–70. Cahn and Meskin, pp. 358–69.

———. "On the Concept of the Beautiful." 1970. Beech, pp. 78–81.

Alber, Jan, Henrik Skov Nielsen, and Brian Richardson, editors. *A Poetics of Unnatural Narrative*. The Ohio State UP, 2013.

Aldama, Frederick Luis. *Postethnic Narrative Criticism: Magicorealism in Oscar "Zeta" Acosta, Ana Castillo, Julie Dash, Hanif Kureishi, and Salman Rushdie*. U of Texas P, 2003.

———. *A User's Guide to Postcolonial and Latino Borderland Fiction*. U of Texas P, 2009.

Aldama, Frederick Luis, and Patrick Colm Hogan. *Conversations on Cognitive Cultural Studies: Literature, Language, and Aesthetics*. The Ohio State UP, 2014.

Andermahr, Sonya. *Jeanette Winterson*. Palgrave Macmillan, 2009.

Andreasen, Liana Vrajitoru. "*Blood Meridian* and the Spatial Metaphysics of the West." *Southwestern American Literature,* vol. 36, no. 3, 2011, pp. 19–30.

Annan, Gabriele. "Devil in the Flesh." *The New York Review of Books,* 4 Mar. 1993.

Armstrong, Paul B. *How Literature Plays with the Brain: The Neuroscience of Reading and Art.* Johns Hopkins UP, 2013.

Arnold, Edwin T. Foreword. *Notes on* Blood Meridian, by John Sepich, pp. xi–xvii.

Arnold, Edwin T., and Dianne C. Luce, editors. *Perspectives on Cormac McCarthy.* Revised ed., U of Mississippi P, 1999.

Attridge, Derek. "Once More with Feeling: Art, Affect and Performance." *Textual Practice,* vol. 25, no. 2, 2011, pp. 329–43.

Axelrod, Mark. "An Epistolary Interview, Mostly with Alasdair Gray." *Review of Contemporary Fiction,* vol. 15, no. 2, 1995, pp. 106–15.

Aylesworth, Gary. "Postmodernism." *The Stanford Encyclopedia of Philosophy,* 30 Sept. 2005, https://plato.stanford.edu/entries/postmodernism/.

Baines, Jennika. "'Un-Understandable Mystery': Catholic Faith and Revelation in *The Third Policeman.*" *Review of Contemporary Fiction,* vol. 31, no. 3, 2011, pp. 78–90.

Bartezzaghi, Stefano. "Calvino at Play: Rules and Games for Writing in Space." Translated by Martin McLaughlin. Grundtvig, McLaughlin, and Petersen, pp. 122–40.

Beach, Christopher. "Recuperating the Aesthetic: Contemporary Approaches and the Case of Adorno." Soderholm, pp. 94–112.

Beckley, Bill, and David Shapiro, editors. *Uncontrollable Beauty: Toward a New Aesthetics.* Allworth Press, 1998.

Beech, Dave, editor. *Beauty.* Whitechapel Gallery and MIT Press, 2009.

Beedham, Matthew. *The Novels of Kazuo Ishiguro.* Palgrave Macmillan, 2010.

Bell, Alice, and Jan Alber. "Ontological Metalepsis and Unnatural Narratology." *Journal of Narrative Theory,* vol. 42, no. 2, 2012, pp. 166–92.

Bell, Alice, and Marie-Laure Ryan, editors. *Possible Worlds Theory and Contemporary Narratology.* U of Nebraska P, 2018, https://www.nebraskapress.unl.edu/university-of-nebraska-press/9780803294998/.

Bell, Clive. *Art.* 1913. Book Jungle, 2009.

——. "Art." Cahn and Meskin, pp. 261–69.

Belsey, Catherine. "Postmodern Love: Questioning the Metaphysics of Desire." *New Literary History,* vol. 25, no. 3, 1994, pp. 683–705.

Benezra, Neal, Olga M. Viso, and Arthur Danto. *Regarding Beauty.* Smithsonian Institution, 1999.

Bernstein, Stephen. *Alasdair Gray.* Associated University Presses, 1999.

Black, Shameem. "Ishiguro's Inhuman Aesthetics." *Modern Fiction Studies,* vol. 55, no. 4, 2009, pp. 785–807.

Blood, Anne J., and Robert J. Zatorre. "Intensely Pleasurable Responses to Music Correlate with Activity in Brain Regions Implicated in Reward and Emotion." *Proceedings of the National Academy of Sciences (PNAS)*, vol. 98, no. 20, 2001, pp. 11818–23.

Bloom, Harold. *How to Read and Why*. Touchstone, 2000.

Bloom, Harold, editor. *Italo Calvino*. Chelsea House Publishers, 2001.

Bohman-Kalaja, Kimberly. *Reading Games: An Aesthetics of Play in Flann O'Brien, Samuel Beckett, and Georges Perec*. Dalkey Archive Press, 2007.

Bohrn, Isabel C. et al. "When We Like What We Know—A Parametric fMRI Analysis of Beauty and Familiarity." *Brain and Language*, vol. 124, 2013, pp. 1–8.

Bold, Alan. *Modern Scottish Literature*. Longmans, 1983.

Boldy, Steven. "*One Hundred Years of Solitude* by Gabriel García Márquez." Kristal, pp. 258–69.

Booker, M. Keith. *Flann O'Brien, Bakhtin and Menippean Satire*. Syracuse UP, 1995.

Bowers, James. "Reading Cormac McCarthy's *Blood Meridian*." *Boise State University Western Writers Series*, vol. 139, 1999.

Boyd, Brian. *On the Origin of Stories: Evolution, Cognition, and Fiction*. Belknap Press, 2010.

Bray, Joe, Miriam Handley, and Anne C. Henry, editors. *Ma(r)king the Text: The Presentation of Meaning on the Literary Page*. Ashgate, 2000.

Brink, Tila Tabea et al. "The Role of Orbitofrontal Cortex in Processing Empathy Stories in 4- to 8-Year-Old Children." *Frontiers in Psychology*, vol. 2, Apr. 2011, pp. 1–16, http://journal.frontiersin.org/article/10.3389/fpsyg.2011.00080/full.

Brown, Steven et al. "Naturalizing Aesthetics: Brain Areas for Aesthetic Appraisal across Sensory Modalities." *NeuroImage*, vol. 58, 2011, pp. 250–58.

Brown, Stuart, and Christopher Vaughan. *Play: How It Shapes the Brain, Opens the Imagination, and Invigorates the Soul*. Avery, 2010.

Burke, Edmund. "A Philosophical Enquiry into the Origin of Our Ideas of the Sublime and Beautiful." Cahn and Meskin, pp. 113–22.

Burns, Christy L. "Fantastic Language: Jeanette Winterson's Recovery of the Postmodern Word." *Contemporary Literature*, vol. 37, no. 2, 1996, pp. 278–306.

Busby, Mark. "Rolling the Stone, Sisyphus, and the Epilogue of *Blood Meridian*." *Southwestern American Literature*, vol. 36, no. 3, 2011, pp. 87–95.

Busl, Gretchen. "Rewriting the *Fiaba*: Collective Signification in Italo Calvino's *Il castello dei destini incrociati*." *The Modern Language Review*, vol. 107, no. 3, 2012, pp. 796–814.

Buss, David M., editor. *The Handbook of Evolutionary Psychology*. Wiley, 2005.

Butler, Rex, editor. *Art after Deconstruction: Jeremy Gilbert-Rolfe*. Editions Three, 2011.

Cahn, Steven M., and Aaron Meskin, editors. *Aesthetics: A Comprehensive Anthology.* Blackwell, 2008.

Caillois, Roger. *Man, Play, and Games.* 1958. Translated by Meyer Barash, The Free Press, 1961.

Călinescu, Matei. *Five Faces of Modernity: Modernism, Avant-Garde, Decadence, Kitsch, Modernism.* Duke UP, 1987.

Calvino, Italo. *The Castle of Crossed Destinies.* 1969. Translated by William Weaver, Vintage, 1977.

———. *Invisible Cities.* 1972. Translated by William Weaver, Vintage, 1997.

———. *Six Memos for the Next Millennium (The Charles Eliot Norton Lectures: 1985–86).* 1988. Translated by Patrick Creagh, Vintage International, 1993.

———. *The Uses of Literature.* 1982. Translated by Patrick Creagh, Harcourt Brace, 1986.

Campbell, Neil. "Liberty beyond Its Proper Bounds: Cormac McCarthy's History of the West in *Blood Meridian.*" Wallach, pp. 217–26.

Cannon, JoAnn. "Literature as Combinatory Game: Italo Calvino's *The Castle of Crossed Destinies.*" *Critique: Studies in Contemporary Fiction,* vol. 21, no. 1, 1979, pp. 83–92.

Cant, John. *Cormac McCarthy and the Myth of American Exceptionalism.* Routledge, 2008.

Carrigan, Henry L., Jr. Review of *Never Let Me Go,* by Kazuo Ishiguro. *Library Journal,* Jan. 2005, p. 98.

Carroll, Noël. *Philosophy of Art: A Contemporary Introduction.* Routledge, 1999.

Carter, Angela. *The Bloody Chamber.* 1979. Vintage Books, 2006.

Cavallaro, Dani. *The Mind of Italo Calvino: A Critical Exploration of His Thought and Writings.* McFarland, 2010.

Cela-Conde, Camilo J. et al. "Dynamics of Brain Networks in the Aesthetic Appreciation." *Proceedings of the National Academy of Sciences (PNAS),* vol. 110, 18 June 2013, pp. 10454–61, http://www.pnas.org/content/110/Supplement_2/10454.full.pdf.

Célérier-Vitasse, Joëlle. "The Blurring of Frontiers in Arundhati Roy's *The God of Small Things.*" *Études Anglaises,* vol. 61, no. 1, 2008, pp. 68–82.

Changeux, Jean-Pierre. *The Good, the True, and the Beautiful: A Neuronal Approach.* Translated by Laurence Garey, Yale UP and Éditions Odile Jacob, 2012.

Chatterjee, Anjan. "Neuroaesthetics." Shimamura and Palmer, pp. 299–317.

Clissmann, Anne. *Flann O'Brien: A Critical Introduction to His Writings (The Story-Teller's Book-Web).* Gill and Macmillan, 1975.

Comer, Todd A. "A Mortal Agency: Flann O'Brien's *At Swim-Two-Birds.*" *Journal of Modern Literature,* vol. 31, no. 2, 2008, pp. 104–14.

Conniff, Brian. "The Dark Side of Magic Realism: Science, Oppression, and Apocalypse in *One Hundred Years of Solitude.*" *Modern Fiction Studies,* vol. 36, no. 2, 1990, pp. 167–79.

Cooper, Simon. "Imagining the Post-Human." Review of *Never Let Me Go*, by Kazuo Ishiguro. *Arena Magazine*, vol. 81, Feb.–Mar. 2006, pp. 19–20.

Costelloe, Timothy M., editor. *The Sublime: From Antiquity to the Present*. Cambridge UP, 2012.

Craig, Cairns. "Going Down to Hell Is Easy." Review of *Lanark*, by Alasdair Gray. *Cencrastus*, vol. 6, 1981, pp. 19–21.

———. *Out of History: Narrative Paradigms in Scottish and British Culture*. Polygon, 1996.

Crowther, Paul, editor. *The Contemporary Sublime: Sensibilities of Transcendence and Shock*. Academy Editions, 1995.

Culler, Jonathan. "Literary Competence." Tompkins, pp. 101–17.

Currie, Mark. *About Time: Narrative, Fiction and the Philosophy of Time*. Edinburgh UP, 2007.

Dalfonzo, Gina R. "Lucky Pawns." Review of *Never Let Me Go*, by Kazuo Ishiguro. *National Review*, vol. 57, no. 11, 20 June 2005, pp. 53–54.

Danto, Arthur. *The Abuse of Beauty: Aesthetics and the Concept of Art*. Open Court, 2003.

———. "The Aesthetics of Brillo Boxes." 2003. Beech, pp. 60–65.

Daugherty, Leo. "Graver False and True: *Blood Meridian* as Gnostic Tragedy." Arnold and Luce, pp. 159–74.

Davis, Charles. "Introduction: 'To See with Our Own Eyes': Hogarth between Native Empiricism and a Theory of 'Beauty in Form.'" *The Analysis of Beauty*, by William Hogarth. Fontes 52, 2010, http://archiv.ub.uni-heidelberg.de/artdok/1217/.

Dehaene, Stanislas. *Reading in the Brain: The New Science of How We Read*. Penguin, 2009.

de Juan, Luis. *Postmodernist Strategies in Alasdair Gray's* Lanark: A Life in 4 Books. Peter Lang, 2003.

Derrida, Jacques. "Parergon." 1978. Translated by Geoffrey Bennington and Ian McLeod. Morley, pp. 41–46.

Desai, Anita. "A Shadow World." Review of *Never Let Me Go*, by Kazuo Ishiguro. *New York Review*, 22 Sept. 2005, pp. 48–51.

Detloff, Madelyn. "Living in 'Energetic Space': Jeanette Winterson's Bodies and Pleasures." *English Language Notes*, vol. 45, no. 2, 2007, pp. 149–59.

Detweiler, Robert. "Games and Play in Modern American Fiction." *Contemporary Literature*, vol. 17, no. 1, 1976, pp. 44–62.

Deveny, John J., Jr., and Juan Manuel Marcos. "Women and Society in *One Hundred Years of Solitude*." *Journal of Popular Culture*, vol. 22, no. 1, 1988, pp. 83–90.

Dewey, John. "Art as Experience." 1934. Cahn and Meskin, pp. 296–316.

Dewsnap, Terence. "Flann O'Brien and the Politics of Buffoonery." *Canadian Journal of Irish Studies*, vol. 19, no. 1, 1993, pp. 22–36.

Dickson, Lisa, and Maryna Romanets, editors. *Beauty, Violence, Representation*. Routledge, 2014.

Dole, Nathan Haskell, editor. *Aesthetical and Philosophical Essays*, vol. 7, by Friedrich Schiller, F. A. Niccolls, 1902.

Doležel, Lubomír. *Possible Worlds of Fiction and History: The Postmodern Stage*. Johns Hopkins UP, 2010.

Donoghue, Denis. *On Eloquence*. Yale UP, 2008.

———. *The Practice of Reading*. Yale UP, 1998.

———. *Speaking of Beauty*. Yale UP, 2003.

Donohue, Keith, editor. *Flann O'Brien: The Complete Novels*, by Flann O'Brien. Everyman's Library (Alfred A. Knopf), 2007.

Duncan, Ian. "Allegory and Cruelty: Gray's *Lanark* and Lindsay's *A Voyage to Arcturus*." McCracken-Flesher, pp. 43–54.

Dutton, Denis. *The Art Instinct: Beauty, Pleasure, and Human Evolution*. Oxford UP, 2009.

Eatough, Matthew. "The Time That Remains: Organ Donation, Temporal Duration, and *Bildung* in Kazuo Ishiguro's *Never Let Me Go*." *Literature and Medicine*, vol. 29, no. 1, 2011, pp. 132–60.

Echevarría, Roberto González. "*Cien años de soledad*: The Novel as Myth and Archive." *MLN*, vol. 99, no. 2, 1984, pp. 358–80.

Eco, Umberto, editor. *History of Beauty*. 2nd ed. Translated by Alastair McEwen, Rizzoli, 2005.

———. *The Role of the Reader: Explorations in the Semiotics of Texts*. Indiana UP, 1979.

Eddins, Dwight. "'Everything a Hunter and Everything Hunted': Schopenhauer and Cormac McCarthy's *Blood Meridian*." *Critique: Studies in Contemporary Fiction*, vol. 45, no. 1, 2003, pp. 25–33.

Egan, Jennifer. *A Visit from the Goon Squad*. 2010. Corsair, 2017.

Elias, Amy. *Sublime Desire: History and Post-1960s Fiction*. Johns Hopkins UP, 2001.

Ellam, Julie. *Love in Jeanette Winterson's Novels*. Rodopi, 2010.

Erickson, Daniel. *Ghosts, Metaphor, and History in Toni Morrison's* Beloved *and Gabriel García Márquez's* One Hundred Years of Solitude. Palgrave Macmillan, 2009.

Etlin, Richard A. "Architecture and the Sublime." Costelloe, pp. 230–74.

Evans, David H. "True West and Lying Marks: The Englishman's Boy, *Blood Meridian*, and the Paradox of the Revisionist Western." *Texas Studies in Literature and Language*, vol. 55, no. 4, 2013, pp. 406–33.

Evans, Michael. "The Second Horseman: The Philosophy of War in *Blood Meridian*." *Quadrant*, vol. 55, no. 4, 2011, pp. 80–88.

Falconer, Rachel. *Hell in Contemporary Literature: Western Descent Narratives since 1945*. Edinburgh UP, 2005.

Felecan, Oliviu, editor. *Name and Naming: Synchronic and Diachronic Perspectives.* Cambridge Scholars Publishing, 2012.

Field, Michele. "Jeanette Winterson: 'I Fear Insincerity.'" *Publishers Weekly,* vol. 242, no. 12, 1995, pp. 38–39.

Finney, Brian. "Bonded by Language: Jeanette Winterson's *Written on the Body.*" *Women and Language,* vol. 25, no. 2, 2002, pp. 23–31.

Foster, Thomas, Carol Siegel, and Ellen E. Berry. *The Gay '90s: Disciplinary and Interdisciplinary Formations in Queer Studies.* New York UP, 1997.

Friedman, Susan Stanford. "Spatial Poetics and Arundhati Roy's *The God of Small Things.*" Phelan and Rabinowitz, pp. 192–205.

Frye, Steven, editor. *The Cambridge Companion to Cormac McCarthy.* Cambridge UP, 2013.

Funk, Wolfgang, Florian Gross, and Irmtraud Huber, editors. *The Aesthetics of Authenticity: Medial Constructions of the Real.* Transaction Publishers, 2012.

García Márquez, Gabriel. *Living to Tell the Tale.* Translated by Edith Grossman, Vintage, 2004.

———. *One Hundred Years of Solitude.* 1967. Translated by Gregory Rabassa, Penguin, 1972.

Garlick, Steve. "Uncanny Sex: Cloning, Photographic Vision, and the Reproduction of Nature." *Social Semiotics,* vol. 20, no. 2, 2010, pp. 139–54.

Gaut, Berys. "The Ethical Criticism of Art." 1998. Cahn and Meskin, pp. 589–601.

Gifford, Douglas. "Private Confession and Public Satire in the Fiction of Alasdair Gray." *Chapman,* vol. 50–51, 1987, pp. 101–16.

Gilbert-Rolfe, Jeremy. "Attractiveness and the Uncontrollable: An Update." Butler, pp. 13–32.

———. *Beauty and the Contemporary Sublime.* Allworth Press, 1999.

Gilmore, Leigh. "An Anatomy of Absence: *Written on the Body, The Lesbian Body,* and Autobiography without Names." Foster, Siegel, and Berry, pp. 224–51.

Gilson, Étienne. *The Arts of the Beautiful.* 1965. Dalkey Archive Press, 2000.

Godwin, Mike. "Remains of the DNA." Review of *Never Let Me Go,* by Kazuo Ishiguro. *Reason,* vol. 37, no. 5, 2005, p. 56.

Gray, Alasdair. *Lanark: A Life in Four Books.* Canongate, 1981.

Green-Lewis, Jennifer, and Margaret Soltan. *Teaching Beauty in DeLillo, Woolf, and Merrill.* Palgrave Macmillan, 2008.

Grice, Helena, and Tim Woods, editors. *'I'm Telling You Stories': Jeanette Winterson and the Politics of Reading.* Rodopi, 1998.

Griffin, Clive. "The Humour of *One Hundred Years of Solitude.*" McGuirk and Cardwell, pp. 81–94.

Griffin, Gabriele. "Science and the Cultural Imaginary: The Case of Kazuo Ishiguro's *Never Let Me Go.*" *Textual Practice,* vol. 23, no. 4, 2009, pp. 645–63.

Groes, Sebastian, and Barry Lewis, editors. *Kazuo Ishiguro: New Critical Visions of the Novels*. Palgrave Macmillan, 2011.

Grundtvig, Birgitte, Martin McLaughlin, and Lene Waage Petersen, editors. *Image, Eye and Art in Calvino: Writing Visibility*. Legenda (MHRA and Maney Publishing), 2007.

Guillemin, George. "'See the Child': The Melancholy Subtext of *Blood Meridian*." Lilley, pp. 239–65.

Guyer, Paul. "The German Sublime after Kant." Costelloe, pp. 102–17.

Haidt, Jonathan. *The Righteous Mind: Why Good People Are Divided by Politics and Religion*. Allen Lane, 2012.

Harris, Andrea L. *Other Sexes: Rewriting Difference from Woolf to Winterson*. State U of New York P, 2000.

Hart, Stephen M. "Magical Realism in the Americas: Politicised Ghosts in *One Hundred Years of Solitude, The House of Spirits,* and *Beloved*." *Journal of Iberian and Latin American Studies*, vol. 9, no. 2, 2003, pp. 115–23.

Hart, Stephen M., and Wen-chin Ouyang, editors. *A Companion to Magical Realism*. Tamesis, 2005.

Harten, Doreet LeVitte. "Creating Heaven." 1999. Morley, pp. 73–76.

Heath, Malcolm. "Longinus and the Ancient Sublime." Costelloe, pp. 11–23.

Hegel, Georg Wilhelm Friedrich. "The Philosophy of Fine Art." 1818–35. Cahn and Meskin, pp. 180–92.

Hensher, Philip. "School for Scandal." Review of *Never Let Me Go*, by Kazuo Ishiguro. *The Spectator*, 26 Feb. 2005, pp. 32–33.

Herman, David. "Toward a Formal Description of Narrative Metalepsis." *Journal of Literary Semantics*, vol. 26, no. 2, 1997, pp. 132–52.

Herman, David, Manfred Jahn, and Marie-Laure Ryan, editors. *Routledge Encyclopedia of Narrative Theory*. Routledge, 2005.

Higgins, Kathleen Marie. "Whatever Happened to Beauty? A Response to Danto." 1996. Beech, pp. 31–35.

Hillman, James. "The Practice of Beauty." Beckley and Shapiro, pp. 261–74.

Hobsbaum, Philip. "Alasdair Gray: The Voice of His Prose." *Review of Contemporary Fiction*, vol. 15, no. 2, 1995, pp. 147–54.

Hogan, Patrick Colm. *Beauty and Sublimity: A Cognitive Aesthetics of Literature and the Arts*. Cambridge UP, 2016.

———. "Literary Aesthetics: Beauty, the Brain, and *Mrs. Dalloway*." *Literature, Neurology, and Neuroscience: Historical and Literary Connections*, edited by Anne Stiles, Stanley Finger, and François Boller. *Progress in Brain Research*, vol. 205, 2013, pp. 319–37.

Hogarth, William. *The Analysis of Beauty*. 1753. Fontes 52, 2010, http://archiv.ub.uni-heidelberg.de/artdok/1217/.

Holmberg, David. "'In a Time before Nomenclature Was and Each was All': *Blood Meridian*'s Neomythic West and the Heterotopian Zone." *Western American Literature*, vol. 44, no. 2, 2009, pp. 140–56.

Hooker, Richard. "Sublimity as Process: Hegel, Newman and Shave." Crowther, pp. 42–53.

Hopper, Keith. *Flann O'Brien: A Portrait of the Artist as a Young Post-Modernist*. 2nd ed., Cork UP, 2011.

Huizinga, John. *Homo Ludens: A Study of the Play-Element in Culture*. 1950. Beacon Press, 1955.

Hume, Kathryn. *Calvino's Fictions: Cogito and Cosmos*. Clarendon Press, 1992.

———. "Calvino's Framed Narrations: Writers, Readers, and Reality." *Review of Contemporary Fiction*, vol. 6, no. 2, 1986, pp. 71–80.

Humicke, Robin, Marc LeBlanc, and Robert Zubek. "MDA: A Formal Approach to Game Design and Game Research." Northwestern University, http://www.cs.northwestern.edu/~hunicke/pubs/MDA.pdf.

Hutcheon, Linda. *A Poetics of Postmodernism: History, Theory, Fiction*. Routledge, 1988.

Imhof, Rüdiger, editor. *Alive-Alive O!: Flann O'Brien's At Swim-Two-Birds*. Wolfhound Press, 1985.

Irvine, Dean J. "Fables of the Plague Years: Postcolonialism, Postmodernism, and Magic Realism in *Cien años de soledad* [*One Hundred Years of Solitude*]." *ARIEL: A Review of International English Literature*, vol. 29, no. 4, 1998, pp. 53–80.

Ishai, Alumit. "Art Compositions Elicit Distributed Activation in the Human Brain." Shimamura and Palmer, pp. 337–55.

Ishiguro, Kazuo. *Never Let Me Go*. 2005. Vintage International, 2006.

Ishizu, Tomohiro, and Semir Zeki. "A Neurobiological Enquiry into the Origins of Our Experience of the Sublime and Beautiful." *Frontiers in Human Neuroscience*, vol. 8, Nov. 2014, pp. 1–10, http://journal.frontiersin.org/article/10.3389/fnhum.2014.00891/full.

James, Caryn. "Is Everybody Dead around Here?" Review of *Blood Meridian*, by Cormac McCarthy. *New York Times*, 28 Apr. 1985, p. 31.

James, Nick. "The Art of Letting Go." Interview with Kazuo Ishiguro. *Sight & Sound*, vol. 21, no. 3, 2011, p. 39.

Jameson, Fredric. *Postmodernism: Or, the Cultural Logic of Late Capitalism*. Duke UP, 1991.

Janaway, Christopher. "Part II: Modern Theories. Introduction." Cahn and Meskin, pp. 163–66.

Jarrett, Robert L. *Cormac McCarthy*. Twayne Publishers, 1997.

Jennings, Jay. "Clone Home: Jay Jennings on Kazuo Ishiguro." *BookForum*, Apr./May 2005, p. 44.

Jernigan, Jessica. "Time Passes." Review of *A Visit from the Goon Squad*, by Jennifer Egan. *The Women's Review of Books*, vol. 28, no. 2, 2011, pp. 3–5.

Johnson, David B. "The Postmodern Sublime: Presentation and Its Limits." Costelloe, pp. 118–34.

Johnson, Galen A. *The Retrieval of the Beautiful: Thinking through Merleau-Ponty's Aesthetics*. Northwestern UP, 2010.

Josyph, Peter. *Adventures in Reading Cormac McCarthy*. Scarecrow Press, 2010.

Kafalenos, Emma. "The Polysemy of Looking: Reading Ekphrasis alongside Images in Calvino's *Castle of Crossed Destinies* and Vargas Llosa's *In Praise of the Stepmother*." *Poetics Today*, vol. 33, no. 1, 2012, pp. 27–57.

Kanske, Philipp. "On the Influence of Emotion on Conflict Processing." *Frontiers in Integrative Neuroscience*, vol. 6, July 2012, pp. 1–4.

Kant, Immanuel. *Aesthetics*. "Critique of Judgement." 1790. Translated by J. C. Meredith. Cahn and Meskin, pp. 131–60.

———. *Aesthetics*. "From 'Critique of Judgment.'" Translated by J. H. Bernard. Adams, pp. 377–99.

Kawabata, Hideaki, and Semir Zeki. "Neural Correlates of Beauty." *Journal of Neurophysiology*, vol. 91, 2004, pp. 1699–705.

Keen, Suzanne. *Empathy and the Novel*. Oxford UP, 2007.

Kelly, Michael, editor. "New Criticism." *Encyclopedia of Aesthetics*. 2nd ed., *Oxford Reference*, 2014.

Kerr, Sarah. "*Never Let Me Go*: When They Were Orphans." Review of *Never Let Me Go*, by Kazuo Ishiguro. *New York Times*, 17 Apr. 2005, http://www.nytimes.com/2005/04/17/books/review/17KERRL.html.

Kostkowska, Justyna. *Ecocriticism and Women Writers: Environmentalist Poetics of Virginia Woolf, Jeanette Winterson, and Ali Smith*. Palgrave Macmillan, 2013.

Kreitler, Hans, and Shulamith Kreitler. *Psychology of the Arts*. Duke UP, 1972.

Kristal, Efraín, editor. *The Cambridge Companion to the Latin American Novel*. Cambridge UP, 2005.

Kristeller, Paul Oskar. "Part I: Classic Sources. Introduction." Cahn and Meskin, pp. 3–15.

Laing, Olivia. "Tech No Overload." Review of *A Visit from the Goon Squad*, by Jennifer Egan. *New Statesman*, 18 Apr. 2011, pp. 48–49.

Langer, Susanne. *Feeling and Form: A Theory of Art Developed from Philosophy in a New Key*. Scribner, 1953.

LeBlanc, Marc. "Tools for Creating Dramatic Game Dynamics." Salen and Zimmerman, pp. 438–59.

Lehrer, Jonah. *Proust was a Neuroscientist*. Houghton Mifflin Harcourt, 2008.

Levy, Titus. "Human Rights Storytelling and Trauma Narrative in Kazuo Ishiguro's *Never Let Me Go*." *Journal of Human Rights*, vol. 10, 2011, pp. 1–16.

Lilley, James D., editor. *Cormac McCarthy: New Directions*. U of New Mexico P, 2014.

Lindenmeyer, Antje. "Postmodern Concepts of the Body in Jeanette Winterson's *Written on the Body*." *Feminist Review*, vol. 63, 1999, pp. 48–63.

Longinus. *On the Sublime*. Translated by H. L. Havell, Project Gutenberg, 2006, http://www.gutenberg.org/files/17957/17957-h/17957-h.htm.

———. "On the Sublime." Translated by W. R. Roberts. Adams, pp. 76–102.

Lyotard, Jean-François. *Lessons on the Analytic of the Sublime*. 1991. Translated by Elizabeth Rottenberg, Stanford UP, 1994.

———. *The Postmodern Condition: A Report on Knowledge*. Translated by Geoff Bennington and Brian Massumi, U of Minnesota P, 1984.

Mackie, Penelope, and Mark Jago. "Transworld Identity." *Stanford Encyclopedia of Philosophy*, Autumn 2013, http://plato.stanford.edu/archives/fall2013/entries/identity-transworld/.

Makinen, Merja. *The Novels of Jeanette Winterson*. Palgrave Macmillan, 2005.

Markey, Constance. *Italo Calvino: A Journey toward Postmodernism*. U of Florida P, 1999.

Masters, Joshua J. "'Witness to the Uttermost Edge of the World': Judge Holden's Textual Enterprise in Cormac McCarthy's *Blood Meridian*." *Critique: Studies in Contemporary Fiction*, vol. 40, no. 1, 1998, pp. 25–37.

McCarthy, Cormac. *Blood Meridian: Or, the Evening Redness in the West*. Vintage International, 1985.

McCracken-Flesher, Caroline, editor. *Scotland as Science Fiction*. Bucknell UP, 2012.

McDonald, Keith. "Days of Past Futures: Kazuo Ishiguro's *Never Let Me Go* as 'Speculative Memoir.'" *Biography*, vol. 30, no. 1, 2007, pp. 74–83.

McGuirk, Bernard, and Richard Cardwell, editors. *Gabriel García Márquez: New Readings*. Cambridge UP, 1987.

McHale, Brian. *The Cambridge Introduction to Postmodernism*. Cambridge UP, 2015.

———. *Postmodernist Fiction*. Methuen, 1987.

Mercier, Vivian. *The Irish Comic Tradition*. 1962. Oxford UP, 1969.

Merritt, Melissa McBay. "The Moral Source of the Kantian Sublime." Costelloe, pp. 37–49.

Messud, Claire. "Love's Body." Review of *Never Let Me Go*, by Kazuo Ishiguro. *The Nation*, 16 May 2005, pp. 29–31.

Miller, Gavin. "Literary Narrative as Soteriology in the Work of Kurt Vonnegut and Alasdair Gray." *Journal of Narrative Theory*, vol. 31, no. 3, 2001, pp. 299–323.

Miner, Valerie. "At Her Wit's End." Review of *Written on the Body*, by Jeanette Winterson. *The Women's Review of Books*, vol. 10, no. 8, 1993, p. 21.

Mittapalli, Rajeshwar. "Caste and Outcast: Dalit Masculinity in Arundhati Roy's *The God of Small Things*." *The IUP Journal of English Studies*, vol. 12, no. 2, 2017, pp. 54–67.

Modena, Letizia. *Italo Calvino's Architecture of Lightness: The Utopian Imagination in an Age of Urban Crisis*. Routledge, 2011.

Moling, Martin. "'No Future': Time, Punk Rock and Jennifer Egan's *A Visit from the Goon Squad*." *Arizona Quarterly*, vol. 72, no. 1, 2016, pp. 51–77.

Morgan, Robert C. "A Sign of Beauty." Beckley and Shapiro, pp. 75–82.

Morley, Simon, editor. *The Sublime*. Whitechapel Gallery and MIT Press, 2010.

Motte, Warren. *Playtexts: Ludics in Contemporary Literature*. U of Nebraska P, 1995.

Murphy, Neil. "Flann O'Brien." *Review of Contemporary Fiction*, vol. 25, no. 3, 2005, pp. 7–41.

Murphy, Neil, and Keith Hopper. "Editors' Introduction: A(nother) Bash in the Tunnel." *Review of Contemporary Fiction*, vol. 31, no. 3, 2011, pp. 9–20.

Nandi, Miriam. "Longing for the Lost (M)other—Postcolonial Ambivalences in Arundhati Roy's *The God of Small Things*." *Journal of Postcolonial Writing*, vol. 46, no. 2, 2010, pp. 175–86.

Nehamas, Alexander. *Only a Promise of Happiness: The Place of Beauty in a World of Art*. Princeton UP, 2007.

Newman, Barnett. "The Sublime Is Now." 1948. Morley, pp. 25–26.

Ngai, Sianne. *Our Aesthetic Categories: Zany, Cute, Interesting*. Harvard UP, 2012.

Nietzsche, Friedrich. "The Birth of Tragedy." Cahn and Meskin, pp. 222–32.

Nolan, Val. "Flann, Fantasy, and Science Fiction: O'Brien's Surprising Synthesis." *Review of Contemporary Fiction*, vol. 31, no. 3, 2011, pp. 178–90.

Ó Háinle, Cathal G. "Fionn and Suibhne in *At Swim-Two-Birds*." *Hermathena*, vol. 142, 1987, pp. 13–49.

O'Brien, Flann. *At Swim-Two-Birds*. 1939. *Flann O'Brien: The Complete Novels*. Edited by Keith Donohue, Everyman's Library (Alfred A. Knopf), 2007.

———. *The Short Fiction of Flann O'Brien*. Edited by Neil Murphy and Keith Hopper, Dalkey Archive Press, 2013.

———. *The Third Policeman*. (1939–40) 1967. Introduction by Denis Donoghue, Dalkey Archive Press, 2006.

O'Connell, Mark. "'How to Handle Eternity': Infinity and the theories of J. W. Dunne in the fiction of Jorge Luis Borges and Flann O'Brien's *The Third Policeman*." *Irish Studies Review*, vol. 17, no. 2, 2009, pp. 223–37.

O'Gallagher, Niall. "Alasdair Gray's *Lanark*: Magic Realism and the Postcolonial Novel." *Textual Practice*, vol. 21, no. 3, 2007, pp. 533–50.

O'Toole, Mary. "The Theory of Serialism in *The Third Policeman*." *Irish University Review*, vol. 18, no. 2, 1988, pp. 215–25.

Oțoiu, Adrian. "Hibernian Choices: The Politics of Naming in Flann O'Brien's *At Swim-Two-Birds*." Felecan, pp. 295–309.

Owens, Barcley. *Cormac McCarthy's Western Novels*. U of Arizona Press, 2000.

Parrish, Timothy. *From Civil War to the Apocalypse: Postmodern History and American Fiction*. U of Massachusetts P, 2008.

———. "History and the Problem of Evil in McCarthy's Western Novels." Frye, pp. 67–78.

Pavel, Thomas G. *Fictional Worlds*. Harvard UP, 1986.

Paxton, Joseph M., Leo Ungar, and Joshua D. Greene. "Reflection and Reasoning in Moral Judgment." *Cognitive Science*, 18 Apr. 2011, pp. 1–15.

Pearce, Lynne. "The Emotional Politics of Reading Winterson." Grice and Woods, pp. 29–40.

Peebles, Stacey. "Yuman Belief Systems and Cormac McCarthy's *Blood Meridian*." *Texas Studies in Literature and Language*, vol. 45, no. 2, 2003, pp. 231–44.

Perloff, Marjorie. *Radical Artifice: Writing Poetry in the Age of Media*. U of Chicago P, 1991.

Petro, Pamela. "A British Original." Review of *Written on the Body*, by Jeanette Winterson. *Atlantic*, Feb. 1993, pp. 112–15.

Phelan, James. *Experiencing Fiction: Judgments, Progressions, and the Rhetorical Theory of Narrative*. The Ohio State UP, 2007.

———. "Implausibilities, Crossovers, and Impossibilities: A Rhetorical Approach to Breaks in the Code of Mimetic Character Narration." Alber, Nielsen, and Richardson, pp. 167–84.

———. "Narrative Ethics." *The Living Handbook of Narratology*, 9 Dec. 2014, http://www.lhn.uni-hamburg.de/article/narrative-ethics.

———. *Narrative as Rhetoric: Technique, Audiences, Ethics, Ideology*. The Ohio State UP, 1996, https://ohiostatepress.org/books/Complete%20PDFs/Phelan%20Narrative/Phelan%20Narrative.htm.

———. "Rhetorical Approaches to Narrative." Herman, Jahn, and Ryan, pp. 500–4.

Phelan, James, and Peter J. Rabinowitz, editors. *A Companion to Narrative Theory*. Blackwell, 2005.

Phillips, Dana. "History and the Ugly Facts of *Blood Meridian*." Lilley, pp. 17–46.

Pinker, Steven. *The Better Angels of Our Nature: Why Violence Has Declined*. Penguin Books, 2011.

Plotinus. "Ennead I, iv." Cahn and Meskin, pp. 57–63.

Poniatowska, Elena. "Gabriel García Márquez: 'I Tore Up All the Drafts of *One Hundred Years of Solitude* out of Modesty.'" *Review: Literature and Arts of the Americas*, vol. 50, no. 2, 2017, pp. 214–17.

Pontynen, Arthur. *For the Love of Beauty: Art History and the Moral Foundations of Aesthetic Judgment*. Transaction Publishers, 2006.

Posada-Carbó, Eduardo. "Fiction as History: The *bananeras* and Gabriel García Márquez's *One Hundred Years of Solitude*." *Journal of Latin American Studies*, vol. 30, no. 2, 1998, pp. 395–414.

Potkay, Adam. "The British Romantic Sublime." Costelloe, pp. 203–16.

Prager, Brad. *Aesthetic Vision and German Romanticism: Writing Images*. Camden House, 2007.

Prieto, René. "The Body of Political Instrument: Communication in *No One Writes to the Colonel*." McGuirk and Cardwell, pp. 33–44.

Puchner, Martin. "When We Were Clones." *Raritan*, vol. 27, no. 4, 2008, pp. 34–49.

Rabassa, Gregory. "Beyond Magic Realism: Thoughts on the Art of Gabriel García Márquez." *Books Abroad*, vol. 47, no. 3, 1973, pp. 444–50.

———. "Gabriel García Márquez." *Review: Literature and Arts of the Americas*, vol. 50, no. 2, 2017, pp. 242–46.

Rabinowitz, Peter J. "Truth in Fiction: A Re-examination of Audiences." *Critical Inquiry*, vol. 4, 1977, pp. 121–41.

Rader, Ralph K. *Fact, Fiction, and Form: Selected Essays*. Edited by James Phelan and David H. Richter, The Ohio State UP, 2011.

Ramachandran, V. S. *The Tell-Tale Brain: A Neuroscientist's Quest for What Makes Us Human*. W. W. Norton, 2011.

Ramazani, R. Jahan. "Yeats: Tragic Joy and the Sublime." *PMLA*, vol. 104, no. 2, 1989, pp. 163–77.

Rawls, John. *A Theory of Justice*. 1971. Harvard UP, 2009.

Reber, Rolf. "Processing Fluency, Aesthetic Pleasure, and Culturally Shared Taste." Shimamura and Palmer, pp. 223–49.

Redfield, Marc W. "Pynchon's Postmodern Sublime." *PMLA*, vol. 104, no. 2, 1989, pp. 152–62.

Robin, Thierry. "Representation as a Hollow Form, or the Paradoxical Magic of Idiocy and Skepticism in Flann O'Brien's Works." *Review of Contemporary Fiction*, vol. 31, no. 3, 2011, pp. 33–48.

Rosenblum, Robert. "The Abstract Sublime." 1961. Morley, pp. 108–12.

Roy, Arundhati. *The God of Small Things*. Flamingo, 1997.

Ryan, Marie-Laure. "Narrative, Games, and Play." Herman, Jahn, and Ryan, pp. 354–56.

———. *Narrative as Virtual Reality: Immersion and Interactivity in Literature and Electronic Media*. Johns Hopkins UP, 2001.

———. *Possible Worlds, Artificial Intelligence, and Narrative Theory*. Indiana UP, 1991.

———. "Possible-Worlds Theory." Herman, Jahn, and Ryan, pp. 446–50.

Salen, Katie, and Eric Zimmerman, editors. *The Game Design Reader: A Rules of Play Anthology*. MIT Press, 2006.

Santayana, George. *The Life of Reason.* 1905. Edited by Marianne S. Wokeck and Martin A. Coleman, vol. 7, book 1, MIT Press, 2011.

———. *The Sense of Beauty.* 1896. Indiana UP, 2017, https://www.iupui.edu/~santedit/sant/wp-content/uploads/2017/11/George-Santayana-The-Sense-of-Beauty.pdf.

Sawyer, Andy. "Kazuo Ishiguro's *Never Let Me Go* and 'Outsider Science Fiction.'" Groes and Lewis, pp. 236–46.

Sayers, Valerie. "Spare Parts." Review of *Never Let Me Go*, by Kazuo Ishiguro. *Commonweal*, 15 Jul. 2005, pp. 27–28.

Scarry, Elaine. *On Beauty and Being Just.* Princeton UP, 1999.

Schelling, Friedrich Wilhelm Joseph von. "Philosophy of Art." 1802–3. Cahn and Meskin, pp. 170–79.

Scheper-Hughes, Nancy. "Sacred Wounds: Making Sense of Violence." *Theatre Symposium*, vol. 7, 1999, pp. 7–29.

Schiller, Friedrich. *Aesthetical and Philosophical Essays.* Edited by Nathan Haskell Dole, vol. 7, F. A. Niccolls, 1902.

Schjeldahl, Peter. "Notes on Beauty." Beckley and Shapiro, pp. 53–59.

Schneider, Marilyn. "Calvino at a Crossroads: *Il castello dei destini incrociati.*" *PMLA*, vol. 95, no. 1, 1980, pp. 73–90.

Schopen, Bernard. "'They Rode On': *Blood Meridian* and the Art of Narrative." *Western American Literature*, vol. 30, no. 2, 1995, pp. 179–94.

Sepich, John. *Notes on* Blood Meridian. 1993. U of Texas P, 2008.

Shaffer, Brian W., and Cynthia F. Wong, editors. *Conversations with Kazuo Ishiguro.* UP of Mississippi, 2008.

Shaviro, Steven. "'The Very Life of Darkness': A Reading of *Blood Meridian.*" Arnold and Luce, pp. 145–58.

Shaw, Jonathan Imber. "Evil Empires: *Blood Meridian*, War in El Salvador, and the Burdens of Omniscience." *Southern Literary Journal*, vol. 40, no. 2, 2008, pp. 207–31.

Shaw, Philip. *The Sublime.* Routledge, 2006.

Shea, Thomas F. *Flann O'Brien's Exorbitant Novels.* Bucknell UP, 1992.

Sheridan, Kimberly M., and Howard Gardner. "Artistic Development: The Three Essential Spheres." Shimamura and Palmer, pp. 276–96.

Shimamura, Arthur P. *Experiencing Art: In the Brain of the Beholder.* Oxford UP, 2013.

Shimamura, Arthur P., and Stephen E. Palmer, editors. *Aesthetic Science: Connecting Minds, Brains, and Experience.* Oxford UP, 2011.

Shusterman, Richard. *Pragmatist Aesthetics: Living Beauty, Rethinking Art.* 2nd ed., Rowman & Littlefield, 2000.

Sim, Wai-chew. *Kazuo Ishiguro.* Routledge, 2010.

Slade, Andrew. *Lyotard, Beckett, Duras, and the Postmodern Sublime.* Peter Lang, 2007.

———. "Violence and Beauty: Jacques Lacan's *Antigone*." Dickson and Romanets, pp. 87–99.

Smethurst, Paul. *The Postmodern Chronotype: Reading Space and Time in Contemporary Fiction*. Rodopi, 2000.

Smith, Jennifer A. "'We Shall Pass Imperceptibly through Every Barrier': Reading Jeanette Winterson's Trans-Formative Romance." *Critique: Studies in Contemporary Fiction*, vol. 52, no. 4, 2011, pp. 412–33.

Snyder, Phillip A. "Disappearance in Cormac McCarthy's *Blood Meridian*." *Western American Literature*, vol. 44, no. 2, 2009, pp. 127–39.

Snyder, Phillip A., and Delys W. Snyder. "Modernism, Postmodernism, and Language: McCarthy's Style." Frye, pp. 27–40.

Soderholm, James, editor. *Beauty and the Critic: Aesthetics in an Age of Cultural Studies*. U of Alabama P, 1997.

Spolsky, Ellen. "Why and How to Take the Fruit and Leave the Chaff." *On the Origin of Fictions: Interdisciplinary Perspectives*, special issue of *SubStance*, vol. 30, no. 1/2, 2001, pp. 177–98.

Starr, G. Gabrielle. *Feeling Beauty: The Neuroscience of Aesthetic Experience*. MIT Press, 2013.

Stowers, Cath. "The Erupting Lesbian Body: Reading *Written on the Body* as a Lesbian Text." Grice and Woods, pp. 89–102.

Stuart, Andrea. "Terms of Endearment." Review of *Written on the Body*, by Jeanette Winterson. *New Statesman & Society*, 18 Sept. 1992, pp. 37–38.

Sutton-Smith, Brian. "Play and Ambiguity." Salen and Zimmerman, pp. 296–313.

Swanson, Philip, editor. *The Cambridge Companion to Gabriel García Márquez*. Cambridge UP, 2010.

Taaffe, Carol. *Ireland through the Looking-Glass: Flann O'Brien, Myles na gCopaleen and Irish Cultural Debate*. Cork UP, 2008.

Tabbi, Joseph. *Postmodern Sublime: Technology and American Writing from Mailer to Cyberpunk*. Cornell UP, 1995.

Third Earl of Shaftesbury. "Characteristics of Men, Manners, Opinions, Times." 1711. Cahn and Meskin, pp. 77–86.

Tompkins, Jane. *Reader-Response Criticism: From Formalism to Post-Structuralism*. Johns Hopkins UP, 1980.

Tooby, John, and Leda Cosmides. "Conceptual Foundations of Evolutionary Psychology." Buss, pp. 5–67, http://www.cep.ucsb.edu/papers/bussconceptual05.pdf.

———. "Does Beauty Build Adapted Minds? Toward an Evolutionary Theory of Aesthetics, Fiction and the Arts." *On the Origin of Fictions: Interdisciplinary Perspectives*, special issue of *SubStance*, vol. 30, no. 1/2, 2001, pp. 6–27.

Truax, Alice. "A Silver Thimble in Her Fist." Review of *The God of Small Things*, by Arundhati Roy. *The New York Times Book Review*, 25 May 1997, p. 5.

Tsao, Tiffany. "The Tyranny of Purpose: Religion and Biotechnology in Ishiguro's *Never Let Me Go.*" *Literature and Theology,* vol. 26, no. 2, 2012, pp. 214–32.

Turner, Frederick. *Beauty: The Value of Values.* UP of Virginia, 1991.

van de Vall, Renée. "Silent Visions: Lyotard on the Sublime." Crowther, pp. 68–75.

Vaux, Anna. "Body Language." Review of *Written on the Body,* by Jeanette Winterson. *Times Literary Supplement,* vol. 4666, 4 Sept. 1992, p. 20.

Vieth, Ronja. "A Frontier Myth Turns Gothic: *Blood Meridian: Or, the Evening Redness in the West.*" *Cormac McCarthy Journal,* vol. 8, no. 1, 2010, pp. 47–62.

Wallach, Rick, editor. *Myth, Legend, Dust: Critical Responses to Cormac McCarthy.* Manchester UP, 2000.

Wang, Tingting et al. "Is Moral Beauty Different from Facial Beauty? Evidence from an fMRI Study." *Social Cognitive and Affective Neuroscience,* 28 Oct. 2014, pp. 1–10, http://scan.oxfordjournals.org/content/early/2014/10/28/scan.nsu123.full.pdf.

Warnes, Christopher. *Magical Realism and the Postcolonial Novel: Between Faith and Irreverence.* Palgrave Macmillan, 2009.

Waugh, Patricia. *Metafiction: The Theory and Practice of Self-Conscious Fiction.* Methuen, 1984.

Weiskel, Thomas. *The Romantic Sublime.* 1976. Foreword by Harold Bloom, Johns Hopkins UP, 1986.

Weiss, Beno. *Understanding Italo Calvino.* U of South Carolina P, 1993.

Wertz, William F., Jr. "A Reader's Guide to *Letters on the Aesthetical.*" *Fidelio,* vol. 14, no. 1/2, 2005, pp. 80–104, http://schillerinstitute.org/fidelio_archive/2005/fidv14n01-02-2005SpSu/fidv14n01-02-2005SpSu_080-a_readers_guide_to_schillers_let.pdf.

White, Glyn. "The Critic in the Text: Footnotes and Marginalia in the Epilogue to Alasdair Gray's *Lanark: A Life in Four Books.*" Bray, Handley, and Henry, pp. 55–70.

Whitehead, Anne. "Writing with Care: Kazuo Ishiguro's *Never Let Me Go.*" *Contemporary Literature,* vol. 52, no. 1, 2011, pp. 54–83.

Williamson, Edwin. "Magical Realism and the Theme of Incest in *One Hundred Years of Solitude.*" McGuirk and Cardwell, pp. 45–63.

Winterson, Jeanette. "What Is Art For?" 9 Nov. 2000. *The World Split Open: Great Authors on How and Why We Write.* Tin House Books, 2014, pp. 121–40.

———. *Written on the Body.* 1992. Vintage International, 1994.

Wolf, Maryanne. *Proust and the Squid: The Story and Science of the Reading Brain.* Icon Books, 2008.

Wood, James. "The Human Difference." Review of *Never Let Me Go,* by Kazuo Ishiguro. *The New Republic,* 16 May 2005, pp. 36–39.

Wood, Michael. *Gabriel García Márquez: One Hundred Years of Solitude.* Cambridge UP, 1990.

Woodward, Richard B. "Cormac McCarthy's Venomous Fiction." *New York Times*, 19 Apr. 1992.

Zeki, Semir. "Clive Bell's 'Significant Form' and the Neurobiology of Aesthetics." *Frontiers in Human Neuroscience,* 12 Dec. 2013, http://journal.frontiersin.org/article/10.3389/fnhum.2013.00730/full.

———. "The Neurology of Ambiguity." *Consciousness and Cognition*, vol. 13, 2004, pp. 173–96.

———. *Splendors and Miseries of the Brain: Love, Creativity, and the Quest for Human Happiness.* Wiley-Blackwell, 2009.

Zuckert, Rachel. "The Associative Sublime: Gerard, Kames, Alison, and Stewart." Costelloe, pp. 64–76.

INDEX

absurd, 1, 20, 79, 84–85, 175–76
accessibility relation, 44–45, 49, 53
actual world (AW), 35, 42–43, 43n1, 44–45, 47–51, 51n5, 54–55, 55nn6–7, 56–57, 60n10, 64, 167
adaptation, 4, 7, 10–11, 15, 98, 99n2, 100, 135n14, 170, 204. *See also* evolution
Adorno, Theodor, 4, 14–15, 77, 135, 161n32, 164, 189–90
aesthetic, vii, 1–15, 17–21, 25, 27, 34–35, 41–42, 45–46, 54, 57–62, 68, 71, 73, 75–79, 83, 87, 91, 94, 97–98, 100–101, 107, 111, 115–19, 120n16, 121–22, 124–25, 128–29, 129n2, 130–34, 134n9, 134nn11–12, 135, 135nn13–14, 137, 140, 142, 142n19, 143, 145–46, 151, 152n24, 156–57, 158n29, 159–60, 161n32, 163–66, 173, 175, 183–87, 189–96, 198, 200–206. *See also* neuroaesthetics
affective, 2–3, 8n7, 10–12, 19–21, 24, 26, 28, 52, 59–62, 64–65, 71, 76–77, 79, 81, 83, 88, 95, 100–101, 103–4, 119, 123–24, 128–29, 131, 144, 147, 149, 155–56, 190, 205

afterlife, 65, 81, 83, 86–87, 94–95. *See also* posthumous
agency, 79, 109–10, 172, 192
Aldama, Frederick, x, 4, 6, 8, 15, 103, 107, 134n10, 175n9, 189
allegory, 80, 158n29, 194
alliteration, 133, 137
ambiguity, 24, 28, 33–34, 44, 58–59, 64, 66–68, 73, 87–88, 91–92, 204, 206
ambivalence, 49, 80, 95, 131, 178, 200
amygdala, 8n7, 76, 99–100
antimimetic, 164. *See also* mimetic
architecture, 8n7, 56, 62, 77, 93, 127, 132, 132n8, 134, 134n10, 194, 200
Aristotle, 5
art, ix–x, 1–6, 6n6, 9, 11, 14–15, 19–21, 24–25, 29–30, 33–35, 41–42, 45, 60, 63–64, 66, 71, 73–78, 81, 89, 103, 107, 119, 121, 123–25, 129, 129n3, 130–31, 131n6, 133–34, 134nn9–10, 134n12, 135, 135nn13–14, 142, 145–46, 152n24, 156–57, 158n29, 160, 161n32, 164–66,

207

166n3, 178n13, 184–87, 190–98, 200–205
assonance, 133, 139
asymmetry, 98, 109, 166
At Swim-Two-Birds (O'Brien), vii, 12, 41–42, 46–53, 57, 61, 65, 67, 69–70 table 3, 79, 83, 164, 166, 186, 192, 197, 200–201
audience, 15, 17, 20–21, 27, 30, 43, 45, 56, 59–61, 65, 67, 79, 81–83, 95, 104, 134, 146, 148, 151–52, 153n25, 159, 172, 201–2
author, 15, 24, 29, 42, 45, 46n2, 47–48, 57, 68, 69 table 3, 71, 89, 97, 101, 123–24, 142, 145, 152–53, 153n25, 156, 159–60, 167, 172–73, 177, 186, 205
authorial audience, 15, 20, 27, 56, 59–60, 67, 79, 81, 83, 95, 146, 148, 151–52
authority, 10, 98, 104–5, 149, 151, 159, 172, 175. *See also* subversion
autodiegetic, 136, 142, 147
awe, 10, 73, 76, 78, 81, 101–2, 119, 170

Bakhtin, Mikhail, 20, 68n14, 107, 191
Banville, John, 127
Barnes, Julian, 127, 142n18
Barthes, Roland, 21, 122
beauty, viii–x, 2, 2n4, 3, 3n5, 4–9, 11–15, 15n13, 29, 68, 75, 77, 77n8, 93n16, 116, 119, 127–35, 137–39, 142, 142n19, 143, 145–46, 151–52, 152n24, 153, 156–61, 163–65, 167–69, 174, 178–79, 183, 184n15, 185–86, 189–98, 200–201, 203–5
Beckett, Samuel, 19, 84, 95, 144, 191, 203
Bell, Clive, 14, 128, 134, 134n10, 134n12, 190, 206
Belsey, Catherine, 143, 190
Benjamin, Walter, 75
betrayal, 24, 98, 106, 109, 143, 175, 180. *See also* loyalty
biblical, 115, 141
Blood Meridian (McCarthy), vii, 13, 93n17, 97, 101, 111–23, 164, 172, 186, 190–94, 196–97, 199, 201, 203–5

Bloody Chamber, The (Carter), 139, 192
body, 61, 61n11, 63, 67, 85–86, 99, 103–4, 106n5, 108, 111, 117, 117n12, 118, 137–40, 146, 150–51, 169, 172, 193, 195, 199, 202, 204–5. *See also Written on the Body*
Borges, Jorge Luis, 76, 93, 200
Boyd, Brian, 7–8, 15, 24, 32, 34–35, 59–60, 66, 68, 131–32, 191
brain, 4, 6, 8–10, 20, 24, 28, 33, 33n4, 50, 66, 76–77, 87, 91–92, 99–100, 118, 121, 128, 129nn2–3, 131–32, 142n18, 164–65, 165n1, 166, 185, 190–93, 196–97, 202–3, 205–6. *See also* cortex
Burke, Edmund, 12, 72, 75, 75n4, 76, 119, 129, 191

Caillois, Roger, 12, 18, 20–21, 30, 192
Călinescu, Matei, 184, 184n15, 192
Calvino, Italo, 12–13, 19–22, 29–30, 32–34, 34n5, 67, 71, 75, 78, 87–94, 131n6, 164, 190–92, 196–200, 203, 205. *See also Castle of Crossed Destinies, The; Invisible Cities*
care, 10, 98, 100, 105–6, 110, 117–18, 148–51, 155, 158–59, 170–73, 175. *See also* harm
carnivalesque, 20, 68n14, 80
Carpentier, Alejo, 175, 175n9
Carroll, Noël, 14, 14n12, 192
Carter, Angela, 139, 192
Castle of Crossed Destinies, The (Calvino), vii, 12, 22, 29–35, 38–39 table 2, 67, 87, 92, 164, 191–92, 198, 203
catharsis, 121, 184n15
Changeux, Jean-Pierre, 9, 130, 166, 192
chaos, vii, 12, 17–18, 20–23, 25, 31, 42, 50, 52, 67–68, 74, 83, 116, 130, 131n6, 136
character-narrator, 26, 79, 83, 201
characters, 2, 15, 17, 22–27, 29–33, 36 table 1, 41, 46–52, 54, 57, 60, 60n10, 61, 61n11, 63, 65, 67, 69–70 table 3, 79, 82–83, 94–95, 102, 105, 109–12, 115n10, 120, 121n17, 133, 136, 141–42, 145, 152n24, 153, 153n25, 155–56,

158, 166, 168, 168n4, 169n5, 171–73, 179–80, 201

cheating, 18, 98, 105, 144, 171, 175, 178. See also fairness

chronology, 22–23, 25, 44, 53, 55, 71. See also time

co-construction, 46, 66–68, 89, 117, 122, 163

Coetzee, J. M., 127

cognitive, x, 4, 8, 8n7, 9–10, 12, 15, 17–18, 20–24, 35, 41–42, 45, 48, 57, 59, 66–67, 76n5, 79, 82, 95, 98, 130–31, 135, 135n13, 151, 165–66, 185, 189, 196, 205; cognition, 17, 128, 185, 191, 206

cognitive sciences, 9–10, 97, 201

coherence, 8, 12, 21–22, 32, 41–42, 57, 66, 122, 132, 135, 135n13, 138–39, 164, 166, 181

comic, 46, 48–49, 82, 84–85, 94, 95n18, 142, 199

compassion, 98n1, 100, 167, 173

consciousness, 7, 21, 62, 73, 80, 114, 114n8, 120n16, 154, 165, 206

cortex, 8, 10, 20, 42, 77, 99–100, 165n1, 184; orbitofrontal cortex, 5, 99, 128, 191

cosmic, 88, 103, 112–15, 120

Cosmides, Leda, 4, 10, 17, 204

create, 17, 20, 24, 26, 28, 35, 47–48, 55, 55n8, 57, 63, 68, 68n14, 73, 91–92, 100, 109, 120n16, 136, 144–45, 148, 151, 157, 164–66, 166n3, 172, 174, 184, 196, 198

creativity, 20, 89, 121n17, 134, 134n9, 206

cultural, 7, 11, 15, 18n1, 49, 73, 79, 98, 128, 129n3, 134, 134n9, 159, 163, 184, 189, 195, 197, 202, 204

culture, x, 3, 4n5, 17, 18n1, 35, 49, 66, 99, 103, 122, 124n19, 128, 130, 141, 159n30, 193, 197

dance, 25–26, 36–37 table 1, 108, 115, 144, 149

Danto, Arthur, 2–3, 3n5, 129, 134, 185, 190, 193, 196

death, xi, 30–31, 37 table 1, 46n2, 53, 55n8, 58, 63–64, 65n12, 66, 82, 86–87, 97, 103–6, 109, 113–14, 114n8, 115, 115n10, 116, 117n12, 118, 121–22, 122n18, 124–25, 137, 140–41, 142n18, 150–51, 154–55, 157, 163, 168–69, 169n5, 170n6, 175, 175n9, 176, 179–82, 197

default mode network, 5, 76–77

degradation, 98–99, 104–5, 117. See also sanctity

Dehaene, Stanislas, 8–9, 15, 132, 132n7, 165, 165n1, 166, 193

delight, 68, 74, 77, 79, 109

departure, 43, 43n1, 44–50, 53–55, 55n8, 56, 58, 81, 167; departure switching, 54–55, 65

Derrida, Jacques, 77, 77n6, 77n8, 78, 93n16, 193

Desai, Anita, 153, 156, 193

design, 12, 19–21, 24, 28, 31, 41, 44, 54–55, 57, 59, 62–64, 66–68, 82, 87, 93, 98n1, 119, 124n19, 134, 135n14, 156, 159, 197, 202

desire, 7, 24, 28, 62, 73n3, 107–10, 130, 130n4, 131, 150, 169, 171, 182, 185, 190, 194

despair, 65n12, 88, 103, 141, 178, 180, 182

Dewey, John, 4, 131, 135, 146, 193

dialectical, 54, 94, 121, 130, 131n6, 132, 140, 143, 145–46, 149, 153, 156–57, 166, 169, 178; dialecticism, 130–31, 133

Dionysian, 7, 12, 25, 77, 123, 130, 136, 143, 152, 168, 175

disclosure, 25, 146–49, 151, 155

discourse, 4n5, 22–23, 48, 59–60, 63, 65, 81, 99, 104, 124n19, 143, 153, 155, 166, 172–73

disgust, 10n9, 98n1, 99, 99n2, 118, 171

disjuncture, 1, 55, 65, 152

disorder, vii, 17, 21, 57, 72, 135n13, 146

disorientation, 20–22, 41–42, 52, 55, 57, 61, 68, 71, 75, 79, 95, 186

dissonance, 2, 130n5, 171–73

Doležel, Lubomír, 43–44, 194
Donoghue, Denis, 3, 119, 120n15, 121, 121n17, 133, 146, 153, 156, 180, 182, 194, 200
Duchamp, Marcel, 2
Dutton, Denis, 4, 7, 10, 10n9, 15, 17, 98, 129n3, 134, 134n9, 138, 165, 186, 194

Eco, Umberto, 3, 19, 130, 134, 134n11, 194
Edelman, Gerald, 66
Egan, Jennifer, 12, 20, 22–25, 27–28, 36 table 1, 67, 194, 198, 200. See also *Visit from the Goon Squad, A*
eloquence, 133, 139, 141, 143–46, 151–53, 156–57, 164, 167, 179–80, 182–83, 194
embodied. See body
emotion, 8n7, 10n9, 11, 11n10, 14, 17–18, 28, 30, 60, 65, 73, 75, 77, 99, 99n2, 100, 102, 109–10, 124, 128, 129n3, 131, 134n9, 136, 140, 143–45, 147, 149, 151, 153, 155–56, 185–87, 191, 198, 201
empathy, 19, 99–101, 128, 173–74, 191, 198
encoding, 7–8, 27, 34, 151
environment, 15, 49, 56, 198
epistemology, 41, 45, 83, 86, 91, 95
eternal, 86, 95, 103–4, 113, 115, 163–64, 169n5, 177, 183; eternalized, 1, 15, 164, 179–80, 183
eternity, 75, 81–84, 86–87, 95, 163, 200
ethical, 5–6, 9, 93–95, 97, 100, 119–20, 120n15, 121, 121n17, 122–23, 137, 146, 148–49, 152, 152n24, 153, 153n25, 155–57, 159–61, 166, 170–72, 178–79, 186, 195; ethicism, 152, 152n24, 174, 179
ethics, 5–6, 97, 121, 128, 148, 151, 153, 153n25, 160, 166, 171–73, 201
ethics of the telling, 153, 153n25, 166, 171–73
ethics of the told, 153, 153n25, 171–73
evolution, 4, 7, 10–11, 17, 20, 33, 97–98, 98n1, 99, 99n2, 115, 129, 129n3, 132, 132n7, 135n14, 170, 185, 191, 194, 204. See also adaptation
evolutionary psychology, 4, 7, 15, 17, 97, 155, 191, 204

excess, 3, 7, 9, 12, 29–30, 34, 75, 80, 82, 121, 143, 145, 152, 170, 174–75, 179, 181, 184
existential, 67, 79
experiencing-I, 147, 147n21
experiential, 4, 43, 43n1
extradiegetic, 58, 114

fairness, 10, 98–99, 105, 154, 171, 175, 178. See also cheating
fear, 76–77, 82, 82n12, 98, 99n2, 131, 141, 148–49, 151, 154–55, 170n6, 173, 178, 195
fiction, vii, 1–2, 4, 6, 9, 11, 11n10, 12–15, 17–18, 20–21, 35, 41–46, 48, 51n5, 52, 57, 59–60, 61n11, 65–68, 71, 79, 85, 93, 97, 100–101, 110–11, 113, 115, 119, 121–22, 125, 127–29, 146, 160, 164–65, 168, 174n8, 178, 184–86, 189–97, 199–206
fictional recentering, 43, 47, 58n9
fit, 24, 46, 88, 133, 135, 138, 142, 142n19, 143, 145, 151–53, 165, 175, 178n13, 179, 181, 183–84
focalization, 22, 27, 34, 36 table 1, 62, 109–10, 171
form, vii, 5–6, 8–9, 12, 17, 20–22, 26–28, 31, 33, 41, 66–68, 73, 76, 87–88, 91, 93, 120, 122, 128–29, 131–32, 134, 134nn10–11, 135, 139, 142, 142n19, 145–46, 152, 152n24, 156, 159, 164, 166n3, 169, 174, 179–81, 183, 184n15, 186, 193, 196–98, 202, 206
form-drive, 6–10, 12–13, 17–18, 21–22, 24, 28–32, 41–42, 54, 57, 59, 67–68, 88, 119, 122, 127–30, 135–37, 139, 146, 151–53, 156, 160–61, 163–69, 171–74, 179–82, 184–86
formalism, 131, 134, 204
fragment, 1, 9, 11, 13, 15, 21, 24, 27–28, 35, 55, 67, 127, 135n13, 179, 183–84
free indirect discourse, 172–73
Friedrich, Caspar David, 72, 81
functional magnetic resonance imaging (fMRI), 76, 101, 129, 133, 184, 191, 205

futility, 25, 83–84, 86, 145, 151, 157, 178–79

game, 18–21, 23–24, 28–29, 34–35, 42, 44–46, 48, 52, 57, 60, 67–68, 89, 109, 135, 164, 190–93, 197–98, 202. *See also* text-as-game

García Márquez, Gabriel, 1, 14, 127, 163, 165–68, 168n4, 169, 171–73, 174n8, 176, 176n10, 177, 177n11, 178, 178nn12–13, 179, 183, 191, 194–95, 199, 201–2, 204–5. See also *One Hundred Years of Solitude*

Gaut, Berys, 6, 152, 152n24, 155, 195

gender, 136, 159, 166

generativity, 7–8, 34, 88, 141, 166, 166n2, 169, 174, 181

Genette, Gérard, 22

genocide, 11n11, 27, 36 table 1, 102, 146, 172

Gibson, William, 75

Gilson, Étienne, 130, 195

God of Small Things, The (Roy), vii, 13, 93n17, 97, 100–11, 166, 192, 195, 200, 202, 204

grace, 9, 62, 138, 179

grand narratives, 2, 13, 127, 144, 158

Gray, Alasdair, 12, 20, 42, 53, 55–57, 59, 61–65, 65n12, 67, 68n13, 190, 193–96, 199–200, 205. See also *Lanark: A Life in Four Books*

grotesque, 80, 95n18, 113, 116

grouping, 8, 127, 132, 135, 135n14

Haidt, Jonathan, 7, 10, 10n9, 11, 11nn10–11, 13, 15, 97–98, 98n1, 99, 99n2, 100–102, 131, 170, 173, 174n7, 196

harm, 10, 10n9, 98, 100, 105–6, 117–18, 147–49, 155, 159, 170–73, 175. *See also* care

harmony, viii, 5–6, 9, 11–13, 21, 41–42, 68n13, 98, 123, 127–28, 130, 130n5, 134, 134n11, 137, 139, 145–46, 152–53, 156, 161, 164–67, 174–75, 179–82, 184

Herman, David, x, 46, 136n15, 147n21, 196, 201–2

heterodiegetic, 22

historical. *See* history

history, 1, 2n4, 3, 7, 9, 46, 46n2, 51, 51n5, 52, 55–56, 63, 74–75, 83–84, 104, 108–9, 111–14, 120, 120n16, 121–22, 124, 130, 134, 134n11, 163, 167–68, 174, 174n8, 176n10, 177, 186, 190, 192–94, 196–97, 201–2; historiography, 67

Hogan, Patrick Colm, x, 4, 6–8, 15, 24, 27, 68, 133, 134n10, 151, 185, 189, 196

Hogarth, William, 130, 193, 196

homodiegetic, 22, 30, 32, 47

Huizinga, John, 12, 17–18, 18n1, 19, 197

humor, 80, 84, 104, 110, 174, 195

Hutcheon, Linda, 2, 197

ilinx, 20–22, 30, 68n14

imagination, vii, 5, 7–8, 13, 17, 24, 26, 32, 35, 42–43, 45, 47, 53, 57, 59–65, 67, 68n13, 71, 76–78, 80–81, 83–85, 88–95, 97, 99, 101, 103, 105–6, 111, 115, 119, 120n16, 125, 130, 134n9, 137–38, 140–41, 144–45, 153, 165, 167, 169–70, 172, 183, 191, 200

immersion, 59–60, 61n11, 65, 67, 202

incest, 167, 169, 174, 176n10, 178, 181, 205

indeterminacy, 45, 53–54, 58–59, 63, 67, 73, 75, 90, 94, 136, 155

indirection, 7–8, 34, 141, 155

infinite, 9n8, 14, 43, 73, 75, 78, 83–86, 95, 103, 114, 120, 124, 164, 169, 178, 184, 200

injustice, 97, 105, 107, 146, 166, 177–78

insula, 76, 99–100

interactivity, 60, 67, 202

interpretation, 22, 29n2, 30–33, 33n4, 34, 34n5, 35, 44, 52, 54, 58–59, 61–68, 79–80, 89, 91, 107–10, 124, 135, 137, 149, 152, 157, 166–68, 186

intertextual, 57, 177, 179

Invisible Cities (Calvino), vii, x–xi, 13, 71, 78, 87–94, 164, 192

Ireland, 47, 49, 79, 83–84, 204; Irish, 11, 46, 49–50, 72, 79–80, 84, 95, 193, 199–200, 204

irony, 29, 104, 110, 136, 150, 158, 173
Ishiguro, Kazuo, 13, 128, 146, 149, 151–53, 155–56, 156n28, 158, 158n29, 159–60, 190, 192–99, 203, 205. See also *Never Let Me Go*

Jameson, Fredric, 2, 2n4, 3, 9, 74–75, 197
Joyce, James, 2
judgment, 3, 5, 9, 11, 15, 15n13, 18, 38 table 2, 62, 74, 78, 87, 99, 101, 105, 107, 120, 120n15, 121–22, 136, 142, 144, 148–49, 152n24, 153, 155, 157, 173, 184, 198, 201
justice, 10, 30, 38–39 table 2, 95, 99, 121, 158, 202

Kafka, Franz, 172
Kant, Immanuel, 5–8, 12–15, 18, 71, 73, 75, 76n5, 77, 77n7, 78, 78n9, 85–86, 93, 93n16, 102, 115, 128–30, 134, 134n12, 135, 160–61, 196, 198–99. See also imagination; reason; understanding
kitsch, 124n19, 184, 184n15, 192
knowledge, 15, 43n1, 44, 58, 74, 78, 82–83, 85–88, 92, 95, 111, 122–23, 140, 149, 170, 174, 182, 199

Lanark: A Life in Four Books (Gray), vii, 12, 42, 53–67, 79, 125, 164, 193–95, 200, 205
language, 1, 7, 20–21, 28, 47, 60, 67, 72, 80, 83, 89, 92, 104, 115, 119–20, 132, 141–43, 143n20, 145, 152, 159n31, 172, 176, 189, 191, 193–95, 201, 204–5
liberty, 10, 98–99, 105, 115, 117, 149, 151, 159, 161, 171, 175, 178, 192. See also oppression
light, 62, 73, 75, 81, 88, 106, 128n1, 177, 179–82
lightness, 92–93, 93n17, 127, 131n6, 200
limitlessness, 73, 75, 78, 103, 106, 112, 114–15, 124
linguistic, 44, 55, 62, 83, 120n16, 146, 153

literary, vii, 1–2, 2n4, 3–4, 4n5, 7–9, 11–15, 18n1, 25, 27, 35, 43n1, 46, 49, 57–58, 64, 66, 71–72, 74, 76–77, 79, 83, 89, 93, 97, 107, 120, 123–25, 129, 130n5, 131–35, 137, 145, 159, 163–65, 166nn2–3, 184–86, 190–91, 193, 196, 199, 203, 205
literature, ix, xi, 1–2, 4, 4n5, 11, 11n11, 12–13, 21, 29–30, 41, 68, 68n14, 72, 75, 78, 97, 100–101, 122, 124, 127, 163, 173, 176, 184–85, 187, 189–94, 196–97, 200–205
Longinus, 12, 15, 71–72, 72n1, 76–78, 81, 124, 196, 199
love, 3, 15, 24, 28, 38 table 2, 65, 100, 102, 107–11, 115, 120n15, 127, 135n14, 136–45, 148, 150, 152, 157–60, 168, 169n5, 171–73, 178–84, 187, 190, 194, 199, 201, 206
loyalty, 10, 98, 100, 106, 175. See also betrayal
Lyotard, Jean-François, 2, 2n4, 12, 74–77, 77nn6–8, 93, 93n16, 122, 124, 160, 199, 203, 205

magic realism, 175, 176n10, 189, 192, 196–97, 200, 202, 205
massacre, 112, 118, 167, 174–75, 175n9, 176
McCarthy, Cormac, 13, 93n17, 101, 111–14, 114n8, 115, 115n10, 116–21, 121n17, 122–23, 190–92, 194–95, 197–99, 201, 204–6. See also *Blood Meridian*
McEwan, Ian, 127
McHale, Brian, ix, 3, 41, 79, 125, 199
memory, 1, 23–24, 26, 37 table 1, 42, 52, 77, 88, 104, 129, 133, 136–40, 147, 158, 169n5, 170–71, 178n12, 180
Merleau-Ponty, Maurice, 157, 198
metafiction, 31, 48, 56, 67, 205
metalepsis, 46, 79, 186, 190, 196
metaphor, 55, 60, 67, 72n1, 135n14, 137–38, 141, 158n29, 176n10, 183, 194
mimetic, 60, 60n10, 62, 65, 201. See also antimimetic

mind, vii, 4, 8, 10, 13, 21, 32, 50–52, 60–62, 66, 76n5, 80, 86–87, 91–92, 97–100, 102–3, 110–12, 115, 117–18, 120, 131, 139, 151, 164, 171, 192, 196, 203–4

mirror neurons. *See* neurons

mise-en-abyme, 56–57, 85

modernism, 2, 9, 41, 49, 75, 192, 204

moral, vii, 3, 5–6, 6n6, 9–10, 10n9, 11, 11nn10–11, 18, 72–73, 78, 94–95, 97–102, 104–7, 111, 115, 117–21, 121n17, 123, 125, 128, 148–49, 155, 158–60, 164, 166, 170–71, 173–75, 178, 199, 201, 205

moral-drive, 6–10, 12–13, 72, 78, 93–95, 97, 101–2, 105–7, 113, 117–19, 123, 125, 128, 130, 146, 152–53, 156, 159–61, 163–67, 169–75, 179, 185–86

moral intuition, 10–11, 11nn10–11, 97–101, 104–5, 115, 117–18, 148–49, 155, 159, 170–72, 174–75, 178

motif, 84–85, 118, 137, 166, 169

multiplicity, 33, 35, 58, 68, 87–89

Murphy, Neil, ix, 46, 46n2, 79, 134n9, 200

music, 28, 37 table 1, 63, 85n14, 89, 119, 128, 129n3, 138–39, 166n3, 170, 179, 181–83, 185, 191

muted, viii, 11, 14, 22, 30, 103, 108, 127, 133, 144, 146–47, 149, 151, 153, 155–57, 160, 180

Nabokov, Vladimir, 19

narrating-I, 147, 147n21

narration, 22–23, 26–28, 30, 50–51, 54, 58, 62, 64, 103, 105, 114–15, 118, 120, 120n16, 121, 136, 147n21, 153, 167, 172–73, 197, 201

narrative, x, 4, 7, 12–15, 17–18, 20–23, 25–27, 29–31, 34–35, 36 table 1, 42–46, 48, 50–51, 55–56, 58–60, 60n10, 61, 65, 67–68, 79, 81–83, 87, 95, 100, 102, 104, 107, 110, 112, 114n8, 116, 127, 133, 136, 140–41, 144, 146, 151–53, 155, 157–59, 164, 166n2, 171–74, 177, 179, 184, 189–90, 193–94, 196, 198–99, 201–3

narrative audience, 14–15, 17, 20, 30, 43, 45, 56, 59–61, 61n11, 65, 67, 79, 81–83, 95, 151

narrative discourse. *See* discourse

narrator, 22–23, 26, 29n2, 30–34, 46–47, 50n4, 53, 64, 69–70 table 3, 75, 79–82, 82n12, 83, 85–87, 95, 100, 120, 136–45, 147, 152–53, 153n25, 154–56, 159

Nehamas, Alexander, 2–3, 14, 14n12, 15n13, 160–61, 200

neural, 5, 8n7, 10, 33–34, 42, 66, 91, 99, 128, 129n3, 165–66, 185, 198

neuroaesthetics, 4, 6–7, 15, 76, 101, 128, 185, 192

neurobiology, 15, 33, 77, 91–92, 129, 197, 206

neurons, 10, 66, 99–100, 129, 131, 165; neurotransmitters, 10, 100

neuroscience, 4–5, 8n7, 9, 18–19, 24, 76, 128, 132, 135, 184–85, 190, 196–98, 202, 204–6

Never Let Me Go (Ishiguro), viii, 13, 128, 146–60, 164, 166, 172, 192–99, 203, 205

New Criticism, 2, 131, 198

Newman, Barnett, 73, 73n3, 75, 197, 200

Nietzsche, Friedrich, 7, 73, 86, 123, 130–31, 200

nihilism, 119, 123

nonrationality, 122–23, 168

nonsense, 43, 79, 79n10, 94, 168

nostalgia, 104, 107, 109, 167, 169–70, 178, 178n12, 179

nuance, 28, 51, 144–46, 158, 160, 166, 173, 178

O'Brien, Flann (Brian O'Nolan), 12–13, 19–20, 42, 46, 46n2, 47–50, 51n5, 52–53, 67, 71, 75, 78–82, 82n12,

83–87, 93–95, 191–94, 197, 200–204.
See also *At Swim-Two-Birds*; *Third Policeman, The*
object recognition, 8, 91, 131–32, 132n7, 140
One Hundred Years of Solitude (García Márquez), viii, ix, 1, 14, 163, 165–84, 186, 191–97, 201–2, 205
ontological, 12, 20, 35, 41–44, 47, 52, 66, 88, 90, 92, 125, 166, 190
oppression, 90, 98–99, 105, 110, 115, 117, 149, 151, 154–55, 159, 171, 175, 178, 192. *See also* liberty
orbitofrontal cortex. *See* cortex
order, vii, 2, 5, 7–8, 10n9, 12, 17–18, 21–23, 30–33, 38 table 2, 42, 44, 50, 53, 57, 59, 66, 68, 78, 81, 88–90, 94, 100–101, 104–5, 109, 128, 130–31, 131n6, 134, 134n11, 135, 135n14, 136–37, 139, 142, 146, 166
OuLiPo, 20
oxytocin, 10, 100

painting, 2, 9, 56, 63, 72–73, 73n3, 75, 81, 130, 133
paradox, 1, 11n11, 74, 89, 131n6, 133, 145, 148, 151, 173, 175, 181, 183, 194, 202
parallel, 139, 168–69, 179, 183
parody, 20, 29, 49, 83–84, 176–77, 179
participant. *See* participation
participation, 17, 21, 24, 28, 34n5, 42, 44–45, 60, 65, 68, 76, 92, 101, 117, 122, 125, 129n2, 134n11, 163–64, 184
passion, 2, 72n1, 78, 140, 142, 160, 169–70, 181
pattern, 6, 8, 22, 24, 27, 29, 31–33, 42, 48, 66, 68, 88, 92, 127, 129n2, 130n4, 132, 166n2, 168, 174
pattern recognition, 7, 25, 27, 68, 131, 133
Pavel, Thomas, 43–45, 66, 201
Perec, Georges, 19–20, 191
Perloff, Marjorie, 20, 201
Phelan, James, ix, 15, 17, 44, 59–60, 60n10, 61–62, 65, 153, 153n25, 171–72, 195, 201–2

philosopher, 5–6, 14, 72–73, 76–79, 93, 129, 133–34
philosophical, 3–5, 7, 73, 84, 127–28, 134n11, 168, 191, 194, 203
philosophy, 2, 82–83, 131, 190, 192–94, 196, 198–99, 203
Picasso, Pablo, 2
Plato, 5–6, 134n11, 160, 189
play, vii, 7, 11–15, 17–22, 24–25, 28–29, 31–35, 41–46, 48–50, 53–54, 56–61, 66–68, 68n14, 71, 79, 83, 86, 94, 110, 122, 125, 138, 140–41, 144, 161, 163–68, 190–93, 197, 200, 202, 204
pleasure, 1, 4, 11–12, 18–19, 21–22, 24–25, 27, 59, 61, 64–65, 67–68, 77–78, 95, 120n16, 125, 129, 129n3, 133, 134n9, 139–41, 143, 146, 167, 170, 170n6, 174, 184, 186, 191, 193–94, 202
Plotinus, 6, 129, 134n9, 134n11, 201
plural, 6–7, 20, 22, 26, 30–31, 33, 35, 71, 157, 164
poetic, 133, 136, 161, 183
poetic justice, 95, 121
poetry, 2, 15, 72–73, 124, 179
political. *See* politics
politics, 49, 56, 74, 79, 84, 89, 99, 122n18, 124n19, 150–51, 156–58, 160, 163, 167, 174–76, 178, 178n13, 179, 184, 186, 193, 195–96, 201–2
polyphony, 22, 27, 57
possible worlds, vii, xi, 12, 35, 41–44, 47, 47n3, 48–50, 52, 56–57, 61, 67, 69–70 table 3, 135, 190, 194, 202
postcolonial, 103, 107, 110, 176, 176n10, 189, 197, 200, 205
posthumous, 83, 86, 125. *See also* afterlife
postmodern, vii, 1–2, 2n4, 3–4, 7, 9, 12–13, 15, 17–18, 20–21, 35, 41–42, 44, 46, 46n2, 52, 54, 57, 59, 65–68, 71, 73–75, 79, 83–87, 93, 95, 111, 115, 119–20, 124–25, 127, 134–35, 141–45, 160, 164–65, 181, 184, 184n15, 185–86, 190–91, 193–94, 197–99, 201–4

power, 7, 19, 24, 44, 57, 59, 64–66, 74–79, 86, 90, 99, 103, 107, 109, 113, 115, 121n17, 125, 131, 143, 146–47, 153, 156, 161, 166–67, 183, 186
pretense, 17, 20, 43, 46n2, 90
principle of maximal departure, 43, 45, 47–49, 53–55, 55n8, 56, 81
principle of minimal departure, 43, 45, 47–48, 50, 54–55
prolepsis, 25–26, 36–37 table 1, 114
psychology, 4, 7, 10, 15, 17, 19, 97–99, 109, 131, 135n14, 155, 166, 191, 198, 204
Pynchon, Thomas, 74–75, 202

Ramachandran, V. S., 4, 8, 15, 24, 135, 135n14, 202
Rawls, John, 10, 202
read, 1, 8n7, 9, 11–12, 15, 17, 27–28, 31–32, 33n3, 34n5, 35, 44–45, 47–48, 52–53, 59, 61–62, 64, 68, 71, 77, 79, 82n12, 85, 103, 107–12, 115n10, 117, 119–20, 124, 132n7, 135, 140, 142, 145, 153, 156, 165–68, 173, 183–84, 186, 190–91, 193–95, 198–99, 201, 203–5
reader, x, 1, 3–4, 6, 11–15, 17–30, 32, 34, 34n5, 36 table 1, 41–68, 68n13, 71, 78–83, 85–87, 89–91, 93–95, 97–98, 101–2, 105–6, 108–9, 111–15, 117–23, 125, 127, 129, 132, 134–36, 140–41, 143–49, 151–53, 155–59, 163–66, 168, 168n4, 170, 170n6, 171, 173–75, 178, 178n13, 179, 182–86, 194, 197, 202, 204–5
readerly judgment. *See* judgment
real, 14, 17, 24, 42–43, 45, 60, 82, 90, 92, 99, 103, 108, 110, 114–16, 147–48, 150, 152n24, 156, 167, 174, 195
realism, 54, 61, 64–65, 79, 81–83, 94, 111
reality, 7, 17, 42–43, 43n1, 48–49, 51, 56, 64–65, 67–68, 75, 82n12, 83–86, 92, 94, 113, 114n8, 140, 155, 157, 160, 167, 169, 175n9, 176–78, 178n13, 183, 186, 197, 202
reason, 5, 10, 11n10, 18, 32, 74, 77–78, 93, 95, 102, 119, 121, 125, 179, 201, 203

relevance, 6, 8, 8n7, 9, 20–21, 27, 44, 71, 99, 129n3, 131, 135, 151, 152n24
repeated, 51, 51n5, 55, 75, 86–87, 91, 113–14, 130, 130n4, 131, 133, 136, 145, 150
repetition, 8, 86–87, 113–14, 114n8, 122, 127, 131n6, 133, 135n14, 136, 136n15, 137, 139, 150, 163, 168
representation, 34, 54, 56, 60n10, 64, 74–75, 78, 80–81, 88, 90–91, 101, 107, 115, 118–21, 124–25, 129n2, 134n9, 146, 148, 151, 164, 170, 194, 202
reward, 24, 77, 128–29, 129n3, 130–33, 166, 184–85, 191
rhetorical, 17, 59, 177, 182, 201
rhyme, 133, 137
rhythm, 8, 103, 115, 127, 131–32, 135n14, 146, 179
Romantic, 72–74, 85, 130, 202, 205
Roy, Arundhati, 13, 93n17, 100–105, 107, 109–11, 189, 192, 195, 200, 202, 204. See also *God of Small Things, The*
Rushdie, Salman, 93n17, 189
Ryan, Marie-Laure, xi, 18, 20–21, 35, 41–43, 43n1, 44–45, 47n3, 50, 53, 55, 55nn6–7, 58–60, 61n11, 66–67, 68n14, 136n15, 147n21, 167, 190, 196, 201–2

sanctity, 10, 98–99, 104–5, 117. *See also* degradation
Santayana, George, 14, 14n12, 86, 131n6, 134, 134n12, 142n19, 203
Saramago, José, 76, 93n17
satire, 57, 79–80, 167, 174–75, 191, 195
Scarry, Elaine, 3, 130n4, 203
Scheper-Hughes, Nancy, 122n18, 123, 203
Schiller, Friedrich, 5–7, 12–13, 15, 21, 45, 68, 71, 77–78, 93, 93n16, 119, 125, 128, 130, 194, 203, 205
Schopenhauer, Arthur, 85, 119, 194
Scotland, 54–57, 64, 199; Scottish, 11, 55–56, 67, 76, 191, 193
self-reflexive, 27, 31, 54, 57, 59

sense-drive, 6–10, 12–13, 18, 22, 26, 28–33, 42–43, 54, 59, 68, 72, 75, 78, 81, 83, 88–90, 92–95, 97, 102, 105–7, 113, 116–19, 122–23, 125, 128–30, 136–37, 139, 141–43, 152, 159, 161, 163–65, 167–70, 174–75, 175n9, 180–82, 184–86

sensuous, 5, 7, 22–23, 26, 28, 31–34, 57, 68, 119, 137, 140, 145, 152, 159, 169–70, 175

sequence, 22, 32–34, 54, 85, 139, 148, 176, 182

sexual, 25, 48, 80, 98n1, 106n5, 107–9, 140, 144, 159, 169, 169n5, 171–72, 181

Shimamura, Arthur, 2–4, 8–9, 15, 28, 99, 132, 164, 166n3, 192, 197, 202–3

Shusterman, Richard, 3–4, 4n5, 21, 57, 131, 134, 134n10, 135, 135n13, 146, 151, 186, 203

silence, 27–28, 85, 85n14, 92, 103, 106, 116–17, 144, 156–57, 172, 205

skepticism, 3, 13, 107, 127, 145, 202

solitude, 157, 167, 169, 178–80, 183. See also *One Hundred Years of Solitude*

sound, 42, 50, 62, 75, 82, 85n14, 107, 179, 197

spatiotemporal, 75, 86, 90

Spolsky, Ellen, 7, 15, 155, 166n2, 204

Starr, G. Gabrielle, 4, 6, 8n7, 14–15, 76–77, 133, 166, 184, 204

story, 11n10, 22–27, 32, 33n3, 47, 50–51, 58, 62, 68, 82n12, 89–90, 131, 136, 156–57, 158n29, 159n31, 167, 174, 205; storytelling, 20, 42, 66, 142, 198

story-over-discourse meta-rule, 59–61, 63, 65

storyworld, 32, 34–35, 60, 65, 79, 83, 85, 151, 181

structure, 5, 8, 10, 12, 19–20, 24, 26, 28, 30, 34, 34n5, 43, 46, 52, 56–57, 68, 68n14, 72n1, 86–88, 90, 97, 101–2, 104–5, 107, 117, 125, 131, 131n6, 132, 135, 151, 164, 184

style, 22, 26–27, 34, 49, 111, 114–16, 120, 133, 134n9, 153, 155, 179, 186, 204

sublime, vii, 2n4, 3–6, 10–15, 71–86, 88, 91, 93–95, 97–98, 101–4, 106–8, 110–13, 115, 115n11, 116, 118–20, 122–24, 124n19, 125, 129, 129n2, 160, 163–65, 167, 169, 169n5, 170, 185, 191, 193–200, 202–6

subversion, 2, 86, 98, 104–5, 111, 149, 159, 175. See also authority

suffer, 2, 95, 98n1, 100, 105, 107, 119, 121, 122n18, 125, 136, 138, 140, 164, 170, 172–73, 180

surprise, 27, 53, 58, 90, 130, 130n4, 131–34, 134n9, 149, 151, 186

Surrealist, 77; surrealistic, 116

symmetry, 8, 10, 87, 127, 132, 134–35, 135n14, 169. See also asymmetry

target encoding. See encoding

tense, 22, 30, 114–15, 179

tension, 1, 6, 9, 12–13, 18, 22, 30–31, 33, 42, 54, 68, 74, 78, 80, 83, 97, 100–103, 105, 107, 118, 120n16, 122–24, 128, 130–31, 131n6, 132, 143, 146, 148–49, 152–53, 157, 164–66, 166n3, 167–72, 174

terror, 22, 73–74, 76–77, 81, 86–87, 103, 122–23, 154, 170, 170n6

text-as-game, 60–63, 65, 67

text-as-world, 60, 62–63, 65

textual actual world (TAW), 43–44, 47–48, 50, 50n4, 53–55, 55nn6–8, 56, 58, 58n9, 60–66, 69 table 3, 92

textual alternate possible subworld (TAPsW), 47–48, 50–53, 69–70 table 3

textual alternate possible world (TAPW), 44, 47–50, 50n4, 51–53, 57, 58n9, 61–64, 66, 69–70 table 3

thematic, 47, 60, 62, 65, 65n12, 79, 83, 94–95, 100, 119, 124–25, 159, 186

Third Policeman, The (O'Brien), vii, 13, 46n2, 71, 75, 78–88, 93–95, 95n18, 115, 125, 167, 189–90, 200

time, 1, 9, 11n10, 15, 17–19, 22–26, 33, 36–37 table 1, 45, 49–52, 55–56,

58n9, 63, 75, 80, 84, 86–87, 90, 98, 105, 110, 112–13, 115–16, 123–24, 133, 136, 141, 145, 148–49, 154, 157, 160, 163, 166, 170n6, 177–78, 183, 185–86, 193–94, 197–98, 200, 204. *See also* chronology

Tooby, John, 4, 10, 17, 204

transcendence, 73, 73n3, 76, 85–87, 123, 193

transgress, 18, 20, 100, 104–5, 170, 186

transport, 45, 76–78

trauma, 74–75, 106n5, 122, 198

ultrasociality, 10–11, 11n11, 98, 101–2

undecidable relation, 45, 53, 58–59, 62, 67

understanding, 5, 8, 28, 30, 34, 74, 83, 86–89, 101, 119, 122, 143, 151, 159

unity, 8–10, 21, 57, 131, 134, 134n11, 135n13, 138, 146, 179–80

utopia, 87, 93–94, 200

vertigo, 20–21, 30, 57, 67

violence, 15, 74, 78, 102, 104–5, 109–17, 119, 120nn15–16, 121–23, 134, 137, 186, 194, 201, 203–4

Visit from the Goon Squad, A (Egan), vii, 12, 22–29, 34–35, 36–37 table 1, 67, 166, 194, 198, 200

visual, 8–9, 28–29, 32, 34, 38 table 2, 58, 75–76, 92, 116, 128, 129n2, 132, 135n14, 166n3, 185

voice, 49, 57–58, 62, 64, 100, 104, 139, 153, 155–56, 159, 170n6, 172–73, 175, 177, 181, 196

war, 4, 6–7, 11, 11n11, 14–15, 46, 79, 89, 102, 108, 113, 118, 129, 163, 167, 170n6, 171, 177–78, 178n12, 179, 186, 194, 201, 203

Waugh, Patricia, 7, 35, 51, 66, 205

Winterson, Jeanette, 7, 13, 128, 133, 136–37, 139, 141–45, 152, 159, 159n31, 189, 191, 193–96, 198–99, 201, 204–5. *See also Written on the Body*

Wittgenstein, Ludwig, 67

Wolf, Maryanne, 8n7, 132n7, 165, 205

world, vii, xi, 1–8, 12, 14–15, 17–18, 20–22, 30, 32, 33n4, 34–35, 39 table 2, 41–53, 55n7, 56–63, 65–68, 69–70 table 3, 71, 74–75, 77, 79, 82–88, 92, 99–101, 103, 105, 110, 112–15, 115n10, 118, 122–23, 127, 134–35, 142, 147–51, 156, 158, 158n29, 160–61, 164, 167, 169, 169n5, 173, 181–82, 184, 186, 190, 193–94, 199–202, 205

Written on the Body (Winterson), viii, 13, 128, 133, 136–46, 152, 159, 164, 181, 195, 199, 201, 204–5

Yeats, W. B., 73, 73n2, 124, 202

Zeki, Semir, 4, 6, 33, 33n4, 76, 91–92, 101, 128, 129n2, 133, 197–98, 206

COGNITIVE APPROACHES TO CULTURE
FREDERICK LUIS ALDAMA, PATRICK COLM HOGAN, LALITA PANDIT HOGAN,
AND SUE J. KIM, SERIES EDITORS

This series takes up cutting edge research in a broad range of cognitive sciences insofar as this research bears on and illuminates cultural phenomena such as literature, film, drama, music, dance, visual art, digital media, and comics, among others. For the purpose of the series, "cognitive science" is construed broadly to encompass work derived from cognitive and social psychology, neuroscience, cognitive and generative linguistics, affective science, and related areas in anthropology, philosophy, computer science, and elsewhere. Though open to all forms of cognitive analysis, the series is particularly interested in works that explore the social and political consequences of cognitive cultural study.

Eternalized Fragments: Reclaiming Aesthetics in Contemporary World Fiction
  W. MICHELLE WANG

Capturing Mariposas: Reading Cultural Schema in Gay Chicano Literature
  DOUG P. BUSH

Necessary Nonsense: Aesthetics, History, Neurology, Psychology
  IRVING MASSEY

Shaming into Brown: Somatic Transactions of Race in Latina/o Literature
  STEPHANIE FETTA

Resilient Memories: Amerindian Cognitive Schemas in Latin American Art
  ARIJ OUWENEEL

Permissible Narratives: The Promise of Latino/a Literature
  CHRISTOPHER GONZÁLEZ

Literatures of Liberation: Non-European Universalisms and Democratic Progress
  MUKTI LAKHI MANGHARAM

Affective Ecologies: Empathy, Emotion, and Environmental Narrative
  ALEXA WEIK VON MOSSNER

A Passion for Specificity: Confronting Inner Experience in Literature and Science
  MARCO CARACCIOLO AND RUSSELL T. HURLBURT

www.ingramcontent.com/pod-product-compliance
Lightning Source LLC
Chambersburg PA
CBHW020652230426
43665CB00008B/407